SOUTHERN V

1929 – 2004

75 years serving the Isle of Wight

Richard Newman

"Will we get a seat on this one?" – concern shows on the faces of potential passengers for Ryde as they queue in Newport's St James's Square to board a Dennis Lancet. This prewar view shows the Company office with bowed-window as well as the roof luggage rack and ladder on the 36 seater bus.

Southern Vectis (SVOC) coll (courtesy Bus & Coach)

Colourpoint

6 5 4 3 2 1

© Richard J Newman and Colourpoint Books, Newtownards 2004

Designed by Colourpoint Books, Newtownards
Printed by W&G Baird Limited

ISBN 1 904242 24 3

Colourpoint Books
Colourpoint House
Jubilee Business Park
21 Jubilee Road
Newtownards
County Down
Northern Ireland
BT23 4YH
Tel: 028 9182 0505
Fax: 028 9182 1900
E-mail: info@colourpoint.co.uk
Web-site: www.colourpoint.co.uk

Richard Newman

Richard Newman was born in Portsmouth and has worked in public transport for over 37 years, divided almost equally between the railway and bus industries. He worked for Southern Vectis from 1984 until 2001 and undertook the company's 60th anniversary publication. He is a joint director of Newbus, which operated an open-top tour from Ryde and a private hire coach until 2003. Richard has been a committee member of the IW Bus Museum since its inception and is owner or part-owner of a number of preserved Southern Vectis and Southdown vehicles.

Photo credits:

Front cover: 1959-built Bristol LD No 563 is seen entering Newport bus station on a journey from Ryde to Cowes in the late summer of 1987, when on loan to Southern Vectis as part of the 'Vintage Fleet'. Number 563 is owned by the author and can be seen at the IW Bus Museum.

P Savage

Back cover upper: *Route Rouge* livery was eventually applied to all of the 1989/90 batch of Leyland-bodied Olympians. Number 720 is pictured in Ventnor in January 2003.

P Savage

Back cover lower: As celebration of the company's 50th anniversary, the first Mk 3 Bristol VR, No 650 (MDL 650R), received an application of the original Vectis Bus Company colours, continued by SVOC at the takeover in 1929.

SVOC

Contents

Foreword by Alan White, MD, Southern Vectis Omnibus Co

It gives me great pleasure to be asked to write the foreword to *Southern Vectis – 75 years serving the Isle of Wight* and my thanks go to author Richard Newman for giving me that opportunity.

Richard is an ideal choice to write this book. Having spent his working life involved in transport (he was employed in the railway industry prior to his bus career) his interest knows no bounds, and, being in an ideal position to carry out the necessary research, he knows the history of Southern Vectis exceptionally well. He put that knowledge to good use in his time as an employee of the company and again when operating as a competitor!

The seventy-five years since 1929 have been witness to massive changes, both on the Island itself and in the company and its field of operations. The current privatised environment enables local management to take business decisions at the very heart of operations, a far cry from the days of a nationalised industry. Things may be different in volume terms, but the core business has changed little over the decades; taking commuters to and from their places of work or the ferries, school children to and from school and, of course, the holiday-makers from over the water for their annual holiday or day out remain key elements of the service we offer.

Our present day challenges and pressures are greater than ever before, and continue to present the Company's management with opportunities to evolve in response to changing circumstances. The massive growth in the use of the Island's road network, due to an ever increasing number of private car journeys, brings with it problems on a scale unknown to the founders of the Company. However, I am sure, when looking through this book, we shall see that no matter which era of public transport we examine, we find one common theme: the trials and challenges of an industry critical to the development of our communities, our way of life, and our nation have been met with enthusiasm and professionalism by those companies and individuals that put the 'service' into 'public service'.

This book is a tribute to the first seventy-five years of one of those companies . . . Southern Vectis.

After experimenting with several demonstrators, SVOC purchased Dennis once again in 1996 when six small Darts were delivered. The 'local' connection was maintained as they had UVG 'Urban Star' bodywork, built at Waterlooville in the former Wadham-Stringer workshops. Number 815 (N815 PDL) is seen being handed over to SVOC MD Alan White outside Nelson Road depot by Dennis representative David Cheeseman.

SVOC

Historical Foreword by Ron Plater

(who started as a fitter in the family business at Benett Street Garage, Ryde, in 1935
and as Asst Chief Engineer 1959–84 was the second longest serving Company officer)

I joined Southern Vectis Omnibus Company in 1938, at the age of 18 when my father's coach business, IOW Tourist Co Ltd, was taken over by SVOC. It was then the policy for staff that had been taken over to have some traffic experience, and my first season was as a conductor, badge No KK9003. It was a very good introduction to 'public relations', and it served me well in later years. At the end of the season I was transferred to the Engineering Section, where the Chief Engineer was Mr R Augustus, as a trainee fitter.

In May of 1939 I volunteered for the RAF and was called up shortly after war was declared. During the years 1939–46, I served in many countries, taking part in the invasions of Sicily and Salerno (Italy), and Normandy (France).

First class engineering technical training on aircraft in the RAF proved beneficial when, in 1946, I returned to SVOC. In 1984 the National Bus Company was dissolved, and as Assistant Chief Engineer I was made redundant.

In 46 years service with SVOC I saw many changes; I served with eight General Managers and four Chief Engineers. There was not only a friendly family atmosphere working at SVOC, but also a bond of comradeship with all those with whom I had the pleasure to work. I made many friends while serving with the Company, some of whom I am still able to see and visit often, others I keep in touch with.

Thank you Richard for asking me to record these happy memories of days gone by, as we celebrate 75 years of the Island's bus company.

With my best wishes

Ron Plater

Ron Plater (right) worked in the bus industry, including distinguished war service in the RAF, for almost 50 years. He started in the family business in 1935 and retired as SVOC Assistant Chief Engineer. Just before retirement, he is showing Island MP Stephen Ross round Central Works at Nelson Road.

Ron Plater Collection

Author's Note & Acknowledgments

Amazingly, 15 years have elapsed since the volume written at Southern Vectis' 60th anniversary. That book, sponsored by the Company and published by Ensign, is long out of print but in updating the story through the Privatisation era I have endeavoured to find new information for the text and a totally different set of photographs to illustrate the seventy-five years.Throughout that time 'the Vectis' has been an important institution for thousands of Island families who have been employed in the industry or used the buses as passengers. It is to the very many loyal staff who have played their part in the conveyance of both locals and tourists on our holiday isle that this seventy-five year history is dedicated. It is intended as much as a social and local history as a book for those purely with an interest in buses. Sadly, in the fifteen years since the last book, many of the experienced busmen who provided me with so much information at that time have passed away, notably Reg Davies whose work lives on in his photographs taken over a half century with the company, and Gordon Butchers who had such an encyclopaedic knowledge of bus routes and personalities from his days in the Traffic Office.

I am much indebted to Southern Vectis and particularly Stuart Linn, Kate Boyes, Alan White and Paul Wheeler for their help in making available company records and photographic archives; many company employees past and present, including Messrs GVR Batchelor, Les Baldwin, CA Bishop, Maurie Cooper, Bob Downer, Patrick Hall, Brian Horner, Malcolm Johnson, Dave Jolliffe, Gerald Kent, Ben Bartram, Alec Morris, Alan Peeling, Ron Plater and Barry Stewart, for information and advice; in addition, I am grateful to K Amos, JH Aston, AB Cross, Dave Evans, R Johnson, A Norris, JH Reynolds and D Strange for use of their photographs, although most are held now in other collections. Much additional information has been gleaned from the *IW County Press* as well as from the erstwhile NBC *Bus* newspaper. Reference to *The Isle of Wight at War* (Adrian Searle) and to research carried out many years ago by Don Howe, Derek Gawn and Martyn Mullins is gratefully acknowledged. Thanks are also due to The PSV Circle for use of fleet list information and to Paul Savage for photographs and acting as a 'go-between' from the Island to the publisher in Ulster.

I am also grateful to my railway colleague, George Wheeler, for proofreading and to John Golding for some vehicle information.

It is my regret that it has not been possible to include a great deal about Solent Blue Line, the satellite company in Southampton, but I hope that can form the basis of a future volume. I trust this book will be enjoyed by all who read it.

Richard Newman
Ryde, IW.
June 2004

The years before

As early as 1844, Dabell's Hand Book to the Isle of Wight stated the place had "enjoyed popularity as a watering place and summer residence for many years, during which time thousands of delighted visitors had frequented its shores". The guide suggested a selection of tours from the ports of Cowes and Ryde, the latter with overnight stops at Blackgang (where the Chine and Hotel had been opened as an attraction by the Dabell's in 1843) and Alum Bay in its three-day itinerary.

There was a well established communication network by horse and carriage, even before Queen Victoria made Osborne her royal residence and brought even greater popularity to the 'Garden Isle'. The main routes between the East Wight towns were covered by mail coaches, later ousted by the railways. However, there were still regular flows of carriage business, such as that from Ventnor Station to Blackgang, that actually prospered by the opening up of railway lines. In fact, it was 1927 before Daish's Hotel Mews in Shanklin replaced their four-in-hand coach by a motor charabanc. Mr BH Bullock, at Havenstreet, had disposed of his carriage business and bought a small Dennis bus in August 1926.

The Island was well served by a 55$\frac{1}{2}$ mile railway network, serving 35 stations, which developed between 1862 and 1900 and survived intact until 1952. Lines constructed were Ryde–Cowes, Ryde–Ventnor, Newport–Sandown, Newport–Freshwater, Brading–Bembridge and Merstone–Ventnor West, mostly by individual promoting companies, which eventually amalgamated into three, later absorbed into the Southern Railway at the 1923 Grouping. Several other proposed lines were, perhaps fortunately, never built (such as the Yarmouth & Ventnor Railway or the Shanklin & Chale scheme of 1885). If late-Victorian plans for a Newport–Carisbrooke horse tramway, or the coastal electric tramway from Ryde to Seaview, had come to fruition this could have led to a municipal involvement in the Island's transport network.

In 1905 the first motorbus service was started by the IW Express Motor Syndicate, with Milnes-Daimler double-deckers, but although an Island company it did not win the support of local people. Its high fares were criticised, although it did offer a 5/- (25p) Special Day Ticket "to traverse the whole Island in one day, breaking journey when and where he chooses" – the precursor of today's Rover tickets; their proclamation was somewhat exaggerated as Express buses did not regularly run west of Blackgang or Carisbrooke! Single-deck charabancs were used from 1906 but the whole undertaking ended up in receivership in 1907 and in the hands of motorbus entrepreneur Douglas MacKenzie, general manager of Sussex Motor Road Car Co, who, in 1909, founded Worthing Motor Services. If the IWEMS had not been beset with financial and other problems it could have become the Island's main operator under MacKenzie's direction, as he also became manager of Southdown Motor Services.

The conveyance of passengers along Island roads was left to a handful of operators running hire-cars or charabancs (such as Creeth at Nettlestone, who ran steam vehicles, commencing in 1909), horse-drawn vehicles or the carriers, who played an important part in the island's economy, bringing produce from outlying villages to Newport on market day and, as time went on, allowing the conveyance of a few passengers as well. It was some of these carriers who formed themselves into bus operators in the 1920s.

World War I brought restrictions and requisitioning to the excursion business but the availability of ex War Department chassis brought impetus to coaching by 1919. When Frank Dodson visited the Island as a tourist and had to walk from Whippingham station to Osborne House (and back), he saw the potential for a bus service. The result was Dodson & Campbell's Vectis Bus Company, which began operations with three Daimler Y type buses (DL 2446–8).

Although outside the scope of the seventy-five years, the Dodson Brothers' Vectis Bus Company laid the foundation of the bus company reconstituted in 1929. Services commenced on 24 October 1921 from Newport to East or West Cowes and from Cowes (Park Gates) to Gurnard (Tinker's Lane) and within a month was also operating from Newport to Ryde, followed by Newport to Sandown (via Arreton or Godshill), Carisbrooke, Ventnor (via Godshill and Niton) or Totland (via Brook or Yarmouth) or Ryde to Shanklin, all in 1922. Thus was formed the core network of routes still running today.

The Dodson family had been involved in building buses in northwest London since horse bus days and had associations with London bus operators. This gave the experience to gain supremacy over the local businesses that started bus operation on the Island in the 1920s. After Campbell had left, Frank Dodson left London for the Island to manage the family business with the competitive aggression that characterised the pioneering years of bus operation.

He had obtained parking at Somerton Aerodrome (and later garages at Somerton and Newport), together with an office at No 19 St James's Square, immediately adjacent to the Newport departure point. Daimler Y or CK type chassis, with bodies constructed by the family firm, became standard; many of these had started life as World War I lorries. There was also a short-lived Thornycroft and a batch of Vulcans which saw no more than five years' service before the bodywork was lengthened and placed on other chassis. At the time these buses were delivered, VBC were describing themselves as "District Vulcan Agents for cars or commercial vehicles". In later years small Guy or Chevrolet buses were also bought, followed by batches of Associated Daimlers, to allow an increased seating capacity of 32.

In their guide for 1922–23, the Vectis Bus Company had boasted that:

> It speaks well for the care displayed by the management, and skills and efficiency of the drivers, that not a single accident or injury to any persons has been recorded. This alone is a remarkable tribute to the thoroughness of an enterprise that bids far to revolutionise the Isle of Wight.

Perhaps this statement was premature, for a bus overturned, with steering gear failure, on the dangerous corner at Stonepitts, Binstead in October 1923, although without injury to the sole passenger or crew. Although damaged the bus was back in service the same day!

Inevitably, VBC buses met with other accidents. After an unfortunate fatality in April 1925, when a cyclist descending Institute Hill, Niton lost control and fell under the rear wheels of a bus coming up the hill, there was another overturning five months later, at Shalcombe Cottage, Chessell. The VBC bus, working the midday Freshwater to Newport journey, skidded on the wet road, hit the bank and overturned. Luckily, there were no passengers aboard and the crew, although shaken, were unhurt. The passengers and crew of a bus heading in the opposite direction removed the wheels of the crippled bus so that other traffic could pass. The bus was righted and towed back for repairs by Somerton Garage staff later in the day. In February 1926 a motorcyclist and his pillion passenger, returning from watching a football match in Shanklin, were both killed in a head-on collision with bus DL 3028 (perhaps a jinxed vehicle as it was later to be destroyed in the Somerton depot fire), on the brow of Skew Bridge, Lake. However, in this case, the bus was moving at only 10 mph and driver Frank Sampson was exonerated of all blame by the coroner at the subsequent inquest.

As early as February 1923, Cowes Urban District Council had discussed the policy of VBC to "send a bus off perhaps a quarter of an hour before time and then send another to chase it. Double the number of buses were running up and down Newport Road, wearing out the road and adding to the annoyance of residents". The bus company was to be asked to adhere to the timetable and not to run intermediate buses.

At this time there was little regulation, apart from the issue of licences by the councils to operate within borough boundaries and authorities threatened to withhold the licences if the 'chasing' tactics did not cease. This was all part of VBC strategy and, although Dodson gave assurances when called before the councils, he had no intention of changing his policy against other bus operators running on the same roads. Newport Council were also concerned at overcrowding after 76 people were seen alighting from one vehicle at the Square in Newport; at this time no vehicle had more than 32 seats! Their fears were well founded when, early in 1929, an Enterprise bus overturned at the foot of Union Street, Ryde, with unfortunate fatal consequences.

Dodson had complained to the Ministry of Transport about the councils' withholding of licences but had been told to "make his peace with the council". Ventnor council had hoped he had "come to his senses" but in 1927 he bought four more 'chasers'! The situation was worse than ever and the chairman of a joint Sandown, Shanklin and Ventnor council meeting, called to discuss the problem, stated "The Vectis Buses come along in pairs to squeeze the other buses out". At Ryde, a councillor who had watched a VBC vehicle negotiating the bend towards Binstead at 35 mph, in a race with a rival, said "that was not chasing but racing".

Even prosecution made little difference; a Vectis driver was fined 10/- (50p), or seven days imprisonment, for dangerous driving in overtaking a rival bus on a corner in Mill Hill Road, Cowes. VBC road staff knew that if their bus reached the Square in Newport behind the opposition they would be summoned to Dodson's office and sacked, although usually reinstated soon after. This situation was repeated throughout Britain, so legislation to regulate the bus industry was inevitable for public safety.

Vectis had survived a devastating fire at its Somerton Garage on 2 October 1927. The premises were divided into three sheds, workshops, stores and offices but No 1 Garage, containing nine or ten buses, became a raging inferno in minutes, after the discovery of the fire at 2.15am. Staff efforts to extinguish the blaze were fruitless and, as the phone was located in an office already engulfed by the flames, the Cowes UDC fire brigade had to be summoned by messenger. Thirteen buses were reduced to mangled skeletons but the duty staff courageously saved nine vehicles, which were pushed or driven out onto the main road – including the last one out, "a big vehicle of the older type", which was almost red hot when removed from the furnace. Petrol fumes from the fuel tanks may have been the cause, but ignition of two underground petrol tanks, one of which had an uncovered top, was prevented by the firemen. In that week's newspaper, VBC announced:

> . . . there are still 21 vehicles remaining, sufficient to maintain the service. 10 more buses of the most modern type are now on order, 4 of which are for delivery at the end of the week. The public are assured that no effort will be spared to provide sufficient accommodation on all routes pending the replacement of the lost buses.

IW Associated Buses (a consortium of Boxall's, Casey's, Enterprise and Wight Star) came to the rescue, despite being rivals, while three Dennis single-deckers were hired from the London General Omnibus Co. A dozen vehicles had been garaged at the other Vectis Bus Company depot at Pyle Street.

Throughout the 1920s, Vectis had added routes from Ventnor to Niton, Newport to Niton via Chale and Blackgang, Shanklin to Bonchurch & Ventnor and Freshwater to Alum Bay to its network but had withdrawn from the Newport–Yarmouth–Freshwater road after April 1925 when Brown's Bus Service commenced.

In 1928 the Railway (Road Powers) Act was placed on the statute book, enabling the 'Big Four' railway companies to acquire up to 50% interest in the major bus concerns. The Southern Railway invested heavily in all operators within its territory – from Kent to north Cornwall – making working agreements for bus/rail co-ordination, and one of those was to with be the Vectis Bus Company. Local councils had received letters from the Railway regarding its intention to apply to Parliament for incidental powers to run road motor vehicles. After the frequent clashes between VBC and the councils, they were hardly likely to oppose a takeover.

Southern Vectis ADC 416, No 29 (DL 5577), is pictured here in the wooden-floored Somerton garage. The nearby Vectis Bus Co garage had been destroyed by fire in 1927.
RH Davies/SVOC

Putting the Southern into Vectis:
1929–39, expansion years

Frank and Leonard Dodson anticipated the industry changes and allowed the Southern Railway (SR) to buy into the Vectis Bus Company from March 1929, when Gilbert Szlumper (Asst to the SR Chairman) and Charles de Pury (Asst for the IW Railways) became Board members. The nominal share capital of VBC was £2400, divided into ordinary shares of £1 each and held by the two brothers, who were directors, with a minority shareholding by a third brother, Christopher. After the initial association with the SR, Frank Dodson had to submit a balance sheet and trading/profit and loss accounts for the year ended February 1929, together with schedules for assets and other statistics, as demanded by the accountant at Waterloo. The assets were:-

	Valued at
Freehold garage & land (including Pyle Street, Newport)	£3206
36 Motorbuses & equipment	£22431
Plant & machinery	£1492
Fixtures & fittings	£242
Stocks	£2698

The main garage at Somerton (Cowes) – a roomy building with space for 75 buses and incorporating machine shop, washing shed, with power washing machine, and electric lighting from its own garage plant – was on a twenty-one year lease at £600 per year. Pyle Street Garage, in central Newport, accommodated 20 buses and consisted of a front entrance area, on an eleven year lease at £100 per year, with a rear freehold area, including two cottages (vacated) for a possible extension, bought for a total of £2400. The office at No 19 The Square was rented for £25 per year from brewers Mew, Langton & Co, while there was also a rental paid for a property at Fountain Yard, Cowes. Interestingly, VBC also owned a 150' x 260' parcel of land at Hunnyhill, on the northern fringe of Newport, bought for £550, for a proposed central garage, before Pyle Street was purchased or Somerton was leased.

'Fixtures & Fittings' included the Somerton Garage clock, valued at £4 17s 6d and, at No 19, a settee, typewriter, Boots filing cabinet and Burroughs adding machine (valued at £25)!

Monthly takings were between £2500 and £4500, depending on the season and the company had made profits of £7100 (year ended February 1927), £9865 (1928) and £4865 (1929). The monthly wages bill averaged £1500 and, additionally, there were the salaries of Dodson and his clerk, Miss Griffiths. In addition to the vehicles listed under the assets, six more ADCs were on order for delivery in spring 1929.

Dodson's accountants, CJ Weir & Co of Coleman Street, London, recommended an asking price of £69,510 2s 3d for the Company, based on assets and goodwill taken at a five year basis on the average profit of the previous three years. Alternatively, they suggested the Railway should acquire half of the 2400 ordinary shares at a price of £27,500 and to assure the holders of the other 1200 shares a return of not less than $137\frac{1}{2}$%. Weir's proposed Dodson should enter into an agreement to continue as Manager, so long as the Railway

The first new buses bought by Southern Vectis after the takeover from VBC were Dodson bodied AEC Reliances delivered in 1930. This view of DL 6830 illustrates the dual doorway, ornate lined livery and footsteps giving access to a roof rack for luggage or cycles.

RHD/SVOC

No photographs of Nettlestone garage in Southern Vectis days (1930-37) seem to exist but this view of two steam buses (OS 41 and LN 4850) shows the fairly basic, timber-framed, corrugated iron structure, in the Creeth era. The building still exists in 2004 although no longer operated by Creeth who regained the garage, for their agricultural business, after SVOC opened the Park Road, Ryde garage.

RHD/SVOC

Company should desire, at a fixed salary plus a percentage of the net profits.

On 27 August 1929 The Southern Vectis Omnibus Company Ltd was registered as a private company, with a nominal capital of £150,000 in £1 shares, to acquire the VBC and its 42 buses. Frank and Leonard Dodson, plus the two Southern Railway officers, comprised the directorate. Frank Dodson, the "capable, experienced and enterprising Manager", would continue in the position under the new regime.

Although the SR could now appoint its own directors, Sir Herbert Walker, the dynamic and progressive General Manager at Waterloo, insisted his directors should act without railway bias. Standing Joint Committees were established from 1930 to bring together road and rail officers for discussion on fares policy and aspects of joint facilities to benefit the public and these continued for more than 50 years. SVOC continued much as it had done before – and still was accused of 'chasing' the small operators – but in October 1930 the Road Traffic Act was announced by the Minister of Transport. This legislation reduced the number of licensing authorities from 1300 to 12, under the direction of a full-time Chairman, to be known as an Area Traffic Commissioner. In order to produce a co-ordinated and efficient network of services for the public, each company would have to deposit its schedule of timetables and prove its right to operate, before a licence would be granted.

Even before this far reaching Act become law, four operators on the Island had sold out to SVOC. These were Bullock's 'Surprise Bus Service' (operating between Newport and Ryde via Havenstreet, acquired September 1929), FW Casey, Ryde (running a Newport–Wootton–Ryde service, acquired November 1929), AE Creeth & Sons (Premier), Nettlestone (Ryde–Nettlestone–Seaview, acquired January 1930) together with the leased Seaview garage in a former chapel and the bus services of the IW Tourist Co (Ryde–Seaview–St Helens and Seaview to Shanklin, acquired June 1930) bringing a total of 19 buses into the SVOC fleet. Only the Creeth premises at Nettlestone Green were used by SVOC as a garage. The timber-framed, corrugated iron shed, in a cramped location, had seen much pioneering experimentation over the years for Creeth's had operated, and rebuilt, steam buses, which had run on the Seaview route as late as 1922. Creeth continued to run their elderly fleet, including a 'steamer' converted to petrol, for a couple more months before SVOC drafted in new buses.

Following the 1930 Act, the Traffic Commissioners had an enormous workload and it was June 1931 before the first IW sitting was held at Newport Town Hall, to deal with some 77 applications for stage carriage, excursions or tours. SVOC was represented by a barrister of the Temple, Mr E Gilbert Woodward, in its 24 service applications. It was pointed out that SVOC had provided seven shelters out of surplus revenue and wished to establish more for its patrons but the presence of small, irregular operations delayed the carrying out of the company's wishes, as profits were reduced. He stated that some small operators had been absorbed and others thought they would like to be absorbed – at a price – so they picked out a remunerative route and ran against SVOC at busy times hoping to be bought out. Eventually most operators were granted at least part of the network applied for, although the outcome was not publicised at the hearing.

An unfortunate fatal accident between an SVOC bus and motorcycle in Victoria Road, Cowes, was followed in August 1931 by a strike, involving some 100 conductors and a few drivers, over the dismissal of the crew. By now many of the staff had joined the National Union of Railwaymen but Frank Dodson recruited replacement staff and his handling of the situation did not impress Waterloo, especially as the Ministry of Labour were allegedly asked to intervene.

Dodson was persuaded to take a holiday, which enabled the Railway's Road Transport Liaison Officer to second a Mr Sutton, of Thames Valley Traction, for the purpose of producing a report on Southern Vectis in November 1931. Besides identifying failures in accountancy matters, the report made criticisms of all manner of operating issues, lack of staff uniforms, purchase of materials, ticket inspection and timekeeping. It criticised excessive 'garage mileage', even though it had been reduced from 1628 to 1236 miles per week by the opening of an extension to the Pyle Street garage accommodating six buses. A 'dormy shed' (outstation) was suggested for the Shanklin district and the acquisition of land nearer the centre of Newport was proposed for a building to include works, garages and more spacious offices. This would permit 'The Square' office and Pyle Street garage to be given up.

SVOC Chairman Gilbert Szlumper endorsed the report with the remark that it should be put "into cold store" until the "major question" is settled. What that was can only be speculated upon but it seems the SR was anxious to remove Dodson from his position. In June 1932 it was announced he should retire to be replaced from 1 July by Walter A Budd, previously the Portsmouth district manager for Southdown. At the same time the registered SVOC office would become 19 St James's Square, Newport (instead of Waterloo Station) and Leslie T Duncan would replace AE Usherwood (who had been Waterloo-based) as Secretary. The Dodson Brothers' shareholding actually passed to the Southern Railway, giving it 100% ownership for a couple of months, before the shares were sold to the Tilling & British Automobile Traction group for £27,700.

Mr Budd was a total contrast to his predecessor and, as General Manager, was to steer the company through difficult times in the next thirty-one years. He introduced a timetable book from October 1932 incorporating, for the first time, the service numbers that continued largely unaltered until recent years. Route numbers had been shown in various guide publications and for internal licensing purposes but most vehicles were incapable of carrying them. Monthly leaflets had previously been published by the company to advise timings, while the *IW County Press* had incorporated bus and rail information in a directory, which even included local telephone numbers.

Also in 1932, Mr Budd introduced a new livery – based on the classic apple green and cream, with dark green relief, used by Southdown – to replace the Vectis Bus Company red, blue and white. By the end of the year, he had convinced the Board of the need for uniforms and these were issued to operating staff in April 1933. Even inspectors had not received a uniform which led to some embarrassment when they inspected tickets!

However, one of the most popular moves was the setting up of an Employees Advisory Committee (really a management/ staff meeting) which met for the first time on 13 October 1932 and was attended by George Gawler (driver), Maurice Finlayson (conductor) and Harold Simmonds (engineering staff). The GM referred to such consultative meetings as having been a great success on the mainland and he had confidence it would prove to the mutual advantage of both management and staff. He requested that operating staff showed every attention and courtesy to passengers and gave helpful information. The first item raised was a request from drivers to have the illuminated VECTIS sign above the windscreen on the ADCs altered, as it obstructed vision when making a left-hand turn! George Gawler also asked for bucket seats to be considered for the driving cab, as the seats used were very hard and had no proper back to them! Both items were quickly dealt with by Walter Budd although bus No DL 6155 somehow was missed so was mentioned at a subsequent meeting.

The meetings were to take place once or twice per year to

Several operators were acquired during SVOC's first months of existence, including Creeth at Nettlestone. DL 1614 was a former National Steam bus, rebuilt by Creeth as a double-decker and further rebuilt to a petrol-engined single-decker when their steam service – the last in Britain – finished in 1922. Seen at Nettlestone Green, in front of the Creeth House and waiting room.

RHD coll/SVOC

discuss a variety of issues such as privilege tickets (agreed from January 1933), holidays, hours and rates of pay, working conditions, rota lines, destination blinds, seniority and the conveyance of bicycles or parcels. Conductor Reg Luff, later to become the long standing National Union of Railwaymen secretary, raised the latter question and asked if an additional delivery charge could be made as customers were expecting the parcels to be delivered right to their shops!

At the second meeting (November 1932), the seeds were sown for the formation of the SVOC Sports and Social Club which, supported by the management, has continued to prosper to this day. One staff request – equal pay for drivers and conductors, raised by Conductor Hutchings in October 1933 – met with a firm refusal from Mr Budd, who was far from satisfied with the way some conductors carried out their duties. He had seen some sitting on the back seat instead of paying attention and being on the look out for intending passengers.

The effects of the recession were still being felt in 1932 and Mr Budd had to lay off 48 road staff at the end of that season. This situation was to be reversed within a few years as the company looked to those unemployed in the South Wales 'Special Area', as well as students on vacation from the Welsh universities, for training as conductors to cope with the heavy summer traffic. Locally, SVOC (and other operators) provided buses free of charge to convey children of the unemployed in Cowes and East Cowes for their annual treat in June 1933.

In January 1933, SVOC had commenced negotiations with the Royal IW Agricultural Society for land adjoining their Nine Acres Showground as a site for a new garage, works and head office. Site preparation began in mid-August providing valuable work for the Island during that winter. Designed by architect Frank Chiverton, of Newport, the new building was to have a floor space of 183' x 154' and garage accommodation for 100 vehicles with space for an extension. The front facade was of Monks Park stone and red brick with roofing of brindled tiles, while the interior of the offices (and Staff & Social Clubroom) was of polished teak.

The depot was originally known as Westfield, after the the former dairy on land it replaced, but later became Nelson Road after the thoroughfare on the Trafalgar housing estate, as it was then called. Lord Mottistone opened the new building on 20 June 1934 and at the celebration luncheon (chicken and ham salad followed by strawberry savarin) toasts were proposed by the Chairman, Gilbert Szlumper and director, Sidney Garcke. The new depot replaced both Somerton and Pyle Street, but the latter remained in company ownership until about 1948 (although requisitioned, and later bombed, during the war).

New AEC Reliance buses had been introduced by SVOC in 1930–31, followed by an AEC Regal (displayed at the Commercial Motor Show and known as 'The Silver Ghost') in 1932. Two small batches of Tilling Stevens (a type favoured by Southdown) arrived in 1932–33, followed by an influx of Dennis vehicles (Lancets, Aces and Lances, all built at Guildford) in 1934–36. This had allowed the last of the old VBC Daimlers to be withdrawn in 1933 and even the ADCs of 1928 came off the road in 1934, by which time no bus was older than five years.

More small operators had sold out to SVOC – Hilton Dyer's Central Bus Service from Godshill in June 1932 (Newport to Shanklin route); Basil Bolwell's Regel of Lake (Shanklin—Wroxall–Ventnor) and Hayles' Supreme, Ryde (Newport–Havenstreet–Haylands–Ryde), both in July 1933; AE King, Carisbrooke (three Newport local routes) from March 1934 and AL Morris, Ventnor (Ventnor Local Service) from May 1934. Only two buses (both from Supreme) were actually operated by SVOC.

Reg Augustus, who had started with VBC, was appointed in 1932 to the role of Engineer, a position which he would occupy for thirty years, until retirement in 1962 – the longest serving officer in the company's history. George Taylor, who had been Chief Clerk and then Traffic Superintendent from 1932, departed in 1934 and was replaced by strict disciplinarian Roger Wakeling, who had previously been with London Transport. He took up the appointment as Traffic Manager in 1935 and became a familiar sight observing bus departures from The Square, while mounted on his horse.

In 1933 work was progressing on the creation of a Ventnor to Freshwater Bay Marine Drive and, as part of this, a new inland Niton to Blackgang road was opened. This replaced the old road below the cliff at Big Rock, which had been swept away by a huge fall in 1928 – the loss of three route miles in an afternoon. The new road allowed service 10 (Newport to Ventnor) to revert to its former route, although the diversion that had been used – between Chale Green and Niton – retained a skeleton service. Although the Chale to Freshwater Bay section of the Military Road was still being constructed, SVOC made application at the Traffic Commissioners' sitting in July 1933 for a coastal route from Ryde to Alum Bay, while Brown's Bus Service applied for an Alum Bay to Ventnor service along the same road but the Chairman refused to devote time to the applications as the road was not ready.

The April 1934 sitting dealt again with the SVOC application for the Ryde to Alum Bay service (calling at Ryde Airport to connect with air services from Portsmouth, Southampton or Croydon), even though the section beyond Brook Chine on the Military Road was incomplete, as the route around Compton Farm was being diverted further inland because of the unstable sandstone cliffs. Despite 28 objections and the fact that part of the Military Road was only nine feet wide, the 'Coastal Service' application was granted but small 20-seater buses were specified. After the Compton to Freshwater Bay section of the road was completed, IWCC Chairman Sir Godfrey Baring performed the opening ceremony in March 1936. In that season's timetable the service was able to run via Compton rather than inland via Tapnell. The service, precursor of the present day *Explorer*, was numbered 26 and used new Dennis Aces, nicknamed 'Pigs' because of their tapered, snout-like bonnets. Throughout fare was 3/9 (19p) single, 6/6 (32½p) return.

Until 1935 only single-deckers had been operated by

Built in 1933, the Westfield garage and offices at Nelson Road, Newport, were the height of modernity when opened. The upper storey originally housed the staff canteen but few major alterations have been carried out since this 1950s view.

RHD/SVOC

Dennis Lancet No 508 (DL 9008), bound for Bembridge on service 8, stops to set down at the Weston Hut on St John's Hill, Ryde. The building immediately to the right of the bus still survives as the Trade-on furniture store but the road has been widened. After being on a bus route for more than seventy years, this road is now served by only one regular journey per day.

RHD/SVOC

White cap covers were worn from May until the end of September so this pre-war view of Lancet DL 9703 waiting to leave The Square for Alum Bay, with three members of the road staff, was taken on a summer's day.

RHD/SVOC

The Island's roads are often closed to remedy slippage or erosion because they are lightly constructed on clay. In this view near The Mirables in the Undercliff, passengers on the Daimler bus have reached 'the point of obstruction' and must walk beyond towards Niton.

RHD/SVOC

The acquisition of Walkden's Bus Service of Sandown in 1936 introduced the Morris make to the SVOC fleet. DL 7569, built in 1931, was one of a pair of Strachan-bodied Viceroys. Seating 24, it became fleet number 300 and lasted until 1938. It is seen in Walkden livery, thought to be photographed adjacent to Morton Common Railway Bridge which had then recently been converted to double track.

RHD/SVOC

SVOC but at the November Traffic Commissioners' hearing, Traffic Manager Roger Wakeling presented a case for double-deck operation. He stated there was a need to avoid duplication as the demands of the public still grew. The peak season was absurdly short, although it had been extended during that summer by the Fleet Review, but with a stable Government and increasing trade the Island could see a future large increase in holiday-makers. SVOC wished to introduce double-deckers to the Ryde to Cowes & Gurnard and Ryde to East Cowes routes but the County Surveyor considered sections of road at the top of Hunnyhill, Quarr Hill, Lushington Shute, Fairlee Road and Whippingham as unsafe for the operation. Mr Wakeling called Arthur Creeth to give evidence that he had safely run a double-decker carrying 60 people back in 1913. The application was allowed and six 56-seaters were ordered. The first two were delivered by towboat to Yarmouth in May 1936 and the first journey, driven by the Traffic Manager, was an evening peak run from Newport to Gurnard.

Traditional coloured tickets for each value, validated through a Bell Punch machine, had been in use since VBC started operating but, when the coastal service 26 was introduced as a one-man operation in 1934, a small number of TIM ticket machines were introduced and fixed to a plate on the Dennis Aces. Such machines were used by Southdown so Walter Budd was no doubt keen to introduce them to the island. A flimsy paper roll was inserted into the machine, the dial set for the appropriate fare and stage and the handle rotated to issue an ink-printed ticket. The Bell Punch system was replaced by Automaticket machines (tickets for which were also produced by the Bell Punch firm) in 1937/8. Use of these machines involved the journey details being written by the conductor directly onto the ticket held in the machine before one copy was actually issued to the passenger. As time went by, the machines frequently jammed up necessitating the use of emergency tickets which, to this day, are in the same format as the Automaticket issues. The machines were in use until replaced by Setrights in 1951.

The acquisition policy continued with several of the larger independent operators now selling out to Southern Vectis. Next was Brown's Bus Service which had run since April 1925 from Carisbrooke (where the registered address was at Clifton House and the garage nearby behind the church). After acquiring Hilton Hall's West Wight Bus Service in 1930 they also had a garage in Princes Road, Freshwater. This property, 12 buses and 11 of the 14 staff were taken over from 1 March 1935, together with five routes (numbered 21–25 in the SVOC network) following an SVOC application in December 1934, through the Traffic Commissioners, to run them. These were basically variations on the Newport–Yarmouth–Freshwater route, either via Newbridge or Shalfleet, plus a summer only route from Totland to Alum Bay. In an official newspaper announcement, Capt JS Brown expressed his sincere appreciation of the generous support afforded them in the last ten years; Brown's had never sustained an accident involving serious injury to a passenger in that time.

A year later (March 1936), Walkden's Bus Service at Sandown with eight maroon and cream liveried buses and routes from Shanklin to Brading & Ryde and Sandown to Bembridge sold out. Their garage at the corner of Broadway and Avenue Road (in use since about 1929) remained operational for four vehicles from the takeover until about June 1937, when they were moved to Eames' premises at Shanklin. Their two most modern vehicles, both 26 seater Leyland Cubs, proved useful sized vehicles for SVOC and survived in the fleet until 1950. Walkden's had ordered two Leyland Tigers for the 1936 season but cancelled the order because of the takeover.

In 1937 two operators succumbed; first was CAG Coffen, who ran the Pioneer service at Ryde, acquired from Hunter six years earlier. In that time, Mr Coffen had operated 350,000 miles without any accident involving serious injury, carrying nearly two million passengers on the town services to Elmfield and Haylands (Butts Road), plus a summer only, fine weather, route to Mersley Down (Kiosk). The town services became SVOC routes 20 and 30 (with the 20 receiving a short-lived extension to Ryde Airport) and the Downs service was incorporated into a revised 27 (Ryde to Alum Bay via The Downs, Newport and Calbourne).

In May, SVOC agreed to buy the Shanklin-based coach operation of HG (George) Eames and, with the Traffic Commissioners' approval, 12 coaches in the operator's brown/buff livery, excursions and tours from Shanklin and Brighstone Holiday Camp and an express service to that camp from Ryde were acquired from 1 July 1937. Also included were offices at Clarendon Road, 93 High Street and 46 Atherley Road and a coach house fronting Collingwood Road. There was also extra land fronting Carter Avenue which was earmarked for a future extension. Mr Eames continued as local manager and the 12 coaches still continued in their former livery with the Eames fleetname for several years.

In June 1938 the IW Tourist Co, operating a dozen grey-liveried coaches, mostly of Dennis manufacture, on excursions from Ryde and Shanklin, came to a similar arrangement with SVOC. The Tourist (whose slogan was 'For the Best and the Surest, book with the Tourist') had its main garage in the former malt house at Benett Street, Ryde (with an adjacent garage). There was also a booking office in Shanklin at 8 Regent Street (with a small garage). Frank Plater, who in thirteen years on the island had taken a prominent role in local

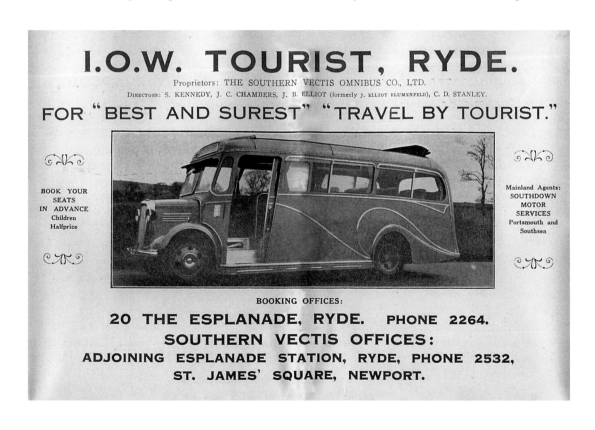

Although a handful of charabancs had been taken over with the operator purchases of the early 1930s, the acquisition of HG Eames of Shanklin in July 1937 was the first entry of SVOC into coaching. A dozen coaches and an Armstrong Siddeley limousine were purchased. Most were built on Dennis chassis, including No 11 (DL 9719), new for the 1935 season and seen at the Duple Coachworks, Hendon, before delivery. The Eames name, brown and cream livery and rising sun motif were retained for a while before Southern Vectis fleet names were used.

A Norris/SVOC

affairs, ran the business from No 20 The Esplanade, Ryde, which was now to be leased by SVOC as an enquiry office and conductors' paying-in room but remaining in the ownership of the Plater family.

In the short term the Tourist name was retained on vehicles and publicity. The office at 8 Regent Street, Shanklin, was also retained by SVOC, but the garage premises in Ryde were not required, as SVOC had just opened its new depot in Park Road.

The final prewar acquisition was the Carisbrooke business of Colson's, with four small capacity buses and routes out of Newport to Carisbrooke and Gunville or Carisbrooke Castle. The purchase was made in March 1939 and included the transfer of three drivers. The business had started in 1920 and Messrs FA & A Colson opened the route to Carisbrooke in 1921.

The former Creeth garage at Nettlestone had become impossibly congested as the dimensions of vehicles increased and in May 1937 a site in Park Road, Ryde, opposite the Gas Works, was earmarked for a 30 vehicle garage and accommodation block, beneath the approach to the railway bridge. The Southern Railway owned the site, which had been occupied by an orchard and old cottage, and it was to remain a leasehold property for over fifty years. The new Ryde depot was opened without ceremony in March 1938 and the Creeth premises at Nettlestone reverted to the family for the continuation of their engineering business. Attention was then turned to Shanklin where a garage, in similar style, to accommodate 50 vehicles was constructed on the land acquired from Eames. The new Shanklin depot, adjacent to the coach house and approached from Carter Avenue, was opened in May 1939.

Since 1929, Sandown-Shanklin UDC had constantly complained about the presence of buses in Clarendon Road and had eventually directed that spare vehicles be moved to St Paul's Avenue (which was also suggested as the departure point for Sandown services). Mr Eames had offered a piece of his land for use as a bus station but the price was too high for the Council. In January 1939 Mr Budd informed the Council that he would experiment to keep spare buses away from Clarendon Road but it was to be many years before a bus station was built.

Publicity for the company was always endorsed "in association with the Southern Railway" and a further liaison occurred in August 1938 when the SR Advertising Department became contractors to the bus company for the "exclusive privilege of affixing advertisements on eight double-deck and 32 single-deck vehicles (two sides, roof spaces, side windows (for double sided window bills), bulkhead spaces and step risers), as well as in all waiting rooms and company-owned shelters, except those solely connected with the tours of Eames and IW Tourist". Darby's Advertising Agency had been responsible for adverts from Vectis Bus Company days (at a rate of £32 per bus per year at the time of the takeover), when painted boards were bolted to the cove panels of the roof on Daimlers and ADCs.

SVOC often had to provide rail replacement buses, particularly over the Newport–Sandown line which ran parallel with the rivers Medina and Eastern Yar and was subject to frequent flooding. Ryde Tunnel was also prone to serious floods, so necessitated bus replacement. One of the worst derailments involved the early morning mail train to Freshwater at Great Park Bridge in January 1939, resulting in Newport—Freshwater replacement buses for several days.

As part of the Tilling & BAT group, SVOC was now encouraged to purchase the standardised Bristol chassis and Eastern Coach Works bodywork specified in its policies. All new buses from 1937, for fleet expansion and renewal, were of this combination – the policy to continue for forty-five years. There were a few exceptions to this rule – two Dennis Falcons in 1939, when small capacity buses were needed and, for the same reason, three Bedford WTB/Duple coaches. The Bedford association – fairly unusual in a Tilling company – continued from 1947 until 1980, as lightweight coaches were perfectly adequate for local tour work confined to the Island.

Southern Vectis had changed dramatically in its first ten years of existence. The fleet had increased from 42 to 112 and the number of passengers had risen from 2¼ to 6½ million. In his way, Frank Dodson had achieved much but his successor as General Manager, Walter Budd, had become a well-respected figurehead and who was about to face six dramatic years ahead.

(continued on page 33)

This very early (1936) colour view depicts a Margham bodied Morris TX taken over from R Walkden Ltd, Sandown. DL 6302 was a 20 seater and had just received a repaint at Nelson Road into apple green and cream but did not survive long enough to receive a fleet number. It was sold to a farmer at Wroxall.

RHD/SVOC

St James's Square, Newport, was always the hub of the Southern Vectis network before the bus station was opened. Bedford OB No 219 and 'LB' No 731 are amongst the vehicles visible in this 1960 view, looking north towards Weeks' Restaurant, which was a popular meeting place for lunch or afternoon tea.

SVOC

Every year until about ten years ago, a procession of SVOC open-toppers would cross to the mainland en route to London for charter to various firms as transport to The Derby at Epsom Downs. The famous duo of K types, Nos 702 (CDL 899) & 703 (DDL 50), reach the end of Newport High Street at the start of their long journey, passing buildings east of County Hall, including the Prince Regent public house, that have long disappeared.

J Reynolds/SVOC

Lightweight Bedfords were ideal for Island tours and consequently accumulated only limited mileage. SB8 No 247 (VDL 855), in Tilling cream/green, stands outside the Pier Gates at Ryde.

K Amos/Author's collection

Coachmen had their personal vehicle which was kept immaculate at all times. Ted Hodges, who had the misfortune to be involved in two overturning accidents on LB type double-deckers, neither of which was his fault, was allocated Bedford SB No 242. Ted was a great character who enjoyed more than 20 years retirement tending his large garden at Wootton and regularly visiting Newport canteen to keep in touch with company news.

RHD/SVOC

SVOC was an early purchaser of the Bristol LHS type but was unusual in having their batch of four buses supplied in 1969 bodied by Marshall of Cambridge. This maker's view of No 835 (NDL 771G) shows the bus prior to delivery. After sale in 1981, Nos 834 and 835 worked for Rev Ian Paisley's Martyrs Memorial Church in Belfast but were eventually scrapped by Gerry Beattie at Hillsborough, Co Down.

SVOC

THE
SOUTHERN
VECTIS

OMNIBUS COMPANY LIMITED

(IN ASSOCIATION WITH ~~Southern Railway~~

BRITISH RAILWAYS

TIMETABLE

27th Sept., 1948—1st May, 1949

3ᵈ

From 1946 the timetables of Tilling Group companies featured a painting of a bus, in a pictorial setting, by a retained artist. Southern Vectis used this view of Bristol L5G DDL 53 against a backdrop of Shanklin Old Village (left) and Godshill church (right) until the winter 1949/50 edition.

The first overall livery for the Company was a striking design for Red Funnel's Cowes-Southampton shipping services. 'LA' No 567 (VDL 844) was positioned on The Parade at Cowes for this official view in March 1974 but was repainted just over a year later.

Red Funnel/SVOC

The NBC leaf green livery could appear scruffy and faded after a while, especially if it had been touched up after accident repairs. Bristol FLF Lodekka 70 seater No 605 (BDL 581B) descends Staplers Road, Newport, on the busy 1A Ryde–Cowes 'rounders' in April 1982. St Paul's Church is in the background.

Author

The Bristol LH was a rugged vehicle intended to have a short life span under NBC policy. Number 829 (PDL 491H), seen at Sandown Library in 1978, did not survive the 1981 fleet reduction but still operates today as a well-maintained mobile home.

Author

The last rear entrance Lodekka to be delivered was withdrawn from the bus fleet early to become a driver trainer (No TB 1, ex No 573, YDL 318). As such it was painted in the yellow livery chosen by NBC for such vehicles. It is parked on the Newport Bus Station lay-by.

D Strange

By the mid 1970s the National all-white coach livery had made its appearance on the Island, although some vehicles retained the Fountain fleetname and livery. Number 426 (MDL 599G), the last of the six Bedford VAM coaches bought new in 1968, is seen negotiating the narrow, winding road amidst the thatched cottages of Shanklin Old Village.

SVOC

The last Bedford coaches bought new were three YMTs with Willowbrook bodies delivered in 1980. Number 128 (EDL 269V) arrived in the distinctive orange and cream with Fountain Coaches fleetnames although the other two were in NBC white. Seen at the Island's most northerly location, Egypt Point, near Cowes, it was sold after ten years, at auction. The bodies were considered inferior to Plaxton products.

SVOC

23

After use by the Badger Vectis operation at Bournemouth, two Bristol REs were sold locally to Seaview Services. The oldest, former No 862 (PDL 493H) is seen with No 863 (TDL 563K), then still in use with Southern Vectis, at the shared Seafield Garage in Sandown.

Author

As it had been refloored, No 628 (SDL 638J) was chosen to represent its type in the 'Vintage Fleet' rather than being despatched to Southampton to inaugurate Solent Blue Line operation. It is seen at Steephill Court Road, St Lawrence, on a section of route that can no longer be served by full size vehicles following the cliff fall.

Author

Although it is hoped to deal with Solent Blue Line more fully in a future volume, the mainland venture remains an integral part of Southern Vectis plc and initially all vehicles were licensed to SVOC. The 1990 intake of Leyland-bodied Olympians (Nos 728/9/31-4) all went to SBL and are seen being accepted by Peter Shelley (Commercial Director) and Stuart Linn (SBL MD at that time) at Barton Park, Eastleigh. The Workington factory that produced them subsequently closed down.

SVOC

The company achieved national publicity with its bright pink 'punishment' minibus for misbehaving school children but the paint was actually leftover from an overall advert for Blackgang Chine applied to two vehicles. Bristol VR No 679 (FDL 679V) is seen on an enthusiasts tour in Quay Street, Newport, just before transfer to Solent Blue Line in 1998.

Author

Some of the Bristol VR fleet survived long enough to carry the parchment/holly green livery, such as No 683 (DPX 683W, re reg. 934 BDL) deputising for the usual open-topper on service 43 at Shanklin Esplanade in July 2001. This area of sea front, including the cliff lift, sustained bombing in World War II. Number 683 was converted to open-top in the subsequent winter and remains in seasonal use.

Author

The early Olympians that had not been transferred to Solent Blue Line all underwent mid-life interior refurbishment which included soft trim and coach-style seating. Number 692 (WDL 692Y) was painted in parchment/holly green latterly and is seen at Sandown library, on an *Explorer* duty, during October 2001. This vehicle had carried London-style advertisement panels, the position still being visible although the edging had been removed.

P Savage

Few liveries had the impact of the Big Dipper purple and lime green 'Battenburg Cake' style application. Number 506 (UFX 858S), a convertible VR in winter guise, which later passed to Westbrook Travel, is seen at Freshwater Bay.

P Savage

Popular former Shanklin depot superintendent George Farrow (centre) performed a variety of duties for the company, including managing Badger Vectis, before retirement. Amongst his farewell gifts was a painting of Shanklin Garage in its heyday, presented at Ryde Bus Station by his colleagues, behind Bristol LHS No 202 in a special variation of the emerald green livery.

Author

One K-reg and two M-reg Olympians received the red livery, which carries yellow 'Route Rouge' branding, after the initial repaints. Number 748 (M748 HDL), working service 2, prepares to stop outside the Hollies Tea Garden in the tourist mecca of Godshill.

D Evans/SVOC

The third generation of minibuses were more spacious, 23 seat Iveco 59.12s purchased in 1996/7. Eight were taken into the fleet and have accumulated high mileages in all day service so are scheduled for replacement in 2005. Number 246 (P246 VDL) ascends from Blackgang Chine, passing the St Catherine's Quay museum complex. From 2001 fares could be paid either in sterling or with Euro notes. As evidenced by No 246 most vehicles carry blue vinyls, with yellow lettering, promoting this facility.

Author

Southern Vectis Coaches was forced to make economies by reducing its fleet in line with the changing market but also bought three good quality secondhand vehicles in 1997/9. These Volvo B10Ms had Plaxton 'Excalibur' coachwork and wore the last version of the white livery with distinctive vinyls. Number 904 (WDL 748, ex N668 VJB), ex Horseman of Reading, is posed at Yarmouth Bus Station. It still resides on the Island but is owned by Kardan Travel who now undertake franchised coaching for Southern Vectis.

SVOC

Deliveries in 1998 were eight more Volvo Olympians with Northern Counties bodywork but specifically to work the *Island Explorer* – round the Island in just under four hours. These are still in front line service and No 755 (R755 GDL) is seen in Brighstone Village passing the 12th century church of St Mary. The livery has since been simplified to just the darker shade of blue and fewer vinyls.

D Evans/SVOC

The company regularly attends the annual Isle of Wight Agricultural Show at Northwood. In 1998, when Volvo Olympian No 754 (R754 GDL) was almost new and displayed the full set of *Explorer* vinyls preventing the application of adverts, Southern Vectis jointly sponsored bringing *Thrust*, the world land speed record car, to the show. Note the tree protection bar on No 754, designed to prevent damage to the front pillar; most bars, though, were quickly ripped off by offending foliage.

SVOC

Seven Volvo B7TLs arrived in 2002 and carried *Explorer* vinyls. Number 105 (HW52 EPU) is actually on a return Tesco working to Ventnor and has just set down at 'Miss Black's', a quaintly-named request stop in Brading named after a long deceased teacher of pianoforte who lived nearby. These Volvos are the largest double-deckers ever operated and have sustained hefty costs for replacement glass because of the overhanging trees on many rural roads.

Author

Solent Blue Line received the new vehicle allocation in 1991 but as Leyland then ceased building bodies the company turned to Northern Counties of Wigan for the 1993 batch of nine buses, Nos 735–43 (K735–43 ODL). These have been undergoing a mid-life refurbishment although two, Nos 742 and 743, have been converted to open top for the Alum Bay service. Number 743 is seen here arriving at the Needles Old Battery terminus on 1st April 2004, during its first week in service as an open-top.

P Savage

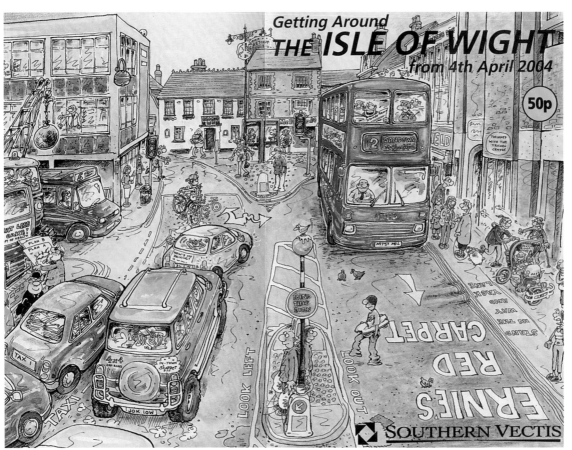

Since 1989 the cover of the summer timetable, has featured humourous artwork by *IW County Press* cartoonist Besley. The 2004 edition features Volvo Olympian No 751 on the 'red carpet', the contra-flow bus lane which runs through St James Square and South Street. This removed bus services from Newport High Street and was promoted by Cllr Ernie Fox, holder of the Council transport portfolio, hence 'Ernie's Red Carpet'.

SVOC

Additional secondhand purchases of midibuses were made from Stagecoach Devon in 2001. Iveco K724 UTT, seen in the Ryde Depot paintshop, swopped its Stagecoach stripes for the Oxford blue livery before entering service as SVOC No 257.

SVOC

Grey clouds and blue skies 1939–51
(World War II and the post-war boom)

Fine weather meant a busy August 1939 for the Island but everyone knew that the European situation was heading towards war. Indeed an ARP exercise had been held in the East Wight in the Spring.

As Newport carnival drew to a close so the first troop movement demand was placed before the company for 250 men to be conveyed, with their kit, to anti-aircraft sites all over the Island, after arrival at Ryde Pier Head at midnight. In a five hour operation, office staff drove the buses and made use of the Ryde Pier tram.

Holiday makers returned home immediately but on 1 and 2 September, a total of nearly 10,000 school children should have been evacuated to the Island as it was regarded by the Government as a 'safe' area at that time. Only just over half that total actually arrived from the mainland. They were mostly conveyed to their new homes by train from Ryde Pier Head, but there was still work for SVOC conveying those for locations distant from railway stations. Considering the Island was so close to potential bomb target areas of Portsmouth and Southampton, the Government attitude was incredible, for as they thought it 'safe' they did not even consider the provision of air-raid shelters necessary at first. As events were to prove over the next six years, the Isle of Wight was a highly vulnerable target with its Cowes shipyard complex and radar station high on St Boniface Down above Ventnor. In the $4^1/_2$ year period of bombing, 214 of the population were killed and 274 seriously injured with some 11,000 buildings being destroyed or damaged, including two SVOC properties, in some 125 attacks (out of some 1600 air-raid alerts).

At the declaration of War (3 September), SVOC employed almost 400 but although bus driving was a reserved profession about 100 members of staff, including many conductors, joined the forces for the duration of the War. The conductors called up were soon replaced by the recruitment of conductresses who performed their duties well on overcrowded buses and in blackout conditions. Passenger behaviour was often criticised but the 'clippies' won praise for their ability to deal with the crowds.

Several conductresses were undergoing training as drivers towards the end of the war but were not, in the event, required as hostilities came to an end, permitting drivers to return to their positions. It was several years into the war before conductresses were supplied with a full uniform but then received a jacket and skirt or trousers. They were also issued with torches to illuminate their fare-tables and to differentiate the coins, but there was often difficulty in obtaining batteries! From 1943, the conductresses were represented on the staff committee by one of their number, Miss AE Wales, while others followed. At the end of the war, as the male staff returned, platform staff were to be stood off by juniority but many of the ladies were to remain as SVOC employees for many years.

Indeed the staff shortage was such that it would be five years before retirement age needed to be enforced amongst road staff.

The first wartime timetable (from 7 September 1939) ruthlessly curtailed the service with the withdrawal of through Ryde to East Cowes journeys (except for workers timings), no service between Bembridge and Sandown (service 29) or from Newport to Gurnard or via Brighstone to the West Wight. Shanklin–Bonchurch–Ventnor and Newport–Merstone–Ventnor (largely duplicated by the railway) were also taken off. Whiteley Bank and Binfield Corner, both rural locations, became important connectional points.

By March, 1940, when the next timetable was published, the situation had been slightly relaxed with some reinstatement on most of the withdrawn routes. For SVOC, priorities had changed and their main task was the conveyance of workers to and from the factories and shipyards at Cowes and East Cowes – for example a convoy of 13 buses left Ryde at 7.10 each morning for East Cowes. At the height of the war, J Samuel White, one of the two major shipyards, alone employed 4300 (the other builder was Saunders-Roe, while there were a number of smaller firms at Cowes). Workers travelling after 9pm had to be in possession of passes issued by the Regional Transport Commissioners as the only others permitted to use the late buses were the military. Such documents were not fully abolished until 1946.

The other main flow of passengers was the forces, either travelling to Newport for evening entertainment during their off duty time or for official troop movements, for which special vehicles would be procured. By June 1943 there were 17,000 men garrisoned on the Island and this number increased further with the build up to D-Day in 1944. Hotels, large houses and holiday establishments were taken over by the military including Puckpool Holiday Camp, which became HMS *Medina* and housed the Fleet Air Arm.

Many soldiers were stationed in the West Wight and it was customary for the two Bristol K5G 56-seat double-deckers CDL 899 and DDL 50 to work the last Freshwater journey out of Newport on service 12, loaded with servicemen egging the drivers on to 'race' along the Forest Road.

The Island had become a prohibited area so no one could visit unless they had official business, just as it was difficult for residents to travel to the mainland. This remained the situation until the War Office removed the movement restriction in August 1944, but certain beaches still remained closed and no unauthorised photography allowed.

At the start of war total blackout was immediately introduced and white lines painted in the centre of main roads. By January 1940, all vehicles had to have headlamp masks, permitting only a meagre beam of light and a 20 mph speed limit enforced during blackout in built up areas. All buses had

Few photographs could be taken in wartime but this close up of a Dennis Lance's cab shows the shabby state of the well used fleet. After war service, these buses were the source of staff complaint. Note the mudguard is painted white to assist visibility in darkened streets under the blackout, while the livery is a drab grey. *SVOC*

white paint applied to the front mudguards and the lower rear panels to assist visibility but they had to operate using side and rear lights only in blackout conditions. This was the 'Phoney War', when the main fear was a gas attack, but the Dunkirk evacuation in June 1940 changed everything. School children evacuees had been despatched back to the mainland and the 6th Black Watch arrived on the Island requiring transport. A contingent of drivers, under Fred Stephens, was seconded and remained with the batallion on 24-hour call wherever they were required. The drivers were actually paid by the Army rather than Vectis and had to sleep on the cushions in their bus. They dashed home for a bath and a change of clothing when there was an opportunity and spent much of the time at Fishbourne where the battalion was billeted.

The Island received regular attention from enemy aircraft from June and the invasion of the Channel Islands at the end of that month put the Garden Isle in the front line as the Battle of

Britain began. There was a real risk of invasion and as Hitler plotted 'Operation Sealion' through that summer he envisaged one of the invading enemy forces coming ashore in Sandown Bay. The SVOC head office switchboard at Nelson Road was constantly manned and the telephonists were amongst those with knowledge of the password if an invasion by the enemy had occurred. Vehicles would then have been summoned – on one of the occasions they were called for, they arrived at the rendezvous before the troops!

The Ventnor radar station was an obvious early target for the Luftwaffe but all Island towns received attention in the bombing, often from aircraft returning from mainland air raids. Although bus drivers made the decision whether to keep going or not if there was an air raid, buses frequently had to stop, allowing passengers to disembark and take cover in the nearest shelter or in roadside undergrowth. The Island railway service were often interrupted by bombing, or the presence of unexploded bombs, and Southern Vectis was called upon to provide the replacement service.

The Dunkirk retreat had resulted in the abandonment of numerous military vehicles and to meet the shortage operators were to have buses and coaches requisitioned. In the spring/early summer of 1941, SVOC lost 36 vehicles (out of a fleet of 116) in this way. The men from the Ministry of Transport visited most operators at this time and took away their best vehicles. In the company's case they lost their six AEC Regal luxury coaches as well as 12 Dennis Lancet buses, six small capacity Dennis Aces, the entire batch of six Tilling-Stevens buses, three elderly AEC Reliances and the AEC Regal 'Silver Ghost' bus. After a couple of years use by the War Dept, they became surplus to requirements and, in a letter to Tilling Headquarters at Crewe House in December 1944, SVOC stated they were not looking for the oldest, nonstandard vehicles to be returned, although if the post-war vehicle shortage had been anticipated the attitude might have been different.

By this time, six 5xx series Lancet buses had returned, in such a decrepit condition they had to be rebodied, under special dispensation, at the Irthlingborough (Northants) temporary factory of Eastern Coach works, who had moved away from vulnerable Lowestoft. The austerity bus bodies, of steel panels rather than aluminium and on framework of unseasoned timber, lasted eight or nine years until the vehicles were retired by SVOC. Three more Lancets were located and returned, but one of these never ran again. The chassis was hung on the wall of the Shanklin coach house in case it was required for spares. This was probably the vehicle located in a derelict state in the depths of the New Forest. Only one AEC Regal coach was returned; three were never found while the other two had been sold off elsewhere (including one, after war service in Ulster, to the Northern Ireland Road Transport Board).

An agreement had been made in May 1939, between the Tilling member companies, that inter-company hiring would take place at a moment's notice to cover for any extensive wartime vehicle loss. The company was thus fortunate to receive four old Leylands on hire from Wilts & Dorset, as well

Although most of the requisitioned Dennis Lancets were returned in the latter years of the War, most had seen such hard usage that they needed rebodying, which had to be specially authorised at this difficult time. ECW built the utility specification 35 seat bodies such as that on No 501 (DL 9001), seen at Sandown (Hotel) terminus in July 1949, at their Irthingborough Works in 1944, as their main plant at Lowestoft had become too vulnerable.
AB Cross/B Stewart colln

as six AEC coaches from Thomas Tilling Ltd, London.

In March 1943 it was announced that SVOC was to have nine producer gas buses – part of a programme by the Tilling group to convert a total of 651 and save two million gallons of fuel per year. Early in the war, the two Bristol J type saloons (800/1) had been converted with gas producer units being located in the rear luggage locker, necessitating the removal of the back seats, but they were not too successful and converted back. Four Regals (three Tilling loans and the other SVOC owned but new to Tilling) were fitted with trailers to convey the fireproof chamber for the burning of anthracite. Designed by Tilling chairman Sir Frederick Heaton, the system was not really a success and the remaining five conversions did not take place. The buses operated from Shanklin Garage on service 6 (Newport–Shanklin–Ryde) but they would crawl uphill and the experiment lasted little over a year. The trailers were sold off to farmers at Newport market in 1944–45.

The allocation of four Bristol K type double-deckers in 1944–45 assisted the Company in its shortage but the offer by the Traffic Commissioners at Reading of six Guy Arabs was politely declined by Walter Budd as they would have been nonstandard!

As a precaution against loss of important company records in bombing, the Tilling Group arranged for all such documents of its member companies to be photographed with specialist equipment and dispersed away from the originals. The Southern Vectis document negatives still survive today in the head office!

Southern Vectis had two of its properties requisitioned – the disused Pyle Street, Newport, garage and an enquiry/booking office at 8 Regent Street, Shanklin, which was taken over by Scott Jackson as a factory engaged on Government work. The Osborne Steps (Shanklin) coach booking office was also in the midst of area largely under military jurisdiction. Southern Vectis had taken the precaution of renting Padmore House, Whippingham, which would have become the head office in the event of bombing damage to Nelson Road. However, Padmore House was quite near to the Saunders-Roe Folly Works, which was producing 40% of the country's plywood requirement for the aircraft industry and, in fact, was damaged by bombing in May 1943, so could have been vulnerable.

Protection for the SVOC Nelson Road depot and offices came from the Home Guard and No 4 Platoon of the Newport Home Guard was formed almost entirely of SVOC staff, both traffic and engineering, who drove buses by day and at night were fire-watching (for incendiaries were very common and from 1941 buses carried bags of sand to extinguish these), on ARP or first-aid duties. This platoon won trophies for their shooting prowess. Like the rest of the country's Home Guard, they were stood down by Government edict in November 1944 although they were still liable to recall if necessary.

The persistent bombing raids continued for nearly four years – with everything from high explosive to V1 Doodle-bugs (unmanned flying bombs) being directed at the Island but no buses were lost and vehicle damage was limited to strafing by machine gun fire or blast effect. By far the worst attack of the war was the specific attack on 4/5 May 1942 on the shipyards and factories of Cowes, East Cowes and the surrounding area, including Somerton Aerodrome and Folly Works. The dropping of incendiaries was followed by high explosive bombs with devastating results. For a time the workers' services were not required but production was restarted quite quickly and a new factory, known as Forest

Works, in Parkhurst Forest, provided an extra destination for the buses. To assist the staff situation certain Saunders-Roe or JS White shipyard employees were trained as drivers on the vehicles hired to their employers. However, the staff committee complained of alleged dangerous and inconsiderate driving by certain of those drivers and indeed a serious accident occurred in Sandown High Street when an ex-Tourist Dennis Lancet collided with several shops.

'Tip and run' bombing raids affected all towns and some rural areas but it was the Sunday afternoon raid on Shanklin (3 January 1943) that wreaked havoc in the resort. The Catholic church was bombed while a service was in progress and the Glo'ster Hotel and Garage in Landguard Road, used by the National Fire Service and adjacent to the SVOC garage, was also flattened. The roof was blown off the bus garage and the coach house also damaged. Repairs had almost been completed when another raid, on the morning of 17 February, destroyed property in the same area and once again damaged the roof of the bus garage.

Later in the war, efforts were made, through Tilling headquarters, to contact Mr Davies, owner of the Glo'ster Hotel site and by now living in Stroud, Glos, to see if he would sell the property. To prevent him thinking Southern Vectis was the interested party, the services of a Bristol Tramways Co official were obtained to make the approach, but he was unwilling to sell. Eventually the site passed via the council to SVOC for use as a bus station.

In another 'tip and run' in February, this time on Ryde, Hazelwood House, which had been one of the Black Watch billets at the time SVOC was providing transport for them, was

destroyed. In another serious raid by eight aircraft on Newport's central area, on the morning of 7 April 1943, the requisitioned former bus garage in Pyle Street was badly damaged.

Ironically, from January 1943, visitors to the Island had been permitted although no one was allowed to take up residence and this relaxation coincided with the serious raids. No extra transport facilities were available and the general injunction against unnecessary travel to the Island was still applicable. The ban on pleasure visits was reimposed and every visitor had to leave by 10 April or face prosecution.

In the meantime a weekend exercise to test alternative communication in the event of an enemy airborne invasion was held in late March. The Regional Transport Commissioner had in fact directed further service curtailment and the discontinuation of duplicates.

Black out conditions led to a series of rhymes in the regular SVOC newspaper advert, such as the following:

> A careless man, Ezekiel Clowne,
> He would not keep his torchlight down!
> He flashed it in the driver's face,
> Really a most regrettable case.
> Ezekiel now will never see
> The Brave New World that's going to be.
> LOOK OUT IN THE BLACKOUT.

This problem had led to a request at the management/staff committee that the Officer Commanding troops stationed on the Island should enlighten his men about the dangers of walking in the road during the blackout period.

Before the war, buses had stopped wherever required,

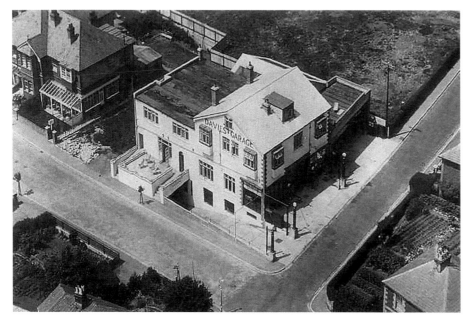

Shanklin bus station was constructed on a site bombed during World War II. Davies' Glo'ster Hotel and Garage (who operated coach excursions) was the building destroyed and is seen in this prewar commercial view. The houses in the top left were bought by Southern Vectis in 1943 for staff accommodation.

M Johnson collection

although the question of fixed stopping places had been raised by the staff committee on a number of occasions. Now it became even more critical in the interest of fuel economy and to avoid confusion by employees and the public after dark. Management had not met with any success in negotiating with local authorities (and the police) in peacetime so it was unlikely they would consider the question under the circumstances. However by 1942 fixed stops were provided on routes 4 and 5 (to East Cowes) but only by the painting of BUS STOP on the road, as it was impossible to obtain materials to fabricate bus stop flags or posts. Unfortunately, the inferior quality paint quickly wore off the road surface. Compulsory or request bus stops were progressively added to other routes and adverts requested passengers to alight at their nearest fixed stopping point (and not to expect to be taken right home) in the interest of saving fuel and rubber.

A scheme was also being prepared early in 1943 for queue and bus stand signs at Ryde Esplanade. In the same year a request had been made for shelters to be provided in St James's Square (Newport). Mr Budd had approached the Bristol Tramways General Manager for specifications of a Glover austerity design shelter but Newport Council declined the proposal.

Because of the need for extra capacity, regulations for the conveyance of bicycles, dogs etc, were tightened up. Dogs were charged for from late 1941, with the provision that they should only be conveyed in the upper saloon on double-deckers; also charged were "folding mailcarts and perambulators" while smoking in double-deckers was to be more strictly controlled. Most of the single-deckers were fitted with roof racks and it was part of the drivers duty to assist with the placing of cycles.

Early in 1944 the Island was in the forefront of D-Day preparations with a consequent increased troop presence. Another top secret operation was PLUTO (Pipe Line Under

The Ocean), centred on Shanklin Chine and Sandown Bay, to pipe fuel across the Channel to assist with the recapture of Nazi-occupied Europe. The pipeline ran across the Island from Thorness to Shanklin and many roads were obstructed as the link, devised by Earl Mountbatten, was constructed. The movement of civilians was even further tightened from April as a result.

After a spate of V1 unmanned flying bombs, fortunately without too much damage, in summer 1944, the tide was turning with peace in sight. The company proudly announced that their employees had invested more per head in National Savings (for the war effort) than any other road transport group.

VE Day, 8 May 1945, brought tremendous celebrations and everyone looked forward to unrestricted travel, holidays and entertainment. But SVOC could not adapt overnight. The fleet was heavily depleted compared with before the war and many vehicles, particularly the 6xx-series Dennis Lances were in poor body condition after arduous war duties. Over eight million passengers had used the Island buses in 1942. Buses were in a drab state with many in all over grey, khaki or matt brown liveries while those in green and cream, long overdue for the paint shop, still had the roof overpainted in wartime grey to make them less conspicuous.

Three employees, R Cheverton, Henry Jones (both RAF) and George Penny (RASC) lost their lives on war service (and are remembered by a plaque above the main staircase at Nelson Road) while conductress Madge Pike, who lived near Shanklin depot, died in the bombing. Considering the damage caused to parts of the Island, Southern Vectis had been relatively fortunate with no vehicles lost and only one operational depot damaged.

1945 was an arctic winter, similar to 1940, and bus services had been disrupted for several weeks, with vehicles stuck in snowdrifts. Saunders-Roe personnel had also been on strike for higher wages in January so that had an effect on passenger

This lowbridge Bristol KSW illustrates the protrusion of the gangway into the offside of the lower saloon. Unusually, because of the uncertainty surrounding the impending railway closures, SVOC also specified nearside luggage racks.

SVOC

Highbridge double-deckers were restricted to a handful of routes because of the Island's low railway bridges so Bristol G type No 701 (BDL 101) went over to Hants & Dorset's works in Southampton to be rebuilt to lowbridge layout in 1951. Despite such an extensive rebuild, this bus, seen in the Square at Newport outside the Bell Inn, was sold in 1954 with its unrebuilt sister.

AB Cross/
B Stewart colln

numbers on the workers services, but there was already a move towards peacetime normality as the Food Minister invited hotels and cafés to apply for licences to reopen their establishments and, in answer to Capt PD Macdonald, MP for the Island, the Minister for War Transport advised that the bigger ferries would be returned at the earliest possible moment to bring great peace and prosperity back to the Island. SVOC reintroduced service 29 on three days a week (instead of two) from March 1945 – this service had been diverted via Yarbridge during the war, bypassing Yaverland, as the area in

front of Sandown Fort (now the Zoo) was under military control. Services were promised for Easter, but with the proviso of one of the company's rhymes in its regular County Press advert:

> Eliza Jane – she had a dream
> Of buses in a constant stream
> With seats to spare and never a queue
> Alas, poor Liza woke and knew
> That while men fought, they couldn't drive her
> No men – no buses; no seat for Liza.

Meanwhile, Ryde Business Association called upon the local council to run a municipal bus service from the Canoe Lake to Ratcliff Avenue and St John's Hill but this was hardly the time to undertake such a venture.

The Whitsun holiday (at the end of May 1945) was celebrated and there was a large influx of visitors despite poor weather; it was almost like a prewar holiday although restrictions imposed by the railway prevented many day excursionists crossing from Portsmouth. Sadly for SVOC May 1945 also saw the death of Frank Plater, the Ryde district manager since the IW Tourist takeover in 1938. He had come to the Island in 1925 to run the IWT Co having previously set up successful ventures at Littlehampton (South Coast Tourist) and Portsmouth (Southsea Tourist), which had been acquired by Southdown in 1924–25.

The company was unable to introduce its planned summer timetable in June as there were insufficient crews to work the increased services but from June the Minister for War Transport allowed some private hire and the resumption of excursions and tours (provided the mileage did not exceed 70 and 50 miles respectively, crews were available and that it did not interfere with stage service, workers and other essential services). However, for SVOC this meant very few tours could actually be operated because of the staff shortage.

The Island was 'comfortably full' for the August Bank Holiday, despite the effects of a threatened rail strike and the General Manager, Mr Budd, wrote to the local paper to make the public aware of the industry's difficulties. He stated that his staff had to bear continuous overloading and long hours of duty and, because insufficient staff were available, any, but minor, service modifications had been put on one side. As to vehicles, he described the situation as acute because of the shortage of skilled and unskilled workers so that the shortage of labour was worse than at any stage during the War.

At this time the fleet consisted largely of 35 seater single-deckers because many roads were unsuited to double-deckers. In December 1945, Sandown-Shanklin UDC finally agreed to cut the trees between Sandown and Shanklin to allow double-deck operation and soon after a demonstration was given (almost certainly on 'Cardiff Kate' Leyland TD1, UH 7175) for IWCC officials and the Sandown Highways Surveyor as a prelude to converting the busy Ryde–Shanklin corridor.

New buses arrived in May 1946 in the form of two Bristol K5Gs (DDL 985/6) with lowbridge bodies by Eastern Coach Works, featuring a sunken gangway and four-across bench type seats on the top deck. Invited guests and officials, who witnessed the disembarkation of the vehicles from the car ferry *Lymington*, at Yarmouth, were then entertained at a function in the Bugle Hotel. This was to be the standard design of bus purchased new over the next seven years.

SVOC had been lucky to acquire a few secondhand vehicles – the two Cardiff Leylands for £1100 in June 1945, a Dennis Lancet from City of Oxford MS for £275 in May 1945 and another, nicknamed the 'Push & Pull', from Fountain Coaches in April 1946 for £100. Hants & Dorset sold another

old Leyland TD1 (with archaic open staircase body) to the company for £350 but it was rebodied with a lowbridge body by Beadle of Dartford before being sent across. These three secondhand double-deckers were petrol engined and gave endless trouble. with the result that they were fitted with Gardner oil engines in due course.

The lowbridge K type double-deckers, of standard Tilling design and in a corporate green and cream livery were introduced to the Island's trunk routes as rapidly as delivery would permit – seven more of the type arrived in time for summer 1947 and route 10 to the hilly town of Ventnor was converted from single-deck. The 'Summer Programme' issued to staff urged that all concerned made a "very special effort on this occasion" as Ventnor was the last single-deck bastion to be invaded. Elderly residents were sceptical at the use of double-deckers and when they had started running in 1936 people actually used to sit on a roadside seat near the West Hill Road terminus in Cowes expecting them to overturn!

The 'Summer Programme' booklets produced from 1946 laid down in concise and helpful terms service alterations and staff instructions; 'Double-deck operation' warranted a special paragraph in the 1946 issue. Drivers were reminded that "Clearing the routes can never rule out the possibility of an accident which would not occur with a single-deck. Camber will always play tricks. There will always be street lamps of which the post is clear of a single-decker but the lantern not clear of a double-decker". The instruction continued "For the first time in this Company, there will be a LOWBRIDGE ONLY route in operation (Ryde–Shanklin) restricted to 13ft buses. Our 56 seaters are 14ft 6in and they WON'T FIT under the bridge at Morton Common."

It stated this situation called for a 'Safety First' attitude of mind in management and staff to ensure there was never a mistake and advised starting the habit of referring to a 'Highbridge' or 'Lowbridge' instead of a 'Double-decker' and the appropriate designation would be painted in the cab. The initial three lowbridge buses were allocated to Ryde for service 16.

Spring 1946 also saw the reintroduction of one-man operation with 20 seaters on deeply rural routes (such as the 9, Newport–Merstone–Ventnor) or Newport Town service. Drivers who had started driving buses on a Ministry of War Transport permit now had to take their full PSV driving test as normality resumed.

Even in 1946, crew operation with 35-seaters was hardly cost effective, especially in the light of staff and vehicle shortages but councils placed obstacles in the way of the company's bid to overcome the problems by conversion to double-deck operation, because of the need to lop the trees.

January 1947 saw the first Traffic Commissioners' sitting (in Newport Guildhall) for eight years, to consider various services started up in the intervening years on temporary permits (such as Sandown or Shanklin to the Saro works at East Cowes, or Folly Works, started in 1941). Councils now raised emphatic objections because of the narrowness of roads,

There were several unfortunate overturning accidents in the 1950s including this 1954 incident in which Lodekka No 515 (KDL 411), when almost new, toppled off the road at Alvington Shute, near Carisbrooke and ended up in a steep-sided field. Some years later an identical overturning accident at the same spot involved the similar No 520 which was then scrapped. Number 515 displays the original style of fleet number just before plates were introduced. The crew involved in No 515's mishap are featured on page 158.

RHD/SVOC

such as Shanklin High Street, for double-deck operation while other operators, such as Shotter's or West Wight Motor Bus Co, objected that SVOC were swamping the local companies.

Routes were steadily restored to prewar frequencies and seasonal services such as the 26 (Yarmouth to Blackgang) reinstated. Victoria Avenue, Shanklin, and the Undercliff Drive from Ventnor to Niton were particularly sensitive portions of route. Sandown-Shanklin UDC claimed "The beauty of the Avenue would be destroyed" if they cut the trees to open up Shanklin–Whiteley Bank to double-decks, while the Ventnor UDC clerk described the operation through the Undercliff as "Juggernauts driving through Fairyland"! However the Traffic Commissioners allowed the Undercliff application in November 1949, despite a storm of protest.

The company was unfortunate in sustaining four overturning accidents with 'Lowbridge' type vehicles in subsequent years – at Yard Farm, Wroxall; The Mall, Newport; Whitcombe Road and Totland Broadway – but only the first was attributable to road camber. Later two Lodekkas overturned when they came off the road and into a field, in near identical circumstances, at the same location – Alvington Shute, Carisbrooke.

Newport Borough Council expressed concern over the congestion at the St James's Square terminal and proposed a bus station on a site next to the Medina Cinema in Newport High Street, where the IW Electricity, Light & Power Co's showroom had stood before the 1943 bombing. Land ownership difficulties and the looming threat of transport nationalisation (including buses) caused rejection by their General Purposes Committee in September 1947, although a design had been drawn up by Tilling architects. In July 1949 the council adopted another plan to acquire the St James's Street/South Street site in the town. Some buildings in the town were derelict because of war damage and the council proposed commencement at "the earliest opportunity".

Sandown-Shanklin UDC continued to press for the removal of the Clarendon Road (Shanklin) on-street bus stops to the nearby SVOC garage and concluded they should themselves provide a bus station but the matter was unresolved. Even in Ryde, the town council earmarked a site at the Union Street/St Thomas's Street junction when a suggestion of building a bus station was made.

Carnivals and events, for which the Island is noted, were resumed as soon as possible after the war and provided more traffic for the buses. For instance, St Helens Bonfire Night (usually the Island's biggest Guy Fawkes event) had a massive bonfire fuelled by 300 gallons of used sump oil and five tons of old tyres donated by SVOC to burn an effigy of Manny Shinwell (the Government Minister responsible for rationing fuel and power, during the period of coal shortage) from a 40 foot gibbet. Many items were still rationed and the Island's military presence was only gradually decreasing – the men of the 1st Bn The Parachute Regiment departed from Albany Barracks in March 1946.

Stanley Bartlett, a former Creeth's conductor, who steered the company through the war as acting Traffic Manager, departed for Hants & Dorset in 1946 when Roger Wakeling returned from War Service to resume as TM, but he also moved – to Southdown – in 1947. HW Downie became Traffic Manager while RL Whitehead succeeded Ian Patey as Secretary in 1947. In that hot summer, a threatened strike by road staff, in support of a mainland issue, was averted at the last minute by the intervention of the National Union Railwaymen General Secretary. Because of the association with the Southern Railway, the NUR became the chosen union for staff – a situation which continues today under the RMT Union – and No 2 branch, specifically for busmen, was formed during the war years.

From 1947–50, 16 new coaches (29-seat Bedford OBs of the type being bought by most IW coaching companies) were taken into the fleet for the resumption of a coaching programme and some elderly Dennis coaches were pensioned off. Even the application for 34 different tours from Shanklin caused the wrath of Newport Borough Council in January 1947, as they pointed out the inadequacy of stage carriage services compared with 1939, while resources were being used for coaching! Other new rolling-stock bought in this period consisted of some Bristol L type single-deck buses (some seating 39) and three full-front 'Queen Mary' style coaches on Bristol LWL chassis.

The Tilling & BAT group had been split in 1942 because the latter considered more individuality desirable for their subsidiaries. Tilling Chairman Sir Frederick Heaton, who believed in a centralised structure on matters such as liveries, vehicle policies and corporate image, also had definite views on the unification of road and rail transport and supported the Government's nationalisation policies with regard to area transport boards. Heaton had recommended to Tilling shareholders a sale and, in autumn 1948, Thos Tilling sold its road transport interests to the newly-formed British Transport Commission. SVOC was a Tilling subsidiary so now came under State control.

Seen as an effect of nationalisation was the sudden termination (on 1 November 1950) of the contract with H Margham & Sons of Newport, who had been responsible for major coachwork overhaul and repaints of the whole fleet since VBC commenced in 1921. Just one day's notice was given, as SVOC stated all vehicles would in future be sent to the Hants & Dorset works in Southampton for attention. In reality, SVOC carried out their own repair work at Nelson Road and most of the displaced Margham's skilled staff were taken on to continue work on the buses they had always maintained.

By 1950, the fleet had almost returned to prewar standards, although with a much higher age profile, and the staff position had eased but costs had risen sharply although passenger journeys were increasing year by year. Fares increase applications were opposed by the councils and yet weekly ticket fare scales were still based on the 1921 rates! In 1947 the application to raise scholars' weeklies and term tickets was declined even though it was necessary to operate 36 school buses daily compared with 28 in the previous year.

The bodyshop built an excellent carnival float on the deck of converted Dennis Ace lorry DL9013 and the engineering staff are seen manning the vehicle before it was entered into Shanklin Carnival. The then new Central Works at Nelson Road is seen as a back drop. Foreman Harry Green is seen alongside. The tinplate coach motif on the diamond survives today in the bus museum.
RHD/SVOC

Tilling green buses oust the steam trains
Road versus rail in the busy 'fifties and 'sixties

Charles de Pury, Asst Divisional Superintendent of the Southern Railway, had as far back as 1935 assured the Sandown/Shanklin hoteliers that "even a superficial consideration of replacing the Island's railways by omnibuses" ruled out the idea because of the colossal number of buses necessary to cope with the passengers at Ryde. GHR Gardener (Asst for the IW) had spoken in 1948 of the possible use of diesel railcars while in 1947–9 a trial had taken place with a more powerful Brighton E4 tank engine with a view to running heavier trains to speeded-up timings.

For the Railway Executive, the physically-isolated Isle of Wight railway network, with its tight curves and restricted loading gauge, was certainly operationally inconvenient. For a relatively small number of nonstandard steam engines and carriages it required two engine sheds, a locomotive works and a carriage & wagon workshop. Retrospectively, it is thus not too surprising that in May 1951 a Joint Working Party was established between the Railway Executive, Southern Vectis and, later, the Railway Haulage Executive to produce a report on "the steps necessary to provide an adequate transport system in the Isle of Wight on the assumption that all rail passenger services would be withdrawn, except on the section of line between Ryde and Ventnor". In addition, the confidential report, finalised in April 1952, had to consider an alternative scheme which would also retain the Ryde to Cowes services. Messrs Walter, Turk, Cooper-Poole and Gardener represented the Railway, TH Thornton (for the Road Haulage Executive) and Messrs Budd, Downie and Whitehead (for Southern Vectis). Using rail passenger census figures for weeks in April and July 1951, the Committee quickly concluded that the closure of Merstone to Ventnor West, Brading to Bembridge, Newport to Freshwater and Newport to Sandown lines could be handled by substitute bus services without difficulty.

In winter, no frequency increase would be needed on existing bus services while in summer it was estimated the following increases would be required:

Ryde–Newport–Cowes (services 1/1a)

Existing frequency (mins)		Proposed frequency (mins)		Add'l buses	Add'l crews
Weekday	Sunday	Weekday	Sunday		
10	10	7½	10	9	18

Ryde–St Helens–Bembridge (service 8)

Existing frequency (mins)		Proposed frequency (mins)		Add'l buses	Add'l crews
Weekday	Sunday	Weekday	Sunday		
20	20	15	20	2	4

Newport–Sandown (services 14/41)

Existing frequency (mins)		Proposed frequency (mins)		Add'l buses	Add'l crews
Weekday	Sunday	Weekday	Sunday		
30	30	15	15	3	6

Newport–Freshwater (services 12/22)

Existing frequency (mins)		Proposed frequency (mins)		Add'l buses	Add'l crews
Weekday	Sunday	Weekday	Sunday		
20	20	15	20	2	4

Additional journeys would also be needed on service 29 (Bembridge to Shanklin), at business periods (one bus, two crews), on service 28 (Newport to Alum Bay) (two buses, four crews), between Apse Heath and Alverstone (new service, one bus, two crews), for workmen's traffic between Ventnor and Cowes, Ryde and Newport and Freshwater and Cowes (four buses, eight crews) and on Sunday mornings where rail commenced earlier than bus services. The Ryde–Newport—Cowes line option had been included but was known to be highly controversial and in any case the track would still be needed for railborne freight entering the Island through Medina

Wharf, near Cowes – mainly 134,000 tons of coal per year although 60,000 tons of this was gas coal for power stations and due to be diverted to the new Kingston plant opening in 1952, with its own jetty.

Provision of 19 extra buses and 38 crews (including spares) in summer and six extra buses, 12 crews (throughout the year) would cost the bus company capital costs of £98,000 and other annual costs of £11,125. SVOC was not prepared to offer an all-Island 5-day holiday ticket as offered on the trains (15/- (75p) First Class; 10/- (50p) Third) encouraging a regular east–west flow of excursionists. They still had a staffing problem and would need to recruit 40% more seasonal staff if all lines except Ryde to Ventnor closed (20% more if the Ryde to Cowes line was also retained).

Luggage conveyance was also considered and 50 buses (at £65 per vehicle) were recommended for equipping with longitudinal luggage racks on the nearside of the lower saloon or with vertical racks over the rear wheel arches, although this would decrease the seating capacity by six. Retention of the Cowes line would mean only 30 vehicles needed to be so equipped. Whereas the Railway made no charge for folding pushchairs, SVOC (in line with Tilling company policy) charged for them at a quarter of the single fare.

The working party concluded that the Ventnor West branch should close in the autumn of 1952 to save £16,000 and was already covered by the parallel SVOC service 9, Newport to Ventnor. Despite a few objections, the Transport Users' Consultative Committee (TUCC) decided they would not oppose closure as the County Council had raised no objection and the last train ran on 13 September. They also recommended closure of the Bembridge branch from 8 June 1953 (although following an outcry from local councils this was later postponed to September); the Freshwater Line; Newport to Sandown and the stations at Ashey, Wootton and Whippingham (between Ryde and Newport), saving 174 staff if all branches and Ryde to Cowes closed but only 89 if the latter line remained. It was envisaged that some of the displaced staff would join SVOC. At this time the working loss on the entire rail network was given as £121,843 per annum, with interest savings of £92,931 giving an annual loss of £214,774 (but by 1953 the loss was quoted as £271,200). In reality, relatively little of the revenue for rail passengers was actually collected through Island stations as return tickets issued from stations all over the country to the Isle of Wight were relatively difficult to proportion, and yet in 1951 a record number of almost four million passengers had been carried on Portsmouth to Ryde boats.

The IW County Council and Chamber of Commerce soon became aware of the closure moves and met with the Southern Region's Chief Officer, CP Hopkins, at the Charing Cross Hotel in August 1951. Notes for the meeting reported, in anticipation of an expected suggestion for dieselisation, that "Any traffic diverted from buses to railway would be no gain to the British Transport Commission unless bus services were reduced and presumably the Islanders would not approve of this". The Railway anticipated the opposition of the IW County Council and Chamber of Commerce would be "vigorous and aggressive" which could have the effect of causing delay in the implementation of closure proposals.

At the TUCC enquiry held in Newport from 11–13 May 1953, CP Hopkins put the Railway's case for closure, which followed four years of deliberations, in that the closing of selected lines would not inflict any serious injury to the Island's transport system. Ashey would now remain open, officially considered as a 'concession' as it was $1^1/_4$ miles from the nearest bus route. Mr Bushrod (SVOC) assured the TUCC that the buses could meet any increased demand by better frequencies and extra relief vehicles. He outlined the arrangements for luggage racks on their new buses and reported the extension of Sandown–Newport journeys to Cowes (if the railway closed) and Freshwater to Newport to Sandown.

Despite the well-planned presentation of objections by councils and others, the TUCC approved closure of the Bembridge and Freshwater lines (from 21 September 1953) as well as Wootton and Whippingham stations from the same date. It was recommended that the Newport–Sandown line should remain open for at least two years.

The Education Dept of the County Council reacted by taking the schools traffic away from SVOC and placing it with the Railway although their season ticket rates were higher. Mr Bushrod described this action as "another indication of the unfriendly attitude that the IWCC adopts towards this Company". Clerk to the Council, LH Baines, was, however, a leading opponent of the railway closures over the fifteen year period and was determined to pursue every possible means,

Following the introduction of new legislation Bristol Commercial Vehicles increased the width of the standard double-decker from 7'6" to 8'0". Southern Vectis took 15 of the new KSW type in 1952/3 including No 763 (JDL 37), seen on service 8 from Ryde passing the closed Bembridge station, terminus of the short branch line from Brading until September 1953.

Author

although it almost resulted in the laying off of SVOC staff. It was all to no avail, for at the end of the two year period the railway advised the Central Transport Consultative Committee in January 1956 that the financial position of the Newport to Sandown line was even worse resulting in closure from 6 February. Increased frequencies on the bus routes were implemented and a new service (24) inaugurated between Sandown, Apse Heath and Alverstone – described as "a popular riverside place", but at the end of some very narrow roads not previously served by bus. The railway had considered serving Alverstone with a Sandown–Newchurch push-pull train at one stage but SVOC converted another Bedford OB for one-man-operation to work the route.

Several schemes were put forward for railway reopening – such as the revolutionary Bennie Airspeed Railway, a monorail scheme which envisaged 125 mph running by 12 cars serving five stations (and allowing a twelve minute circuit of the Island!) and the 1955 project of IW Travel Ltd, who floated a company with £500 capital to reopen the Freshwater line – but none was taken too seriously. SVOC proved its ability to carry the passengers from closed lines on its improved bus services and, in 1956, the IWCC had been assured by the GM, Southern Region of BR that five years notice would be given of any intention to close the Ryde to Cowes line and about seven years in the case of Ryde to Ventnor. This was reiterated by FPB Taylor (BR's Line Traffic Manager and also a SVOC Director) in 1961.

Although Walter Budd had sat on the Joint Working Party, he only partially oversaw the rail substitution as he retired after twenty-one years as GM in April 1953. His successor was RF Bushrod from Wilts & Dorset who was to steer SVOC through a progressive 4$^1/_2$ years before promotion to Lincolnshire Road Car. From 1 November 1957, RG Howe moved from United Counties to succeed him as SVOC GM. Traffic Manager HW Downie had also left in 1953 to be Transport Manager to the Kumasi Town Council in West Africa and his successor (designated Traffic Superintendent) was Leslie Duncan who had been with SVOC, except for war service, since 1932. Charlie Toogood held the position of Depot Superintendent at Newport and was appointed as his deputy.

When LT Duncan departed to be Asst TM of Western & Southern National in the summer of 1957, he was replaced on the Island as TM by Robert Hanley, who had previously served with Eastern National at Chelmsford. The Chief Engineer was also given an Assistant in the early 1950s and Rod Longley was appointed to that post. During his tenure he built the carnival float on a Dennis Ace lorry, raising a good sum for charity as it toured the various Island events in summer 1956. When he departed at the end of 1956, his successor was Ron Plater, ex IW Tourist and then a fitter for SVOC at Ryde depot.

In this period of expansion more operators had sold out to SVOC. JH Wavell's Enterprise Bus Service had started slightly earlier than the Vectis Bus Co, in March 1921, with one charabanc and then entered bus operation. Later they retreated to the Arreton Valley route, running between Newport and Sandown. Blake's Bus Service, in similar territory but serving Newchurch, had been acquired by Wavell in February 1951 but within a few months the whole operation was sold to SVOC (from 18 June 1951). Six buses (including two ex-Reading utility Guys, which became nicknamed The Flying Birds) and the two routes were acquired but the South Street, Newport, garage was excluded. Their decision to sell had been hastened by a case brought against them by the TGWU in late 1949 that their rates of pay were below the laid-down standard in the National Omnibus Agreement. After involvement with an industrial court in London, it was decreed that Enterprise was not paying wages in accordance with the Road Traffic Act. They also fell foul of the Ministry over vehicle maintenance.

From 16 June 1952, Pink Bros' West Wight Motor Bus Co, sold out their stage carriage operations from Freshwater Bay to

Four Bedford coaches of Bernard Groves, Cowes, were taken over with that business in 1955. The newest was this 33 seat SB model built in 1951. Number 230 (HDL 570) is seen in Newport depot but being nonstandard it was sold in 1960.

RHD/SVOC

Yarmouth (or Alum Bay) and Alum Bay to Yarmouth. They had been the authorised railway carrier for Freshwater station but continued running coaches so no vehicles passed to SVOC. Bernard Groves' coaching operation in Cowes, with four petrol-engined Bedford coaches and a High Street office was the next acquisition (from 8 May 1955) while in 1956 three more operators sold out to SVOC.

Bartlett's of Shanklin were the first, disposing of their local Esplanade–Luccombe bus service after 30 April. Their Bedford OB, performing the last journey, was bedecked with rosettes and a laurel wreath. The regular driver, Bill Silsbury, was given a pewter pint pot by his 'Luccomber' regulars, with a basket of fruit for his aged mother! Shotters of Brighstone disposed of their bus services between Newport and Compton Bay or Gunville from 14 May and these were incorporated within existing SVOC services 12b and 34. Shotter's sold the buses separately and retained their coaching activities. Finally, Nash's Luxury Coaches of Ventnor sold out from 1 June. Included with this old-established business were five coaches and the Pier Street garage.

An increased bus fleet meant the need for extra depot space and between February and May 1950 a paved area was constructed outside Newport depot after the demolition of the air raid shelter and cycle racks. An orchard adjacent to Ryde depot was purchased and, in 1950, plans were drawn up for a single storey extension containing fitters workshops and stores, which were constructed by Westridge Construction, using local bricks from Rookley, in 1951. The parking area was extended at Ryde in 1953 with extra paving which would provide storage for withdrawn or delicensed vehicles. The acute situation at Shanklin depot was eased by the removal of six buses to the new parking spaces at Ryde or Newport but it was not until 1960 that Shanklin had an outside hardstanding area. In the autumn of 1953, planning authority was sought for a hardstanding bus park behind Freshwater garage, in Princes Road.

Although the roof of the original Hilton Hall iron and timber shed had been raised, at the end of the war, to accommodate double-deckers (following Walter Budd's approach to Tilling architect H Starkey on this issue in April 1943) the building accommodated no more than five or six vehicles. With the railway closure in September 1953, 12 buses now needed outstationing at the depot. A cleaner and fitter (for light running repairs) were to be Freshwater-based during the summer months, with increased supervision by the Inspectorate, while a fuel pump was also installed. The new parking area, ready for Whitsun 1954, also allowed garage space for coaches allocated to work the IOW tour for Hants & Dorset passengers. Further improvements were planned utilising SVOC staff over several winters and in early 1959 a new depot with rest and paying in room was opened.

Alterations at Nelson Road had been considered for some time and a draft plan was prepared by early 1954 for the directors' consideration. By now some staff had their own cars but no depot space could be allocated to them and the company investigated renting a portion of Nine Acres Field or the school canteen site for this purpose.

Construction of a new Central Works, costing £40,000, was commenced in April 1955, and consisted of a steel framed 160ft x 105ft building with brick walls and asbestos roof. Built by Frank Batty & Smith, it also possessed five inspection pits, machine shops, welding and blacksmith's bays, paintshop, stores and first aid room. On the upper storey, mess facilities, offices and the trimmers shop were provided. A band saw and sewing machine had previously been installed in the depot to deal with the work that had beforehand been done by outside firms. Most of the old machinery had been over thirty years old but the modern equipment installed in the new works included a calibrating machine, nozzle grinder, new centre

At the start of the 1956 season another coach operator was bought out – Nash's Luxury Coaches Ltd. of Ventnor. Their five coaches were totally nonstandard for any Tilling Company, but they all entered service with Southern Vectis and worked for four or five seasons. Number 104 (HDL 304) was a Harrington-bodied Commer Avenger that later worked on Jersey.

RHD/SVOC

lathe, power press (allowing the sleeving of cylinder blocks), a cylinder boring machine and an electrical test bench.

The new works was opened on 1 February 1956 by Mr HJ Thom, Chairman of the South Eastern Traffic Area licensing authority and the building was described as one of the most modern works in the country. After the inspection and speeches, lunch was taken by the official party at the Gloster Hotel, Cowes. An exchange of land had taken place with Newport Borough Council in June 1955 which allowed SVOC to build a boundary wall at the rear of 4–14 Winston Road, adjacent to Newport depot.

Plans to alter the railway-owned buildings used by SVOC next to Ryde Esplanade station had been drawn up in late 1952 and it had been hoped to have a two-storey, modern rest room and accommodation block in use for summer 1956 but there was difficulty in pushing any improvement scheme, other than renovations and essential legal modifications, past the BR Property Board and it was not until 1974, when a bus station was built, that the old huts were swept away.

The Railway had permitted the placing of a wooden kiosk at Ryde Pier Head for the summer of 1954 (and subsequent seasons). It proved an effective means of boosting SVOC tours from Ryde or Shanklin but even this had featured in a House of

SVOC opened an enquiry office at 32 High Street, Cowes in 1956 and this later became the coaching office. It is still in use as one of the company's travel offices and for a time in the 1990s contained a Post Office.

RHD/SVOC

Commons reference by the Island MP who criticised the BTC for allowing SVOC to have a booking point on the pier as an opportunity to attack the rail abandonment policy. By 1960 a similar kiosk was located at Royal Pier, Southampton, to promote coach tours from Cowes and an annual rental was payable to the Southampton Harbour Board.

The first SVOC bus station was built in Shanklin. The site had been suggested before the war, as the council became irate with the use of Clarendon Road as the town's bus terminal but eventually the bombed site of the Glo'ster Hotel was bought from Mr JG Davies by the Central Land Board for £2286 and resold to SVOC for use as part of a new bus station.

By January 1950, Alan A Briggs FRIBA, the Tilling Group architect who designed all the major new SVOC buildings of this era, produced the first draft plans. The new bus station was estimated to cost £20,000 but the bombing had left the remains of deep basements and a long drop from road level so the first task, from early 1954, was the infilling with consolidated chalk (using two old Dennis Ace buses adapted as lorries for the task) and levelling of the site. The Tilling Board authorised the expenditure in November 1954 and planning approval was granted by the IWCC in November 1955.

The bus station, situated adjacent to the prewar garage, which had itself been reroofed in 1946 following war damage, was to be built by Westridge Construction of Ryde and completion was required by the spring of 1956. It was to consist of three parallel departure platforms and an accommodation block comprising tea bar, staff canteen, lavatories and the Inspector's office. An enquiry office was to be built at the Landguard Road/Collingwood Road corner, a commercially viable site, but the structure put up served as a tobacconists kiosk and newspaper stall. A continuous crack from ground level to the parapet of the depot wall gave cause for concern and delayed the bus station work – although connected with war damage it was worsening and had to be attended to.

Shanklin bus station was opened without ceremony (except for coloured bunting streamers) on 11 June 1956, although 37% of the work remained uncompleted, including guard rails around the boundaries, canopies on the island platforms, tea room, the new enquiry office and the lavatories. Late delivery of the coin-operated turnstile for the ladies lavatory caused some irate correspondence! Floodlights and a public address system were also included in the original specification while the old waiting room was modified with red and white plastic covered bench seating and 3D pictures of local scenes around the wall. Much of the concrete paving in the bus station needed replacing by the spring of 1963 and a new Astralite waiting shelter was also added at the same time.

Another purchase of property, in the summer of 1955, was Hewett's shop at 32 High Street, Cowes, to be rebuilt as a SVOC enquiry office. This needed reconstruction and planning approval was given by Cowes UDC in June 1956. Once again, Westridge Construction were the contractors but the demolition and rebuilding was not without problems. The owner of the adjacent Clarendon Restaurant threatened legal action over part of the

Shanklin Bus Station and garage was a locaion well known to holiday-makers. The original garage is in the background while the bus station, constructed in 1956, is on the site of the bombed Davies Hotel & Garage. The café was situated to the right of the tree and the tobacconists kiosk was also company-owned. The only bus visible is the ex-Enterprise Bedford OB, No 207.

RHD/SVOC

division wall being taken down and the state of the roof, while at No 31 a hole appeared in the wall and the plaster fell off!

The completed office was well appointed, with counters and fittings of Afrormosia teak produced by H Margham & Sons, the Newport coachbuilding firm who had men idle in winter 1957 and were given the contract. Morris' Stores of Newport supplied the furnishings while the novel ceiling of blue and white sailcloth was produced by the famous Cowes sailmaker Ratsey & Lapthorn. At the opening, at Whitsun 1957, when it replaced the old Groves' office at 103 High Street, the SVOC Chairman was less than impressed with the sailcloth ceiling as he thought it would gather dust!

As at Shanklin, Newport Town Council had long been concerned at the congestion caused by buses using St James's Square as a terminal point and had looked at various sites in the town to establish a bus station. At peak times ten buses could be on the stands with another six double banked, which the police also frowned upon. In late 1955 Newport Council earmarked the site of 144 Pyle Street and 5/6 High Street as a possible bus station (but it was later used to build a police station). It had also made a compulsory purchase order on part of the war-damaged South Street site in 1952 although roadworks were needed for bus access.

Maurice Holmes (acting Company Chairman) reported that five million passengers were annually being carried from the Square on 185,000 departures and that "although Southern Vectis almost monopolises the Square, control is seriously hampered by traders' vans and private cars occupying kerb space for varying periods".

Also in 1955 SVOC conceived the idea of building its own bus station and by April 1956 had received Tilling Group approval to purchase property in the Orchard Street, South Street, and St James's Street parcel of land. By October 1958 the total purchase of land had been achieved for £25,652 and the demolition of buildings – including five cottages, the occupants of which had to be rehoused by Newport Corporation – completed by Cheek Bros. The rubble was utilised by SVOC for levelling the new Sandown (Fort Street) Bus Terminal and at Freshwater depot.

The new development was to incorporate seven shops, a newspaper kiosk and an office block, interest in which had already been shown by the Ministry of Works for an Income Tax Office, centralising five scattered locations. The anticipated total building cost of £108,000 was expected to be offset by commercial rentals within fifteen years. Other benefits included the saving of dead mileage to and from Nelson Road garage, reduced hours for conductors who would now be booked on at the bus station rather than the depot, the saving of rent and rates on the Square office, availability of advertising sites and improved client facilities in new private hire and enquiry offices (as the office at No 19 was on the first floor).

Early plans produced by the Tilling architects envisaged a central platform unloading on one side and loading on the other, based on the design of Bath bus station. Later it was considered the administration block, containing enquiry office, waiting room and café would be in the centre of this island platform with six loading points on the South St side and six on the station side, with a substantial parking area south of this. The council had begun South St road improvements in autumn 1958 and these were finished by early 1959 with the result that GM RG Howe described the council as being 'almost violent' at the delay.

By this time, construction costs had risen to £113,688 and the tender for the work had been won by Westridge Construction Co of Ryde. Legalities, such as an altered right of way to the adjacent Bright & Minns laundry, had to be resolved and the layout was completely altered with the accommodation block being situated on the southern boundary, at right angles to the office building. Two parallel loading platforms, facing west, were to be provided with the 24 space lay-by for spare buses now positioned next to the widened South Street. A fully automatic electrical floor warming system (later to prove none too successful) was provided, while the GEC post-top lanterns chosen to illuminate the stands were of a design used on Birmingham's Ring Road. The concrete framed buildings of the bus station were infilled with red or rustic blue brick outer walls.

Other notable features were the continuous covered platform, attractive enquiry, booking and left luggage office,

Soon after the opening of Newport's bus station in May 1962, several double-deckers are in evidence, including one on a town service journey to Camp Hill. The skyline has changed dramatically; Safeway and Marks and Spencer have replaced the old market site and BRS garage while most of the buildings in Orchard Street, to the right, have been demolished.

Bus & Coach/SVOC

restaurant and café, waiting room seating up to 40, toilets, bookstall, shops, administrative offices, well-equipped staff canteen and staff cycle store.

Newport's Mayor, Ald EWG Hands, JP opened the new bus station on 18 May 1962 and the invited guests then took lunch (Potage Minestrone, Scotch Salmon, Roast Saddle of local Lamb, followed by Deep Apple Pie and Cream) at the nearby Bugle Hotel, where toasts were proposed by SVOC Chairman Tony Gailey. The first departure from the new stands was one of the latest air suspension Lodekkas (No 567), bound for Ryde.

The release of crew canteen facilities at Nelson Road allowed office expansion work to commence in October 1963. After the first floor had been refurbished, the general office and ground floor offices received attention in autumn 1964.

Loading of buses in Avenue Road, Sandown (outside The Tap and the Sandown Hotel) also created congestion so the chance was taken to purchase a piece of land in Fort Street for use as a bus terminal. This came into use for terminating services (such as 12, 14, 22, 26, 41 and 43) for the summer of 1959 and was an open area of land devoid of passenger facilities but kept buses away from the busy town centre in summer.

In Ventnor, buses terminated in Albert Street outside the Town Hall and a property opposite, at 2 Albert Terrace had been bought in 1954 as a booking office. This had a flat above, sublet to Inspector Bill Bradbury (ex Colson's staff) who supervised Ventnor arrangements. The Nash acquisition in 1956 provided a six-coach garage and small office at 22/23 Pier Street but the Albert Terrace office continued to function until the end of 1961. A new Pier Street office had been built

'in house' by SVOC staff in 1957. In 1958 SVOC bought the adjacent shop with flat above (22a) with a view to extending the garage in due course, and, in the short term, let the shop as the Tropicana Coffee Bar.

Soon after the Nash takeover, Mr Bushrod asked the Tilling architects whether the garage could be safely adapted to accommodate double-deckers by removing the existing girders, but it was fully rebuilt in winter 1961/2. The freehold of three houses in Melbourne Street, Newport, was also bought in 1957 as they included land adjacent to Nelson Road depot and could have been useful if a Central Works extension was required, while 'Thatcham', at Fishbourne, was acquired as a General Manager's residence in 1960.

Investment continued in the 1958/9 winter with enquiry office improvements, including the modernisation of Shanklin (Regent Street), a new degreasing bay extension in Central Works, fluorescent lighting in Newport and Ryde depots and modern heating at Shanklin depot – all designed to increase efficiency and reduce costs.

In these expansive years the company had reached its zenith in terms of passenger numbers. In 1953, Coronation and Fleet Review year, passenger carryings topped 19 million, rising to $20\frac{1}{2}$ million in 1954 and peaking at 21,885,039, an all time record, in 1956 when fleet strength reached 200.

SVOC was investing in property and improving facilities for passengers and staff. In 1956, when Central Works had just opened and a high proportion of the fleet was less than ten years old, only one breakdown occurred for every 100,000 miles operated – an improvement over the figure of 90,000 in 1955

The Island's Tax Office is a familiar landmark in Newport and is located in an SVOC-owned building at the western end of the bus station. The enquiry office was located on the ground floor and the shop units to the far right were subsequently leased.

J Owen/SVOC

and 77,000 in 1954. Staffing was under control, despite an increased requirement in 1955/6 and at this stage SVOC was looking to Ireland in its seasonal recruitment of road staff. The company undertook to find accommodation for these employees and appealed to permanent staff who might have rooms available in their own homes. Standards were always high and a trade journal reported that SVOC showed "staff courtesy which we have never found exceeded on any other undertaking".

With the increase in private motoring and the introduction of television superceding a night out at a cinema, passenger numbers declined from 1957. Costs increased with fuel tax (in the aftermath of the Suez crisis when fuel availability was limited) and higher wages, while lay-off of some of the Cowes shipyard workforce meant fewer workers' buses for SVOC. A regular round of fares increases, placed before the Traffic Commissioners, began and a summer surcharge was introduced. In 1957, return fares were abolished and short stages eliminated.

The season had also been affected by a couple of strikes which became acrimonious and decreased passenger numbers by $2^1/_2$ million compared with 1956. The first stoppage was on Easter Saturday 1957 over the dismissal of an employee with twenty-seven years service, who had been sick for a long period. Those parts of the Island without trains were isolated as the strike was 100% effective amongst road staff. The housewives of Brighstone clubbed together to hire a private coach to take them shopping in Newport!

Agreement was reached but a national strike in July over pay was more serious. A 3% increase had been agreed with the National Council for the Omnibus Industry in November 1956 but now the Council offer of a further 5% was rejected by the unions who were claiming an extra £1 per week. The matter was referred to the Minister of Labour but a national provincial

bus strike commenced on 20 July, a busy holiday Saturday.

As SVOC (with 725 staff) had a virtual monopoly of stage carriage work, parts of the Island that had lost their railway were at a virtual standstill. A few defiant drivers who tried to take buses out suffered abuse and intimidation and had to receive a police escort. One such driver who operated from Shanklin to Newport and back received a £5 note from a Newport businessman for his courage! The remaining trains were packed and taxis busier than they had ever been. Coaches, from private operators, were hired by firms and holiday camps, while the West Wight Bus Co were granted a short term licence by the Traffic Commissioners to operate coaches from Yarmouth to Totland Bay or Freshwater Bay, but to avoid a clash with pickets the West Wight directors, Messrs Cooper and Pink, drove them. Little Canada Camp, at Wootton, chartered a 'water bus' – the motor launch *Skylark* – to convey campers to or from Ryde Pier!

At Shanklin bus station, strikers who usually paid 3d for tea on the staff side were charged 5d on the public side. The manageress told them "You want more money, so do we!" Also at Shanklin a skirmish occurred as the depot manager, Ernie Kettell, attempted to drive his car, containing staff who wished to work, past the picket. An assault charge against two strikers, who tried to drag him from his car, resulted, but they were found not guilty. After nine days, the strike was over, the union accepting an 11/- (55p) per week increase, but this meant £20,000 per year on the company's wage bill and led to an immediate fares increase application. This was the eighth pay award since 1951; the strike had lost SVOC £13,000 and 200,000 miles.

Although one-man-operation (OMO) had been employed by SVOC for years the GM proposed in winter 1958/9 that it should be introduced (to routes 3, 9, 30 and 40) as an alternative to abandoning unremunerative services. A further £15,000 for another pay award had to be met and another suggestion was the speeding up of some winter services to make them more attractive to the travelling public. OMO was the way ahead – but now using up to 41 seaters rather than the 26 seat Bedfords – so that by the end of 1963 all newly recruited drivers were expected to to take up OMO positions, if required.

The 1950s and 1960s brought Tilling standardisation and modernisation to the SVOC bus and coach fleet and cleared out most of the prewar or nonstandard rolling stock.

The last of the 'LB's, Bristol KSW5G eight foot wide lowbridge double-deckers, were received in 1953. The final batch had 'staggered' upstairs seating, with individual seat backs. At least this made the awkward arrangement more tolerable in that four people could be comfortably seated instead of the poor unfortunate nearest to the offside risking being edged off into the offside sunken gangway on a sharp bend! Some 'LB's also had the lower saloon nearside luggage racks, mirroring the offside gangway protrusion into the saloon ceiling.

In the spring of 1953, SVOC received on demonstration, from Hants & Dorset, one of six pre-production Lodekkas and used it from Newport depot for a fortnight. This bus, an improved version of two experimental vehicles Bristol had produced in 1949/50, featured conventional 'highbridge' top deck 2+2 seating with a middle gangway, but had a dropped chassis frame and so achieved an overall height of 13'5" – low enough to pass through those railway bridges at Morton Common, Lake Hill or Havenstreet that were "Too Low for Highbridge Buses" (By this time the dismantling of the Ventnor West branch removed similar obstructions at Godshill and Whitwell). The outcome was the ordering of 74 Lodekkas between 1954 and 1962, many of which were equipped with luggage racks over the rear wheel arches for rail replacement, although these were removed after 1964.

The traditionally-designed 30-foot FLF Lodekka, with front entrance, was bought from 1964–8 with twenty-two 70-seaters entering the fleet and providing extra capacity on rail substitution, even though staff side representatives found design faults with the FLF and would have preferred a 70-seat rear loader.

By 1952, Bristol had an underfloor engined single-deck chassis (the LS) in production and 11 coaches and one bus were bought in 1952–3 by SVOC. One of the coaches had a Gardner instead of the allotted Bristol engine and was swopped with a Lincolnshire Road Car vehicle that should have been delivered to the Island. This only came to light after a medical student visiting Shanklin from the East Midlands wrote in to point out the error! Probably SVOC would have preferred the superior Gardner model but as that builder could not produce sufficient engines to meet Bristol-ECW requirements at that time supply was shared out and the inferior Bristol AVW engine had sometimes to be accepted.

A later development was the MW type chassis, of which SVOC had two coaches and, later, seven buses. They also selected eight Bristol SUL4A 36-seaters – Albion engined with

a David Brown gearbox – in 1963. These were OMO replacements for the Bedford OB conversions (ex coaches, with Perkins oil engines replacing the original petrol) which were exported to Cyprus. The SU type was supplied to only a few Tilling operators who wanted buses suitable for narrow country lanes.

When the Bedford OBs became inadequate for coaching work, SVOC moved on to the Bedford SB model for its 'lightweight' coach fleet and bought some 28 new over the nine seasons from 1955. These were ideal for low mileage 'Round the Island' tours, as was the Bedford VAL 6-wheeler that introduced the 36-foot length coach to the fleet in 1964.

SVOC had acquired 15 secondhand double-deckers of 1939–41 vintage from Bristol Tramways and Hants & Dorset over the 1955–57 period, as a means of increasing capacity. They replaced prewar L-type single-deckers but usually appeared only in the summer so spent long periods delicensed at the back of Ryde depot. They were a stopgap measure so all were gone by 1960.

In the 1950s, many operators serving seaside resorts cut the tops off elderly buses to provide the novelty of 'open-top' operation for holiday-makers. SVOC experimented by buying four AEC Regents of 1931/2 vintage from Brighton, Hove & District, pioneers of such conversions. Two of these entered service on Shanklin-based services in 1956 (and the others

A handful of pre-production Lodekkas were constructed, including Hants & Dorset no 1337 (LRU 67), which was sent on demonstration to Southern Vectis and ran in service. It is seen at Newport depot having worked in from Ventnor.

RHD/SVOC

A major private hire in the mid 1950s required some 11 coaches for a Round the Island excursion. Passengers arrived at Ryde Esplanade after crossing from Portsmouth by boat and joined their vehicles at Quay Road, then the main coach parking area. Vehicles include four LS type and two of the LWL 'Queen Mary' coaches. The skyline remains similar today but behind the photographer all has changed.

RHD/SVOC

were unused). However, it set the scene for this type of service, which saw a doubling of passenger numbers over 1957/8, so that the famous duo of SVOC's own highbridge K5Gs (CDL 899, DDL 50) were converted to open top in the Nelson Road workshops in 1958/9. They should have been converted to full front, in Hants & Dorset style, completely changing their appearance, but the cost was too high. As open top routes were extended between Sandown Zoo and Ventnor and introduced at Ryde and Yarmouth to Alum Bay, some ten more Bristol K type open-toppers arrived from traditional sources – Brighton, Bristol Omnibus (where they had run at Weston-super-Mare) and Hants & Dorset (who had used them around Bournemouth, Sandbanks and Poole or from Fareham to Lee-on-the-Solent).

The takeover of Enterprise, Groves and Nash had introduced nonstandard makes such as Guy Arabs, Crossleys and a Commer Avenger but some of the 14 acquired vehicles worked about five years for SVOC.

Until 1956, SVOC coaches were, unlike those of most other local firms, not equipped with microphones. The staff side requested this feature to save time and improve the running of tours. As a result the Board agreed to the fitment of three coaches, plus an ex-Groves vehicle which could have a microphone reinstated. It was not until summer 1962 that all coaches were so equipped. From 1961 flashing indicators were fitted to 32 vehicles in a programme that continued over successive years. Side screen boxes (above the platform on double-deckers) were abolished in 1952 and after September 1956 intermediate destination blinds were gradually phased out and no longer in use by 1960.

Several officer changes occurred in the early 1960s – HW Mills replaced RG Howe as GM in 1960 and, following the passing of Charlie Toogood, Brian Horner was appointed Asst Traffic Manager. The long serving Reg Augustus retired at the end of 1962 after thirty years as Chief Engineer and was succeeded by Brian Hancock while Robert Hanley moved on promotion in 1963 to be replaced as Traffic Manager by Tom Jackson. 1965 saw an almost total change in Vectis management with Secretary RL Whitehead (18 years with SVOC) and General Manager HW Mills both retiring, Chief Engineer Brian Hancock moving to West Yorkshire Road Car and TM Tom Jackson departing for health reasons. They were followed early in 1966 by Brian Horner, who was appointed TM of United Welsh. Their successors were Messrs H Harding (as both Secretary and GM), David Searle (as CE), Don Howe, who arrived from Bristol Omnibus to serve as TM and David Dickinson (ATM).

This chapter ends, as it began, with the saga of bus replacement of the Island's railways. A further BR/SVOC Working Party had reported in 1961, including on Ryde interchange arrangements if the railway closed. The question of adapting the railway pier for bus operation had even been examined.

March 1963 saw the publication of the Beeching Report (to identify uneconomic areas of operation on British Railways) and both Ryde to Cowes and Ryde to Ventnor were proposed for complete closure, despite their use by at least 2.8 million passengers per year. There had been an immediate threat to close the lines at the end of 1963 because of the state of Ryde Pier but action taken by Ald Mark Woodnutt MP persuaded BR to carry out £250,000 of work on the pier, as it would still be needed for a diesel train shuttle (using converted Underground stock) running from the Pier Head to a new Esplanade bus terminal. Closure was estimated to mean a fleet increase of 90, from 190 to 280, for SVOC!

Immediately after the Beeching Report, the IW Railway Retention Association was formed by a former Ventnor UDC Chairman to co-ordinate the retention efforts of the MP and councils by organising well attended meetings in all rail-served towns, as well as compiling a 81,733 signature petition for the TUCC hearing which was presented to the Minister of Transport. In February 1964 it was announced that closure would take effect from 12 October 1964 subject to the TUCC 3-day hearing in June at Newport's County Hall. The IWRRA's case stated that:

(1) the railway could be viable if efficiency improved;
(2) that it was the lifeblood of the Island's holiday industry – 50 buses per hour out of Ryde would be needed to replace peak Saturday trains;
(3) road widening would be necessary, destroying the Island's distinctive beauty and putting at least 25% of the cost upon ratepayers and
(4) without the Island's visitors, use of the Portsmouth to Ryde shipping route and the lines from London to Southampton or Portsmouth would decrease.

At the TUCC hearing, the redoubtable LH Baines, Clerk to the IWCC, headed the objectors. He disputed the passenger figures, claiming annual usage to be some 600,000 more at 3.4 million and referred to the 1956 pledge, repeated in 1961 by FPB Taylor, that five years notice would be given for the Cowes line closure and seven years for Ventnor. BR now considered the terms of the 1962 Transport Act relieved them of that obligation. By the second afternoon, the chairman recorded that a 'Prima Facie' hardship case had been made out for both Ryde to Ventnor and the Newport to Cowes section. The Esplanade Bus Interchange scheme was unacceptable to the IWCC and Ryde Borough Council while transfer at Ryde St Johns was unattractive to BR. The meeting was jubilant and at the suggestion of the MP, further evidence from the IWRRA was not presented as they seemed to have won the day with the Ventnor line. Subsequently, South Western Division Line Manager FPB Taylor (also a SVOC Director) put forward his

alternative proposal to terminate the line at Shanklin – and it was now too late for further objections.

The October 1964 closure date was postponed and in July 1965 Minister of Transport Tom Fraser notified the BRB that Ryde to Cowes and Shanklin to Ventnor could close, with the Ryde to Shanklin section reprieved subject to modernisation. SVOC was also advised of the bus service requirements but closure (previously planned for 4 October 1965) had to be put back until after the Traffic Commissioners hearing into the substitute services, at Ryde Town Hall on 6/7 January 1966. Ventnor operators Randall's and Crinage's both applied for Ryde–Ventnor express services but were refused, although SVOC subsequently had their application for a service 16a Limited Stop summer Saturday operation granted.

The SVOC Shanklin–Wroxall–Ventnor rail replacement service (39) was granted, although on a one year licence. The Commissioners had inspected terminal arrangements at Shanklin Railway Station where waiting shelters for 90 people were required and at Ventnor (Albert St), which they saw at a quiet time and were told that Ventnor UDC would be offering land for a bus station to relieve congestion. In fact within a month they compulsorily purchased the Salvation Army Hall and 24 Victoria Street, which were demolished a few months later as part of the proposed bus station site.

The frequent services 1 and 1a between Ryde and Cowes were to be modified with extra journeys to replace trains between those towns, with service 3 (Ryde to Newport) serving Ashey and Havenstreet. BR then announced closure dates of 21 February 1966 (Cowes line) and 18 April 1966 (Ventnor), with last steam trains running the previous day. Electrification of the line between Ryde and Shanklin, costing an estimated £680,500, would take place in winter 1966/7 with a complete closure of nearly three months (during which time SVOC provided the replacement service).

Following the 1966 railway closures, and the subsequent provision of replacement services by SVOC, the vocal support for the Vectrail project to re-open the Ryde to Cowes route caused the bus company great concern. This railcar, the Sadler Rail Coach, seen with its designer Charles Sadler Ashby, on the leased test track at Droxford (Meon Valley line), had visited the Island's Trade and Industries Fair in late 1966 and would have been used if the Cowes line had reopened.

Author

The councils submitted an appeal against the Traffic Commissioners decision but Ventnor UDC, already criticised by the local hoteliers for an ineffectual objection at the hearing, withdrew their appeal. Ald Mark Woodnutt MP had asked for a special adjournment debate in the House because it was not considered the Shanklin to Ventnor bus service would work and it had been established that public expenditure involved in providing a replacement bus service (and road improvements costing £100,000) was greater than modernising the Shanklin—Ventnor railway (the cost of an extra sub-station and equipping with the third rail). He also raised the whole issue in a twenty minute Commons speech and Mr Baines, with Ald Woodnutt, met with the new Minister of Transport, Barbara Castle, who advised she was unable to reverse a closure decision by her predecessor – despite the circumstances of that decision. Mr Harding, SVOC GM, had assured Ventnor hoteliers, before the closure, that the company had sufficient buses and staff to cope but could hire in from local coach operators if required.

Closures went ahead and replacement buses took over but it soon became obvious that the six buses per hour peak Saturday frequency to Ventnor was over provision. Whatever the 1963 census figures had shown, the expected numbers were not there as many visitors no longer chose Ventnor as their destination.

SVOC's 1966 financial results were well below that expected (as a result of service 39) so the company considered making application for a subvention payment. By then a private scheme by the Vectrail Society to reopen the Ventnor and Cowes lines, using diesel railcars of the Sadler Rail Coach Co, had been submitted with IWCC support and the SVOC Directors viewed the proposal as a serious threat. Mr FPB Taylor (the railway appointed director) was asked to communicate the feeling of SVOC to the appropriate rail authority!

The well-fought IW campaign to save the railways had revealed many suspect statistics. BR was obviously anxious to rid itself of the Island lines at all costs; in 1965 it had even proposed financing a new Ryde Esplanade bus terminal at £153,500 and the electrification was carried out at minimal cost as another attempt to close would have been made in 1975. By then the formation of the National Bus Company had ensured the railway and bus companies were competitors. The battle for the Island railways was only partially won but as the Island's MP stated "Of all the battles fought to retain railways, that from the Isle of Wight was the longest and most vigorous." If the Shanklin line had also closed, SVOC might have found itself in a serious financial situation, with a fleet of buses only needed on peak summer Saturdays.

When Ventnor was cut off by a snowstorm in December 1967, telegrams were sent by the local Hoteliers' and Business Associations to the Minister of Transport, Mrs Barbara Castle, pointing out that the alternative to rail transport arrangements to Ventnor had completely broken down, compared with what she had led the public to believe! If snow hits the Island, hilly Ventnor is the first place to lose its buses.

This picture, believed to date from the winter of 1959/60, sums up the nature of bus operation on the Isle of Wight until recent years. Even before the further extension of the Ryde depot yard into a former orchard, it was the company's winter storage area and often at least a third of the fleet was delicensed during the winter. 'LB's, 'LA's and single-deck LLs are evident along with a Bedford OB bus and an ex BH&D AEC Regent open-top.

RHD/SVOC

Leaf green or National white:
The NBC era

The 1968 Transport Act brought a major change to the bus industry. This set up the National Bus Company, Passenger Transport Authorities and Executives in major conurbations and provided for both rural service grants and a New Bus Grant (set initially at 25% but increased to 50% in October 1971) to enable operators to finance the replacement of conventional crew buses by those built for one man working.

The new Act was the work of Minister of Transport Barbara Castle, who had been appointed by Labour Prime Minister Harold Wilson to integrate public transport. Provincial services had been controlled by two major groups which had separated following disagreement in 1942. Some were controlled by the Transport Holding Company, which had taken over the Tilling Group road passenger interests from the British Transport Commission when that was dissolved by the 1962 Transport Act to become more commercial, while the British Electric Traction group consisted of companies like Southdown that had a minority THC holding inherited from the historic railway involvement under the 1928 Act. The BET Group were pressurised into selling their bus company involvement to the THC in November 1967 and the statutory NBC was set up as a commercial organisation that would rationalise duplicated operations and reorganise services to meet the needs of each area. The Act received Royal Assent in October 1968 (but by this time Barbara Castle had moved on to be replaced by Richard Marsh!) to form the new NBC on 28 November 1968. It became operational with a fleet of more than 20,000 vehicles in its subsidiaries throughout England and Wales from 1 January 1969.

Southern Vectis, which had always been one of the smallest, but most profitable, constituents of the Tilling empire, was allocated to NBC's Southern Region initially. The ten regions were reduced to six in 1970 (SVOC was now in the South Eastern Region alongside Southdown, East Kent and Maidstone & District), to three in 1972 (when it became part of a huge Southern Region stretching from Kent to Cornwall) and finally increased again to four regions in 1977 when the Island company became part of a Midlands & West Region stretching north to the Potteries.

At first there was little outward change, at least to the passenger, although a new 'mirrored N' emblem began to appear. In 1971/2, new uniforms were presented for staff in all constituent companies with road staff being supplied with a striking style in Air Force mid-blue. Twelve SVOC staff had been involved in 'wearer trials' before the final design was chosen. Repainting of buses began with Lodekka No 539 in August 1972, which left the paint shop in the leaf green standard livery with white relief and fleetnames in corporate style including the 'mirrored N' motif. It took four years to work through the fleet although a 'temporary' livery with the cream repainted white and new fleetnames applied to the existing darker Tilling green was rapidly applied to all buses.

The leaf green was a difficult colour to apply and even more difficult to match if a vehicle had to be touched up after

Not all the Lodekkas survived long enough to receive full NBC leaf green livery but many were adapted with the cream band overpainted white. New fleetnames were applied and wheels repainted grey. Number 549 (ODL 9) pulls away from Ryde bus station supervised by the duty Inspector, the late Joe Taylor.

D Strange

panel damage! The alternative livery that could be selected by an NBC operator was poppy red. SVOC actually ran an ex Devon General Bristol LHS in red for some months when it was urgently required for the Yarmouth Bridge service, while a driver trainer from East Yorkshire, that was never used by SVOC, also carried that livery. Coaches were painted in white with red and blue lettering, including a large NATIONAL fleetname applied to the body sides, this being the livery chosen for the Corporate Activities Group of NBC, established to promote express tours and company coaching and, later, *National Express* and *National Holidays* work. The ex Shamrock & Rambler fleet managed to retain their orange and cream colours with Fountain Coaches fleetname while SVOC did not intend to paint coaches over eight years old and only used for local work in corporate colours – but this caused comment during the visit of NBC Chairman, Freddie Wood, to the Island. Subsequently elderly Bedford VAL coaches were adorned in white!

The next stage was for the application of suitable signs and fasciae in corporate image style (with the large emblem prominent) to all SVOC buildings – this was undertaken in 1973/4. For the staff, a major improvement was the adoption of a good pension scheme (known as BEST) from April 1974 and the issue of privilege passes for staff and dependants that could be utilised on the services of any other NBC operator, as well as those of SVOC.

The earliest evidence of the new organisation was the merging of the Shamrock & Rambler (THC) Ltd fleet, based in Southampton and Cowes, with Hants & Dorset and SVOC respectively. The old established Shamrock & Rambler business at Bournemouth had been bought out by THC in 1966, with the name retained, and the Ventnor coaching firms of EH Crinage & Sons and H Randall & Sons were acquired in the spring of 1967, probably as a lever to gain a foothold in Isle of Wight coaching. As a result the directors of Fountain Coaches, Cowes also decided to sell out to S&R in November 1967. They also ran coaches in the name of Holmes Saloon Coaches (of Cowes) who they had taken over, with J Groves of East Cowes, after the war.

Crinage, Randall, Fountain and Holmes were all old-established businesses that had been running charabancs from the 1920s or earlier. From 1967 all four trading names were retained, together with liveries although Fountain changed their colours from red and cream to orange and cream.

The Atkey Bros had established coaching from their Fountain Garage using two ex World War I Army chassis bodied as charabancs (Island Queen, followed by Island King by the 1920 season) and had an impressive modern garage, built by director BJ Newnham at Northwood c1935, but this was sold after the war. Fountain expanded to Yarmouth in prewar years with the purchase of the Yellow Cars business. Fountain also ran taxis and limousines and could claim royal patronage as Queen Mary, when visiting the town with King George V during Cowes Week, would hire a limousine for an

The last pair of Bedford VAL coaches arrived in 1971 and were bodied by Plaxton of Scarborough. Delivered in 'Tilling' cream and green, they later received a repaint into 'corporate' National overall white livery before finally becoming Fountain vehicles. Number 410 (SDL 743J) is seen at Little Canada Holiday Camp, Wootton, inaugurating an express service to London (Victoria).

SVOC

afternoon tour to Ventnor and Shanklin, returning over the Downs. BA Baldwin had occupied the post of Traffic Manager with Fountain for many years and he was succeeded by his son, Les, in 1964.

In February 1969, Southern Vectis was advised that certain assets of the Shamrock & Rambler operation on the Island would be transferred to them but it would remain a separate entity under SVOC control. This was part of NBC policy to rationalise operating units for an improvement of coordination and integration. Capital expenditure for the transfer, on 31 May 1969, amounted to £45,329 for the goodwill, 20 coaches (mostly Bedford SBs or VALs, with a few Fords and an ex SVOC Bristol LS6B) and equipment, freehold garages at Church Place, Freshwater (ex Yellow Cars, for six vehicles) and Carvel Lane, Cowes (which also comprised a car park and an office opened in 1951) and leasehold booking office premises in Cowes at 96 High Street and 1 The Arcade (the main Fountain office), plus a lock up office on the west side of Yarmouth Square.

Under the direction of Les Baldwin local operations continued largely as before, with the individual liveries and fleetnames of the constituent operators retained for a few years until new vehicles arrived to replace the old. The Fountain Coaches fleetname remained, with the orange and cream livery devoid of the NBC emblem, and batches of coaches ordered by SVOC henceforward included several appropriately liveried for Fountain. The High Street office was closed and The Arcade office vacated in early 1977 upon refurbishment of the SVOC enquiry office at 32 High Street to accommodate the Fountain staff. The Yarmouth office was also given up in 1977 but by this time a Glasdon portable building, better located to attract passengers arriving by boat, had been positioned on the nearby quay as a booking office.

The new NBC organisation brought more scope for promotion within the bus industry for the company's officers. Chief Engineer, David Searle, departed for Aldershot & District at the end of 1968 and was succeeded by Arthur Bishop, from Brighton, Hove & District some months later. Hebble Motor Services (a former BET company) was the next destination for ATM, David Dickinson, who left SVOC towards the end of 1969 and was replaced in the post by Alan Rolls, who spent $3^1/_2$ years on the Island, before becoming ATM (Planning) at Crosville.

The GM & Secretary, Bert Harding, retired in 1970 and was replaced by Ronald Wade (ex Eastern Counties TM) in the former post and Gary Batchelor, who had joined SVOC as Chief Accountant in August 1968, in the latter. Ray Price, who had worked at Nelson Road since the 1950s was promoted to Assistant Secretary in March 1973. A former Secretary, Ian Patey, was briefly appointed to the directorate in 1971/2, while the railway influence on the Board finally ended in April 1972 with the departure of South Western Divisional Manager Llew Edwards. This association went back to the earliest days of SVOC when Gilbert Szlumper (a Waterloo officer) and Alistair MacLeod (Asst for the IW railway) held positions on the board.

Eirgwyn Jones arrived in 1973 from Bristol Omnibus Co to become the last occupant of the ATM's post and in 1976 Mr Wade was appointed GM of Eastern Counties Omnibus Co (and Divisional Director of the Southern Division, NBC Eastern Region). Michael Wadsworth, previously Hants & Dorset's TM, moved across the water as SVOC GM, a post he occupied with enthusiasm through five difficult years, until he moved as GM of Bristol Omnibus Co. Geoffrey Webb replaced him on the Island during the years 1981–4, having previously managed National Travel (South West) at Cheltenham. He subsequently moved to Hampshire Bus (a division formed by the splitting up of Hants & Dorset) and then Gary Batchelor took the post of GM in addition to that of Secretary that he already occupied.

The Island in 1968–70 is probably best remembered for the three great pop festivals that attracted thousands of music fans in the era of hippies, flower power and love and peace. The first festival, an overnight one day event on August Bank Holiday Saturday/ Sunday 1968 (so in fact the very end of the THC regime) designed to raise money for the IW Indoor Swimming Pool Association, was held in Hell Field at Ford Farm, Fairfields, near Godshill. The acts booked were top bands of the day – The Move, Jefferson Airplane, Fairport Convention and Tyrannosaurus Rex – who attracted a crowd of more than 7000, each paying 25/- (£1.25) for a ticket, but a cold night in a stubble field drove the fans home early and the event was less successful than hoped.

Transport arrangements involved extra ferries to Ryde and trains to Shanklin from where SVOC became involved. In addition to regular service buses thence to Godshill (followed by a long trek), the company provided half-hourly express workings from Shanklin station yard and an hourly express direct from Ryde to the site. Because of the narrow roads at Fairfields, an anti-clockwise circuit for buses and coaches was established, inwards via Rookley and Bleak Down and back via Niton and Whitwell.

The organisers, now calling themselves Fiery Creations Ltd, planned their 1969 event more commercially – this time at Woodside Bay, Wootton, over three days leading up to August Bank Holiday. A spectacular array of performers, including Bob Dylan, The Moody Blues, The Who, Tom Paxton and Julie Felix, attracted some 100,000 people to this IW Festival of Music, but this time the ticket price had doubled to £2 10/- (£2.50)! The site was less than ideal for public transport although Wootton Bridge, served by frequent SVOC services 1, 1a, 1b and 4, was less than a mile away. Duplicates were run but the return exodus involved 80–100 buses and coaches over a twelve hour period to clear the crowds and was hampered by the congested approach roads and the difficulty in turning vehicles. An estimated 70,000 single journeys were made to or from the Festival.

The promoters planned an event of even greater international significance for August Bank Holiday 1970, anticipating an attendance of 200,000, but did not publicly conclude the location – East Afton Farm, Freshwater – until about three weeks beforehand. International singer/guitarist

The Isle of Wight Pop Festival staged at Afton Down near Freshwater over the weekend of August Bank Holiday 1970 was probably the biggest passenger movement the Island has ever seen. With every bus pressed into service, SVOC operated from Ryde, Cowes and Yarmouth to the festival site and hired in from other local coach operators. It was also beneficial to every busman and coachman! This is the field, viewed from Tapnell, at the end of the show as the hippy generation trudged homewards.

RHD/SVOC

Joan Baez, backed by Donovan, Jethro Tull, Chicago, Richie Havens, Jimi Hendrix, Sly & the Family Stone and Procul Harum, amongst many others, performed at the incredible three day event. For the bus company it was an unrivalled operational challenge – on what would in any case have been a busy holiday weekend – but with the advanced planning and cooperation with other local operators, the police and councils, transport arrangements were put together.

Good liaison was established with British Rail, Sealink (who had vessels available through the night from Ryde) and Red Funnel. Express road services were established from Ryde or East Cowes to the site with a special service from Yarmouth to Afton Corner. At the request of the police, Wilmingham Lane was kept free of buses as it was used as a pedestrian route from or to Yarmouth. The Ryde service began on the Wednesday as fans began to arrive in numbers, building up to a maximum of 120–140 vehicles returning from East Afton on the Sunday night/Monday morning after the last performance. This should have allowed for the lifting of at least 4000 during the hours of darkness when the bus fleet would normally have been parked up in the depots. Four vehicles had been allocated to the service from East Cowes which commenced on the Friday while two spare buses were available at Freshwater depot to cover the Yarmouth situation.

The Ryde terminal was at the Esplanade (with loading being undertaken in the spare bus parking area known as The Siding) although during night hours Quay Road Coach Park was utilised, while the south side of the Esplanade was used for parking spare buses. At the festival site an area of hardstanding was established for setting down or picking up, although buses were actually turned at Afton Corner, west of the site. SVOC's last surviving lowbridge buses were relicenced to provide additional capacity while coaches were hired from Moss Motors, Seaview Services, Shotter's, West Wight Bus Co and Towers.

Arrival of the fans at Ryde had actually begun early in the week, as reported in the *Sunday Telegraph* by correspondent John Peyton, who wrote "They started arriving a lot earlier than last year, said the bus driver, as though he was Peter Scott talking about geese!" 11,500 were conveyed on the Thursday, 17,300 (the climax of journeys to the site) on the Friday but only 9,600 on the Saturday. For the return journey some fans left on the Saturday (12,000) or Sunday (4,000) but the main exodus, delayed by a very late programme finish, moved 37,000 overnight on Sunday and through the Bank Holiday.

The delay meant the 140 buses, with crews, were lined up for up to six hours just waiting for the rush. Crewed double-deckers commenced the movement while coaches, either SVOC, Fountain or hired in, brought up the rear guard and were booked by roving conductors. The police allowed two or three buses to depart together every few minutes – laden down with well behaved music fans and all their impedimentia associated with spending several days on an open hillside. At the end of the event all buses were thoroughly disinfected! An estimated 130,000 single journeys had been made over the nine or ten days and the whole transport arrangement, expertly organised and overseen by TM Don Howe, had worked well. Both he and Company Secretary Gary Batchelor, armed with Setright ticket machines, were at the festival site acting as conductors! The whole event depended considerably on the dedication and long hours worked by the busmen; almost every employee was involved and they still have their vivid memories of the operation. SVOC had proved its ability to cope with the most demanding crowd movement.

The new NBC era saw a succession of retirements of members of staff, in all grades, who had served SVOC since the earliest days and, in many cases, the Dodson era of Vectis Bus Co. Those included Insps Pat Gamble (40 years) and Maurie Cooper (45 years), Wages Clerk Reg Davies (41 years – although he had infact been a temporary conductor from

1922 so in reality accumulated 50 years), Traffic Clerk George Langley (46) Drivers Ken Osborne (41), Vic Farrell (41), Stan Rigby (40), HG Cave (46) and Spencer Harris (42), Chargehand Fitter Len Woodward (41), Setright Fitter Arthur Chatfield (42), Fitters Stan Larcombe (43), Bill Clarke (41) and Bert Brading (44). Sadly several members of staff including Foreman Coach Driver Arthur Pardey (49 years) and Inspector Wavell Wale (43), died in service very shortly before their retirement was due.

As the staff was changing so were the vehicles. At the time of the NBC formation, the company was taking delivery of a batch of Bedford VAM coaches for the 'lightweight' fleet, having purchased several batches of the revolutionary twin-steering Bedford VAL coach in previous seasons. For mainland work and extended tours an unusual Duple 'Commander' bodied Bristol RESH6G coach was delivered in 1968 but it proved an embarrassing disappointment; it was underpowered and would not climb hills in Scotland and broke down in the Yorkshire Dales. The problem was not resolved until a new, more powerful engine was fitted.

The Bristol RESL6G was chosen for the single-deck bus fleet in 1967–9, with eight entering service. Some of them regularly worked the tightly timed Shanklin–Ventnor rail replacement but were underpowered on the hills and sometimes had difficulty in reaching Shanklin station to make the connection into the electric train for Ryde! Performance was improved by the fitment of a 5-speed gear box to one example (811), together with improved cab heaters and demisters, but fleet cuts eliminated the type by 1982 so no other RESLs were modified as had been intended. In March 1975, another of the type, no 812, sustained a serious electrical fault while parked up in Newport depot one evening. As smoke poured from the engine, no 812 was shunted to safety by an MW but this could have resulted in another Somerton disaster. As a result all RESLs were rewired.

Five rugged Bristol LH single-decks, with Leyland engines, were bought in 1968/70 for country work but their failure rate was high and SVOC was pleased to see the back of two of them to United at Scarborough in 1977. The company had more success with the shorter LHS6L type – for services along narrow roads in towns and country. The 1969 order was bodied by Marshall, who were also considered for the 1975 order of four vehicles (actually bodied by ECW). One more came secondhand from National Travel (South East) while three more (dual purpose seated) were part of a special late build shared with Western National in 1980. It was planned at one stage to use them as coach feeders.

Following inspection of a Hants & Dorset Bristol RELL6G, nine of the 36 foot buses were ordered in 1970/1 (a tenth was cancelled). The 1972 order featured one more RE – a well appointed RELH coach – which was the front line coach for mainland tours or *National Express* work for almost ten years.

More Bedford VALs had been anticipated for the coach fleet in 1970–2 but in the event only three were supplied – seven VALs, plus one VAM, were cancelled. From 1973 the lightweight Bedford YRT type (later YMT) model became the standard coach for SVOC and Fountain. Twenty-three were bought new up to 1980 (and delivery of another four in 1975 was cancelled). Duple (or Plaxton) built the bodywork, except for the last three which had the problematic bodywork by Willowbrook built to a large NBC order.

SVOC was supplied with 19 Leyland Nationals in 1973/6/7; this was supposed to be the NBC's bus of the future and was built in quantity at a new factory near Workington. The company did not really require more single-deckers and these found even less favour with staff after several skidded across the road in wet weather, in one case (at Whippingham) with fatal result.

The standard double-decker for NBC was the Bristol VRT, with transverse rear engine and a seating capacity of 70 or 74.

Like many NBC operators, Southern Vectis painted VR No 680 (FDL 680V) in a 'Unibus' livery in 1980 when almost new. The advertiser was Moreys, the local timber merchants, and the bus stands at the Southdown Road terminal above Freshwater Bay.

Author

SVOC took delivery of two in 1969 but they were mechanically troublesome at first and, amongst other modifications, had new engine cooling systems fitted. In addition they were slightly higher than the older Lodekkas so could not work the busy service 16 (Ryde–Blackgang) until after the road surface had been scraped under the restricted Morton Common railway bridge in 1976. Four more were expected in 1970 but the order was amended to three and then those were diverted to City of Oxford MS. However, the 1971 order for five (reduced to four by NBC directive) was increased to six by the inclusion of two that should have gone to Crosville! Eventually, over some twelve years, VRT deliveries to SVOC totalled 70 (and would have been 79 but for cancellations), replacing crew-operated Lodekkas. In addition, another 11 secondhand examples were taken in, including three from the Scottish Bus Group who had exchanged an equivalent number of front engined FLFs in a deal negotiated by the NBC affecting a number of subsidiaries. Others were involved in exchanges – with Hants & Dorset who sent six convertible models to the Island, and Bristol Omnibus Co (two).

Just into the privatised era, two more secondhand examples arrived from Devon General, making a grand total of 83 operated, without those in the Solent Blue Line fleet. For many of the Series 3 VRTs supplied from 1977 onwards, the Company took advantage of leasing arrangements negotiated by the NBC with various finance houses including Lloyds Industrial Leasing, Midland Montagu and Hazard. By 1978, Central Works was busily engaged in rebuilding the front floor structure and pillar fixing at the rear and offside of the earlier VRTs. The direct cause was the critical condition of 50% of Island roads, built on clay and prone to cracking up after heavy rain. The attention of the County Surveyor was drawn to the problem but he had already stated $1/7$ of the Island's roads needed complete reconstruction, for which he had no resources. Some Series 3 VRTs less than four years old were now showing signs of rear structure failure while one of the 1969 pair, No 623, had to be written off because of a broken side chassis member. Other chassis repairs had to be undertaken and it was stated that air suspension would be desirable on new double-deckers. More single-deck Leyland Nationals (with air suspension) would not be an acceptable alternative due to summer peak loadings!

At this time (1980) a prototype air suspension B45 double-decker had been built to NBC specification by Leyland and was in service with Ribble. This became the Leyland Olympian and in July 1981 SVOC ordered six for the 1982 Rolling Stock programme. The total bill was £390,000 of which 20% was met by the New Bus Grant. By the following year, only 10% grant was available on the cost of £365,000 for five Olympians and it was phased out altogether by 1984 when six more were delivered.

Central Works had earlier converted of a batch of 1956 Lodekkas to open-top. Complete with front screen to the top deck three buses were prepared for the 1973 season with two more in 1974/5 while an FLF, damaged in a lowbridge accident

at Bracknell, was acquired from Alder Valley to provide a further open-top at Shanklin.

At this stage the future of veteran CDL 899 had been in doubt but it was luckily retained while the secondhand K type open-tops were sold. By August 1975 the average age of the fleet was eleven years (double-deck), five years (single-deck) and seven years (coaches).

The two major property developments in the NBC era involved the opening of bus stations at Ryde and Ventnor. For many years, attempts had been made to reconstruct the substandard railway-owned timber structures used by SVOC at Ryde Esplanade and in 1969 it seemed progress had been made. Meetings were being held between SVOC, BR and the councils to consider a bus station plan submitted by Mr HAF Spooner, NBC Regional Architect. BR's application for an infrastructure grant was refused by the Ministry but it seemed the bus company might obtain a 25% grant towards the capital cost of their element, estimated to be £33,000, but almost to treble in cost before completion. Until the railway station ticket and parcels office were relocated, progress could not be made on the bus station. However the bus bays, depot superintendent's office, Inspector's office and travel office finally became operational on 25 May 1974 and all bus services that had previously started from on-street stops between the plane trees along the eastbound carriageway of Ryde Esplanade now departed from the new bus station. By this date work on the canopy was completed but there was still work on the adjacent railway station to be finished. The layout was 'sawtooth' parking on the stands, with buses reversing out, for which a marshall was provided for the first season. A Dept of the Environment order also had to be obtained restricting the service access road to PSVs.

At the time of the 1966 railway closure there was considerable local pressure for Ventnor station yard to be used as a bus terminal as it had sufficient space for passenger transfers to and from taxis, which Albert Street in the town did not. SVOC was happy to call at the railway station, but en route to the town. Nothing came of this idea but in May 1966 SVOC made an interim payment to Ventnor UDC for use of a piece of land and commenced negotiations for a site comprising a car park, coach shed, the sites of 1–4 Oxford Terrace, 24 Victoria Street and the Salvation Army Hall.

The parcel of land was conveyed to SVOC from the council in August 1967 but planning and progress was slow. A right of way across the site for several householders proved a difficulty that persisted throughout SVOC's ownership of the land. By 1970 the Group Architect had produced plans for a bus station that met with the local authority's approval, in principle. However much infilling and levelling was required, even after demolition of the old buildings, so that surfacing and the provision of waiting shelters was not completed until the spring of 1974. Costing £12,700, the new four stand facility opened for the summer of 1974.

The company had in 1969 tried to purchase the freehold from BR of the land on which Park Road depot at Ryde stood.

Their Estates Dept refused to negotiate and even after the intervention of SV director, George Weeden (also the Railway's Divisional Manager), the selling price was far too high!

The NBC Group had inherited a vast empire of buildings and even in the early 1970s was considering any rationalisation scheme that would raise capital in difficult times, even if it put buses back into busy town thoroughfares. SVOC received a visit from the Director of Property Development in June 1973 and three of their properties – Newport bus station, Shanklin and Cowes (Carvel Lane) coach garage – were earmarked for future development potential, but it was later decided that Newport would only have been considered if the neighbouring local authority car park east of Orchard Street was acquired. Shanklin and Cowes were unsuitable for development at that stage but the latter was suggested for a new coach station. This began discussion with the IWCC Estates Dept who had scheduled the Fountain Coaches Cowes site as part of a central Cowes redevelopment, with a new road cutting across part of the land. Nevertheless, in 1975 the Regional Architect prepared new depot plans which went for planning approval to establish exactly what was proposed for the site.

The Council suggested a bus and coach terminal as part of the development but wanted the coach garage to be sited elsewhere in Cowes. Eventually the planners indicated "a desire for high density residential development on the site while retaining existing amenities" so in 1978 NBC Architects submitted plans for flats over a coach station and car park. The garage deteriorated so was demolished in 1976 but the cleared site continued for coach parking and as a car park for a number of years. The other Fountain garage at Church Place, Freshwater, was vacated in 1977 and let to a local removal firm, as coaches could now be parked on the hardstanding at the SVOC Princes Road depot in the village. A proposed extension to the latter depot to accommodate coaches did not, in fact, reach fruition.

SVOC had sold two of its houses in 1970 (1 Vinings Gardens, Sandown and 'Thatcham' at Fishbourne) but actually purchased another house in 1974 – 9 Collingwood Road, Shanklin, bordering the depot and adjacent to the three similar company-owned houses (bought in 1943), which were mostly let to staff. A couple of other properties, 33 Melbourne Street, Newport and 2 Albert Terrace, Ventnor had been sold in the previous decade while in 1977 the lease was terminated on the coach booking office in Atherley Road, Shanklin.

As fewer bus services terminated in Sandown, the use of Fort Street Bus Terminal ceased after February 1981. The site was considered for residential development and an application submitted to the planners, but South Wight BC was anxious to retain the land for coach parking and it was sold to them in July 1982. Several years later, the area became a six bus overnight outstation for SVOC but it was too close for comfort to Colonel Bogey's nightclub and the author drove back one night to find a bus 'joy-ridden' into the corner of the car park. Luckily, the miscreant could not find reverse on a VRT or the bus would have been stolen!

Another sale (in April 1981) was of spare land at The Orchard, adjacent to Ryde depot. The land had been let since 1953 but it was unlikely this L-shaped area adjoining the houses of Monkton Street would be utilised for parking purposes. A parcel of 0.59 acres was sold to the Council for Small Industries in Rural Areas (of Salisbury) for the building of a factory. Right of joint access was maintained in case the depot entrance on the area leased from BR was at any time lost (for the adjacent open area of the site was freehold property).

The 1970s saw a continuing programme of property improvements although these sometimes were postponed by the financial situation. The existing two pits at Ryde and Shanklin depots were extended in 1970 and a new pit also installed at Shanklin. Similar work was undertaken in 1975 on the four Newport depot pits, together with installation of a new bus wash and roller brake tester. These pit modifications had become essential with the revised dimensions (up to 36 foot in length) permitted for single deckers whereas 30 foot had been the previous maximum permissible length. New bus wash machines were authorised for Shanklin and Ryde depots in 1977/8 although installation took some while because of groundwork complications. The Colt roof ventilation system was fitted at Newport depot, Central Works, Ryde depot and then Shanklin depot over the next few years. As the Health & Safety at Work Act had now become law, attempts were being made to improve working conditions and pit areas were enclosed in the next stage of building work.

Devastating garage fires had occurred at Durham and Hove with the result that the NBC architects insisted on side screens and a rear wall to the pits at Shanklin, to reduce the fire risk, when this was modified in 1979/80.

Expenditure of some £18,300 had been spent on a new Travel Office at Shanklin bus station in the previous winter. The work, undertaken by JCM Shopfitters Ltd, included the replacement of the brick frontage with a full glass shop front and the South Wight Mayor, Mrs Jean Ainsworth, performed the opening ceremony on 5 February 1979. Attempts were made to obtain a ten year lease on a shop next to Ventnor garage for a new Travel Office but these failed and the Architect drew up proposals in 1981 for a larger office to be installed along the south wall of the building fronting Pier Street.

Following the opening of Ryde bus station, a similar 'sawtooth' stand layout was considered as an operational project for Newport bus station as it was thought to be more suited to modern vehicles than the existing parallel platforms but no alteration was ever made. The accommodation block was, however, equipped with a new gas central heating system in 1979 to replace the defective underfloor heating system. Also at Newport bus station, Westridge Construction undertook refurbishment of the Travel Office in the winter 1983/4 and it was launched as a National Travelworld agency in February 1984, when a bus was also unveiled in a mid blue overall advert for the agency. SVOC began another pioneering venture in one of the Newport bus station shops in October 1983 when the VMS Computer Centre was opened (by TV personality John Craven) to sell computers and software.

Shanklin depot's commercial value made it vulnerable under NBC rationalisation in the early 80s and the site was sold for redevelopment as a Somerfield supermarket. When the demolition men moved in, they found the wartime air-raid shelters still intact beneath the concrete forecourt where Leyland National No 872 is seen parked. The other vehicle is a visiting Potteries Leyland Leopard coach.

Author

Since GM Walter Budd had performed the opening of the SVOC Sports & Social Club in October 1934 it had been located on the first floor of the Nelson Road offices. By 1974 it had raised sufficient capital to buy land in South Street, Newport, opposite the bus station, for £12,500 and began the construction of a new clubroom and bar which GM Ronald Wade declared open, immediately before he left the Island in June 1976. With the old clubroom vacated, this allowed for extensive refurbishment of the Head Office at Nelson Road, beginning with the entrance hall. The offices of the ATM, Senior Traffic Assistant and Traffic Dept were now moved from the north end of the building to the ground floor, adjacent to the TM, while a Committee Room and Training Room were subsequently created. The intention was also to allow accommodation for the expanding Vikki Osborne holiday organisation. In 1978/9, an extension had been envisaged by building over the single-storey General Office and Computer Room but was not progressed. At this time computers were a novel development for SVOC, who had purchased an NCR500 machine from Alder Valley in the autumn of 1974 and installed it to run a programme on route analysis.

The last major building development of the NBC era was in the Central Works, which by this time was under the jurisdiction of Mechanical Supt, Vernon Gibbs. The facilities had quickly become outdated as vehicles had increased in size, so production was being hindered. Working conditions in the old maintenance pits were primitive (as they were only three foot deep and three foot wide) but the refurbishment programme, mooted in 1981 and involving pits, stores, paint and bodyshop, was finally completed in June 1984.

SVOC/IWCC relations had not been good because of the rail closure situation but a combination of political legislation and economic necessity in the 1970s eventually cemented an alliance. In 1971, the IWCC, unhappy with SVOC's monopoly of schools work, purchased a small fleet of Strachan bodied Bedford buses, in yellow livery, to convey a proportion of schoolchildren and this meant a loss of revenue to SVOC. The Council also appointed a Transport Officer, and their fleet has increased over the years, although in 1978/9 the 'Yellow Buses' proved so unreliable that SVOC obtained much casual private hire work to cover their school journeys until the original fleet was replaced by new leased Fords.

As provided for in the 1968 Act, SVOC agreed with the IWCC, in December 1971, a rural bus subsidy of £4500 to finance the operation of ten unremunerative routes for a trial six month period. These were the 3/3a (Ryde–Havenstreet—Newport); the 9/10/11 group between Newport and Ventnor; 13a/24 between Sandown & Alverstone; 28 (Newport– Alum Bay); 30 (Newport–Gurnard); 35 (Newport– Porchfield–Cowes) and 43 (Newport–Newchurch–Sandown).

Earlier in the year (May) SVOC had given up running service 19 to Newtown, leaving that hamlet (once the Island's capital and a thriving port until sacked by French invaders in the 14th Century) without a bus until the operation of two rural post buses began in January 1975. The other route served the Yafford area of the West Wight and covered narrow roads unserved by SVOC who thus co-operated in planning routes and fares. Under NBC accountancy, cross-subsidisation of routes, as had occurred in the past, was not encouraged and SVOC was needing to tighten the belt.

A milestone was reached on 17 May 1971 when double-deck OMO operation began, from Newport depot, using recently delivered VRTs but there was union resistance to a blanket OMO introduction. Locally, several years earlier, an Urban Bonus Scheme had been initially rejected because of alleged "mistrust of management", fear of redundancy and the use of OMO double-deckers as rumours circulated of a complete OMO conversion within three years. The GM, had given an assurance that 100% OMO was impracticable for the Island and, in any case, they had too many crew operated buses to effect a rapid changeover. However by 1973 the total staff had been reduced, within a year, from 508 to 472.

In 1973, the company had maintained fares without increase as revenue was in excess of budget but had suffered an unprecedented road staff shortage that had affected stage carriage duplication and excursion operations in both early and late season when students, and school teachers who drove during the holidays, were unavailable. The reduced summer timetable had to be introduced earlier in September than usual.

The fleet consisted of 190 vehicles of which only 146 were licensed in the winter period. One man operation had reached 48.4% of all miles operated, compared with 42.07% in 1972. Staffing improved in 1974, but SVOC had to press the Traffic Commissioners' office because of delays in arranging driving tests and suggested bus companies should have their own tester.

In May 1974 SVOC produced a Public Passenger Transport Report for the Council, who were preparing a submission for their Transport Policies and Programmes document required for 1975/6 and thus welcomed SVOC staff expertise. The IWCC recognised the need to grant aid more loss making services to prevent further decline in bus usage and encouraged experiments, such as express buses, postbuses or minibuses but were very concerned about payments made by SVOC to NBC HQ under its statutory duty. As it was a 'viable undertaking', they felt it was being called upon to contribute more than its fair share with the result that subsidies would have to be found by the council.

Frequent wage awards (made by the National Council for the Omnibus Industry) and subsequent applications to the Traffic Commissioners to increase fares were adding to SVOC's problems but their routine fares application in January 1975 brought an unjustified response from the Chairman of the Commissioners, who said "We are concerned about the age of vehicles being operated by SVOC and the rate at which the company are able to introduce OMO. They should exert pressure on the NBC to ensure that the average age of these vehicles is considerably reduced and OMO is speeded up". He also commented that the company should co-operate more with the councils. The GM refuted the remark, especially as the relationship with most council officers was good, although some members would always be critical as long as a statutory duty to NBC had to be fulfilled. The oldest buses in the main fleet dated back to 1954 but had probably done less miles than mainland rolling stock half their age! Although granted, the February 1975 fares increase was a massive 28%.

SVOC's TM produced a report for the IWCC about the possible introduction of minibus services on the Island but it was not progressed and the Council resisted subsidising SVOC beyond the budget provision and promised to object through the Traffic Commissioners hearing to any service reduction.

1975 proved to be the first year in SVOC's history that it sustained a deficit and in the autumn, in a bid to reduce costs, it applied to withdraw all Sunday morning and late evening journeys (allowing operation on a one shift basis). All councils objected and the application was declined by the Traffic Commissioners. Joint Bus Working Parties were established between SVOC and the IWCC, meeting monthly and producing some beneficial results to both sides.

The company introduced a 'Senior Saver' pass during the winter months from autumn 1976, available for eleven or thirty-four weeks and allowing the purchaser half fare travel. The scheme continued each winter and was extended to a Summer Saver in 1979 with a young persons' Student Saver pass introduced in Sept 1979 and a Jobhunter's Pass in 1982. Previously, the only concessionary fare in operation was for OAPs on supplementary benefit who received books of 5p paper tokens to be exchanged on the bus.

By the 1976/7 year, the IWCC was making a £130,000 grant for loss making services, so SVOC had to show the council, and ratepayers, that it was seeking economies by continuing OMO, which by early 1977 had reached 69% of the total mileage, with the total conversion of Ventnor depot as well as some Ryde duties. At this time the Ryde–Shanklin railway received an annual grant of over £200,000 and in 1977 the IWCC was faced with the possibility of taking on this subsidy or seeing the line closed. BR met with the Council in February 1977, putting forward that the existing rolling stock would need renewal in 1980 with a £4m replacement cost and that there was a parallel bus service which could affect continued Government support for the railway. A continuing concern to SVOC was the disparity between Cheap Day Return rail fares and SVOC's 'singles only' policy.

Town services were the worst loss-leaders and the IWCC used its transport experiments budget to promote a revamped Newport network serving Pan, Whitepit Lane and Priory Park under the *Medinabus* branding. Using LHS midi-buses, it commenced in October 1977 with a flat fare, which speeded up loading. Timetable leaflets distributed house to house helped to promote the improved service which saw a passenger increase of 50% within a year. Ryde was the next town targeted and the *Rydabus* scheme began on 11 December 1977, launched by Cllr Roy Westmore, on routes 6 (Elmfield), 7 (Haylands), 9 (Pell) and 10 (Binstead). A flat 10p fare (or 16p transfer) was offered with improved frequencies and extra coverage of new estates. An eastern Ryde diversion to serve Albert Street and Well Street had to be withdrawn because of sustained residents opposition to buses "shaking their houses"! The service also had to be removed from the Lower High Street precinct but ridership increased by 25% in the first year.

In 1978 Cowes and Ventnor were considered for town services but County and Police objections to using Cowes High Street precinct proved a problem and the next IWCC supported scheme was the *Sandliner*, services 37/38 serving Sandown and Shanklin and launched by South Wight Mayor Ivor Davies in May 1981. This featured a zonal fare system (15p, 25p, 35p) because of the longer routes. In July 1981, the *Rydabus*

The opening of a Tesco store on the old Ryde Airport site in 1981 began to revolutionise Island shopping habits. Several free shopper services were set up and Leyland National No 871 (XDL 795L) stands at Tesco on service 81 at the start of operations, supervised by Chief Inspector Hughie Smith.

SVOC

Vectis Bus Co Daimlers had crossed the Medina river using the Cowes Floating Bridge on off service runs but before the inauguration of the *Cowes Clipper* local service Southern Vectis carried out tests with a Bristol LHS, No 202 (KDL 202W). However, clearances would have been inadequate at certain times and it was several years before the extended service 4, using Iveco minibuses, made the crossing as part of a regular service.

SVOC

Elmfield route was extended to a new Tesco superstore built on the Airport site at the edge of the town; also introduced was a network of four contract services bringing shoppers from other East Wight locations. The last of the town service projects was the *Cowes Clipper* (with suitable maritime motif representing a type of vessel once familiar in the port) which was inaugurated by MP Stephen Ross in February 1982 to serve a route network linking Cowes and Gurnard. Connection with East Cowes via the Floating Bridge had been investigated but the Bristol LHS

buses would have grounded on the ramps at certain states of the tide.

The brightest spot in a difficult period was SVOC's Vikki Osborne holiday division. This had been instigated in 1969 by TM Don Howe as a means of keeping a clerk with plenty of summer work, but little in winter, fully employed. Weekend Winterbreaks were offered, including travel to and from the Island and accommodation, at a choice of five hotels, plus a Rover ticket for bus travel on the Island. The first winter produced a turnover of £2000 but by 1980 this had risen to £0.5 million, involving 50 hotels and some self-catering establishments, in an all the year business. Marketed as the IW Breakaway Holiday, the promotion included a publicity caravan that toured London railway terminals, as BR acted as agents. The developing business at its zenith required a staff of five, including Inclusive Holidays Officer Phyllis McCarthy, who was awarded the MBE in 1982 for her hard work in developing the business but who left SVOC in 1983 to run a post office.

Coaching had also been hit by the recession and lost £52,000 in 1975. The fleet stood at 52 (35 SVOC, 17 Fountain) in August 1976 – the largest number ever owned – but with mileage increased by 20% per vehicle this was reduced to a total of 44 by 1978. Although Island operations would never achieve the mileages operated elsewhere, there was now the basis for a profitable coach operation with lightweight vehicles being retained for a ten year life. Some National Travel holiday tours were being run from the Island – for which a couple of Bedfords had reclining seats – and this total was increasing to 20 per year while there were weekend express workings to Victoria, Southend and, from 1980, Gravesend.

GM Mike Wadsworth considered 25% of the coach fleet should be heavyweight vehicles and ordered two Leyland Leopards, as Bedfords were no longer suitable for mainland work involving sustained motorway operation. His successor outlined in 1981 an urgent need to obtain *National Holidays* and *National Express* work, as well as the operation of more mainland and continental tours, but this would not be obtainable without heavyweight vehicles. SVOC had only its two Bristol RE coaches, nine and thirteen years old respectively, plus the two Leylands on order. Nothing suitable was immediately available from other NBC companies but SVOC required nine such coaches by April 1983. Mr Webb suggested they could either look for returned rental NBC stock, which would be cheap but after 4½ years hard labour could be troublesome, buy nearly new secondhand stock from dealers or

negotiate with dealers for new stock they might have on their hands. (The latter source yielded two Leopards while another secondhand one came from Western National.)

SVOC had pursued a policy of buying suitable Bedfords over previous years – two VAMs from Lincolnshire, six YRQs from Maidstone & District, a YRT from National Travel (SW) and six YRTs from Western National, at book value, but the latter had suffered a series of mechanical breakdowns despite being prepared for MOT at Bournemouth.

A new coach staff agreement to regularise pay and conditions had been drawn up in 1979, as a prelude to merging SVOC and Fountain Coaches into one unit, but because of the impending 1980 Transport Act, bringing deregulation to coaching, they kept their separate identities. *Wightrider* was adopted as a brand name for the touring programme and appeared as a fleet name on the vehicles. Experiments were undertaken with liveries (including red/black/white and orange/black/white) before green/orange/white was chosen as a new standard for the Island based fleet. The two arms of the coaching organisation were increasingly intertwined but still managed by Les Baldwin, who was another recipient of an MBE for his coaching work in 1986.

For many years, SVOC had operated all stage carriage routes on the Island with one exception – the coastal route from Ryde to Seaview which ran along The Duver private toll road and had been run by Seaview Services (previously Newell's) since 1922. By the end of 1977, working director John Higgins wished to retire but had no successors so was looking to sell the two bus, 11 coach operation, which employed seven permanent staff and held a stage and 14 Express licences. The garage property – Seafield Garage in Ryde Road, Seaview – was excluded. SVOC were interested in part of the business but the owners wished to see it sold as a whole. Moss Motors were interested in the coaching but not the bus operation, so there seemed to be scope for a joint acquisition. No progress was made, however, and the delivery of a new coach increased the previous vehicle valuation by Baker West. Relaxation of licensing at the end of 1979 was

An experimental coach livery was white with red and black relief applied as part of the *Wightrider* branding. Number 417 (ODL 174R) waits at Quay Road coach park at Ryde, a site since redeveloped.
Author

Like most NBC operators, SVOC introduced several urban minibus schemes using Ford Transits from the huge batch that the group purchased to rescue town services from financial problems. Number 251 (B251 LDL) of the first batch commenced Ryde's *Wanderer* service to Binstead in March, 1985 and is seen climbing Hillrise Avenue, then newly built to connect two residential estates.

Author

seen to reduce the value of the coaching activities and in the end the whole firm was sold early in 1980 to Albert and Mary Robinson who had then recently started a Ryde coach operation.

1983 proved to be another record low year for SVOC, with a loss of £164,000, and GM Geoffrey Webb submitted his Restructuring Proposal in the late summer to help the company out of its financial problems. These envisaged:

(1) The abolition of Assistant Chief Officers' posts (ATM Eirgwyn Jones was already on the move to Oxford, while Ron Plater (ACE) would take early retirement in January 1984);

(2) The cost of an early advance to 100% OMO – in terms of redundancy payments – was to be calculated (but in fact the expected phasing out did not occur);

(3) Improvements to Newport depot (2 extra pits) would enable Shanklin depot and bus station to be closed by April 1984; the Shanklin site, including four houses, was subsequently sold in Sept 1984 to the British American Tobacco Co (parent company of International Stores) for the building of a supermarket. In addition, Ryde depot was to be reduced to outstation status in September 1984 subject to an extra parking area being found in Newport near to Nelson Road depot (for which sites at Whitepit Lane Chalk Pit and Nine Acres Sports Field were considered), but in fact this part of the scheme did not occur;

(4) Specifications were being exchanged with Hants & Dorset MS in respect of secretarial function.

The proposals cast a considerable shadow over the company, especially the Shanklin closure although most staff were accommodated elsewhere, with disturbance payments being made. The bus station was actually used for another seven to eight months as redevelopment gradually encroached and reduced the available platforms. The nearby railway station yard was favoured by some as an interchange terminal but a lay-by, with shelters, was decided upon for Landguard Road

adjacent to the former bus station site. Shanklin depot had received considerable expenditure within the previous seven years – including bus washer, pits, fire precautions and ventilation equipment – while the Travel Office had been extensively modernised. The building would now be demolished so £30,000 was required to modernise the Regent Street premises.

At the end of 1984, Don Howe (TM) took early retirement and the new appointment to a post now designated Business Development Manager (BDM) was Stuart Linn, who arrived in January 1985 after having previously been manager at Midland Fox's Leicester (Southgate) depot. In the following September, CE Arthur Bishop also retired after forty-nine years in the industry, having served with West Yorkshire, United Counties, Western National and Brighton, Hove & District before joining SVOC. Alan Peeling, formerly with London Transport, was appointed to the engineering post in November 1985 to replace him.

The re-election of a Conservative government in 1983 placed Nicholas Ridley back in the post of Secretary of State for Transport, which resulted in a White Paper being produced in July 1984. It found that only 8% of travel was now by bus (cf 42%, 30 years before), criticised the highly restrictive licensing system and advocated competition as a means of keeping down costs. It proposed reorganising the NBC into smaller subsidiaries and then transferring them to the private sector. The enactment of the new Transport Act on 30 October 1985 made this a reality.

Commercial services were required to be registered by February 1986 after which competitive tenders could be sought. Full deregulation was to take effect from January 1987, when any operator could introduce a local service at 42 days' notice to the Commissioner. This was seen by unions and many others as a death knell to many uneconomic rural services.

A sudden weight restriction on Yarmouth Bridge led to an immediate requirement for small buses and Devon General supplied SVOC with two, including No 201 (LFJ 849W). This is seen in the village of Freshwater wearing the special West Yar Link livery designed by the company's painter, Alan Cooley.

Author

As a final defiant gesture the NBC cancelled most of its 1985 orders for full size buses and made a bulk purchase of 'end of range' Ford Transit vans which were converted to minibuses by Carlyle Engineering for use on high frequency town services making it less attractive for other operators to enter the market. Two 23 seat minicoaches had been ordered in 1984, subsequently changed to three Ford minibuses which converted the Ryde–Binstead routes from 2 March 1985, following a publicity launch during the previous week by strongman Geoff Capes who hauled minibus 250 through Ryde High Street. From May 1985 the programme was extended to a new Newport–Cowes Pontoon service linking into the Red Funnel hydrofoil to Southampton. (The route number (91) coincided with the headcode of BR's Southampton–London trains.) Newport town services, and the link thence to East Cowes, were converted in September, followed in January 1986 by the other Ryde service (to Elmfield and Tesco). This produced a Ryde network which included a frequent service to the Pier Head via the Promenade Pier.

Stuart Linn's regime began with an operational problem caused by the imposition of a 7½ ton limit on the 1860s River Yar swing bridge at Yarmouth from 14 January 1985. The 11/12 service had to be split with the Yarmouth–Freshwater Bay portion being operated by a small Bristol LHS bus – not always adequate for passenger numbers – and the local police threatened prosecution for overloading! SVOC hastily acquired two more of these buses from Devon General to assist with the emergency. Passengers and drivers changed buses, although some workings made the long diversion via Wilmingham to reach their destination or Freshwater depot. Although the

bridge restriction was sudden it was not entirely unexpected as the County Surveyor had warned in 1981 that it was "a substandard structure for modern traffic." The arrangement continued, and affected other West Wight seasonal services, until a new bridge opened in September 1987.

The new BDM had an ability for network design and the 1985 summer timetable brought the most far-reaching changes that had occurred at one time. The Sandown/Shanklin–Newport services continued to Cowes instead of the West Wight, which was now linked to a new service 7 from Sandown to Newport via the Arreton Valley. One of the Ryde–Cowes services now diverted at Newport to Ventnor via Chale and the *Cowes Clipper* branding was dropped. A cartoon character, Professor Decker, appeared in SVOC publicity to promote these and other changes.

In January 1986 the company had expressed interest in operating the River Medina chain ferry linking East and West Cowes on a subsidised basis for a minimum of three years. The Council had lost some £185,000 on the operation in the previous year and was considering its powers to let out the right to operate it but, in the event, this did not happen. In February SVOC registered with the Council the 85% of its network that was considered commercial, leaving the remainder to be put out to tender by the IWCC.

The Council had at last introduced an Islander Travel Card in 1986, allowing local bus or train concessionary travel for all resident Senior Citizens or children aged 14–15, and this was later extended to the Disabled and Young Persons aged 16–18.

East Cowes was selected as an outstation in May 1986 and a piece of council land between Well Road and York Ave purchased as an overnight parking area for three buses and several coaches. This was eventually reduced to a single bus (for a long time this was the last conventional RE single-decker, No 863) and part of the land leased to Southern Water. The land was eventually sold in 1998 after absorption of the East Cowes bus into Ryde's allocation.

As the NBC was prepared for dismantlement, the SVOC Management Team of three – Messrs Batchelor, Linn and Peeling – were now poised to buy their company. Talks were held with financial institutions and staff (as a share purchase scheme was proposed) but it was then found there was a rival bid from Worksop coach dealership Carlton Commercial Vehicles (Notts) Ltd, an ATL subsidiary, whose directors visited the Island to inspect the fleet and property.

The SVOC team had the confidence to submit their offer at an early stage despite the uncertainties facing the bus industry. Their bid was accepted. No longer was there an umbrella organisation to advise on or execute property, vehicle, publicity or other matters.

The new Southern Vectis was on its own.

The outstation at East Cowes was, for a long time, the home of Bristol RELL6G single-decker No 863. In this April 2001 view at Ryde, No 863 is seen wearing the parchment/holly green livery, the only RE to do so. Also visible is the coach-style seating fitted in 1999. Interestingly, No 863 was the last Bristol RE to operate with any of the former Tilling Group companies.

P Savage

Shades of green to red or blue
Back to privatisation

"We've bought a bus company!"
Privatisation Day (8 October 1986) and SV Directors Dick Dabell, Stuart Linn, Alford Collins (Chairman), Gary Batchelor and Alan Peeling celebrate their purchase of the company from the National Bus Company at Padmore House, Whippingham.

SVOC

At 16.30 hours on Tuesday 7 October 1986, Southern Vectis Omnibus Co Ltd reverted to private ownership as the Managing Director & Secretary (Gary Batchelor), Fleet Engineer (Alan Peeling) and Business Development Manager (Stuart Linn) signed the transfer deal, at NBC's London headquarters, with Portfolio Chairman John Hargreaves, for the 130 vehicle fleet, and its properties, for a figure of £1.2m. While the new directors were jubilant at their success in overcoming the rival bid of Tony Lavin's ATL Group, there was obvious regret from NBC at the break-up of its empire.

County Development Capital and the National Westminster Bank helped finance the buyout and shares in the new holding company, Southern Vectis Ltd, were immediately taken up by the management team and some 80 staff members. The aforementioned managers became Managing, Engineering and Commercial Directors respectively, while Ms Kate Boyes became Secretary.

Two local businessmen, Alford Collins and Dick Dabell, joined the Board in a non-executive capacity, Alford Collins as Chairman. A Financial Director, Ian Palmer, was appointed to the Board in the following September. The Company's registered office was transferred to Nelson Road, Newport from their solicitor's address in Pyle Street.

Southern Vectis Ltd had been incorporated on 1st April 1986 as an 'off the shelf' company called RP63 Ltd, the name of which was subsequently changed. The management team had contracted the purchase of the SVOC business from NBC to occur on 14 June, but completion of the deal was protracted. As a result, this became the third sale of the 52 bus operating NBC subsidiaries rather than the first, previous transfers to management teams having involved Devon General (19 August) and Badgerline (23 September). The National Holidays subsidiary had been the first of the NBC's 71 entities (which included engineering operations) to change hands. Southern Vectis Omnibus Co continued to exist as a subsidiary of Southern Vectis Ltd.

To celebrate the victory for the Island, the company provided half fares for all passengers on 'Independence Day' (22 October 1986) when, in a ceremony in Newport bus station, local MP Stephen Ross cracked a bottle of champagne over the wheel of bus No 651, just out of the paint shop in the revised emerald green livery.

On the domestic front, an early meeting with Solent shipping operators Sealink (and in particular James Sherwood, supremo of parent company Sea Containers) brought a desire for a close working relationship resulting in Sealink liveried coaches, minibus connections on Ryde Pier and advertising on catamarans. Southern Vectis expressed a long term interest in Sealink should it ever be for sale, which at that moment it was not.

The company was endeavouring to purchase a house in Melbourne Street, Newport, to give access to an overflow staff car park but eventually only a plot of land that had access through the depot was required.

South Wight Borough Council had made an approach, in association with the fire damaged former town hall next door, regarding Ventnor (Albert Street) Bus Terminal for housing development. Alternative arrangements for bus stop locations and parking would have been necessary, but it would be another five years before the bus station closed.

The Princes Road garage site in Freshwater also interested the council for housing development and would also have required relocation to another parking area. In the event, the acquisition of the West Wight Bus Co created a demand for extra parking and the plan was shelved.

Two non-operational properties – another house in Melbourne Street and the coach garage at Church Place, Freshwater (inherited from Shamrock & Rambler) – were repurchased from National Bus Properties Ltd, to which they had passed in 1985. Both were resold within a few years, being of no operational value, although Church Place had been used for the storage of the Solent Blue Line Bristol LH buses before they were sold.

The new organisation possessed 11 other properties around the Island. Negotiations were already ongoing for the former Fountain Garage site at Carvel Lane, Cowes (identified some years before as part of a town centre redevelopment by the council). Newport bus station had been earmarked ten years earlier by the NBC as being of commercial development value as it was becoming group policy to revert to on-street bus stops in many towns.

At an early stage there was interest in trying to purchase other NBC subsidiaries and of the seven considered, Wilts & Dorset Motor Services, based at Poole and Salisbury, was a particular target. A former SVOC Assistant Traffic Manager, Alan Rolls, was at this time Managing Director of W&D and he was to be included in the bid when negotiations commenced in December 1986. However, the W&D management team was split and the three officers who put forward their own bid became successful purchasers, from five interested parties, when the result was announced by NBC in April 1987.

By this time the best 'prizes' amongst NBC subsidiaries had been sold and prices being offered for the remainder had risen dramatically as 'outsiders' such as Stagecoach or Endless Holdings submitted bids.

Expansion was still an attractive proposition and in March 1987 it was decided to set up a Southampton operation with John Chadwick, recently redundant from Southampton City Transport, as Managing Director. Twelve surplus VRs would be sent from the Island, supplemented by four ex Cambus vehicles acquired through a dealer, and placed in service as crewed vehicles on lucrative town routes to Millbrook, Thornhill, Townhill Park and Weston.

The new subsidiary, Musterphantom Ltd (which traded as Solent Blue Line) commenced on 25 May 1987 with a ceremony at Ocean Village, in Southampton's former dockland, involving Radio Solent presenter Sandy Jones. The yellow and blue painted fleet was based at Lorraine Auto Park in the Chapel area of the city and was running in direct competition with the former municipal authority, which responded with a fleet of ex London Routemasters.

The new operator was well received but from an early stage

The setting up of Solent Blue Line in Southampton in 1987 was an important landmark in the post-privatisation years. The initial fleet was largely made up of 13 to 16 year old VRs including SBL No 27 (ex SV No 630) seen passing the Canute Café, a former ale house that served as an unofficial restroom for the crews in the pioneering years.

Author

maintenance problems created a degree of unreliability, Blue Line possessing no workshop facility of its own and having to send vehicles to a local commercial firm.

Not surprisingly, by August 1987, Southampton Citybus threatened retaliation on the Island and did reach the stage of interviewing potential drivers. They also negotiated with Islandlink, the commercial vehicle successor to British Road Services, for the parking and maintenance of up to 20 vehicles. Local operators Moss Motors and Seaview Services had been approached by Southampton (who even made an offer to purchase Seaview Services) but as neither wished to become involved in a bus war all approaches were refused. If Southampton Citybus had established itself on the Island's busiest routes, there is no doubt it would have become an aggressive situation, but as the summer passed the threat receded and relations within Southampton improved by the end of 1987.

Having been rejected in its Wilts & Dorset bid, Vectis looked to the territory of that 200-bus operator for its next competitive operation. Avon-based Badgerline had become an ally and together they agreed to a joint venture in the W&D Salisbury and Poole territory.

The Salisbury city network, using minibuses from Badgerline, was registered to commence at the end of June 1987 while the Bournemouth and Poole services began on 6 September 1987 using a collection of Bristol RE single-deckers from both Badgerline and Southern Vectis plus some minis and a few double-deckers.

Another 'off the shelf' company, Quayshelfco 175 Ltd, had been obtained for the operation which was branded Badger Vectis. Originally SV would have held 55% of the shares, Badgerline 40% and local management 5% but this was later altered to 20%, 75% and 5%. Garage and maintenance facilities were obtained with Bournemouth Transport at its Mallard Road depot even though the main routes (Poole–Bournemouth–Mudeford) ran through Bournemouth's territory. Other routes ran from Poole to Turlin Moor, Canford Heath and Broadstone.

Three factors affected the operation – a constant staff

shortage, vehicle problems, as the least reliable examples had naturally been selected at each depot for transfer to Poole and the location of the Poole terminal, adjacent to the railway station but separated from the town's shopping centre which was better served by W&D departures. These, combined with determined efforts from Wilts & Dorset to maintain its territory, led to an abrupt demise in March 1988.

The Ryde minibus network had seen a cutback as services to the Pier Head were poorly patronised but from Newport there was extension of the Priory Park service into new housing at Gunville and a new service to a residential part of Wootton from early February 1987. The Wootton service was extended to Fishbourne Car Ferry Terminal once turning arrangements had been resolved.

With the assistance of a Rural Development Commission grant, a minibus service (31) commenced on 23 February 1987 to connect Apse Heath, Alverstone and Adgestone (all in the Arreton Valley) with Sandown and Shanklin, extending to Luccombe and Sibden Hill. Worked by a 16-seat Transit with a regular driver, the route traversed some roads that had never seen a bus service. However after a year the tender was lost to Wiltax.

Two acquisitions were made in Spring 1987. The first was the long established West Wight Bus Co, together with four Ford coaches, for a consideration of £70,000, but the garage in Avenue Road, Totland, and the rest of the fleet was sold separately. The coaches taken over continued to operate in grey livery (with red relief) and a separate West Wight unit was set up under the jurisdiction of the SV Coaching Manager. A complication arose in that Moss Motors considered they had already entered into a contract for the West Wight business and sought a High Court injunction against the West Wight directors.

After the sale of the nonstandard Ford coaches SVOC's three Bedford/Willowbrook coaches maintained the grey livery and West Wight fleetname.

Even at this time the future of the Coaching Unit was under consideration and a coaching business in northeast England was being sought for purchase to provide a regular flow of

Later in 1987, the company embarked upon a joint venture with Badgerline, Badger Vectis, in the Bournemouth area,. The fleet consisted largely of Bristol REs such as TDL 568K (ex SVOC 868) seen in a line-up at Poole Station.

Author

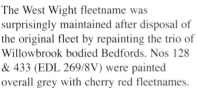

The West Wight fleetname was surprisingly maintained after disposal of the original fleet by repainting the trio of Willowbrook bodied Bedfords. Nos 128 & 433 (EDL 269/8V) were painted overall grey with cherry red fleetnames.

Author

holiday business to the Island. Following the deregulation of coaching in 1980, two of the large independent groups had purchased Island hotels but the coaching unit of Southern Vectis, part of the NBC at that time, would not have been permitted to follow suit, even though this might have maintained its supremacy.

The second purchase, on 15 May, was new territory for Southern Vectis – the acquisition of the AB Wadham (Rentals) self drive business, of 93 Pyle Street, Newport, which operated from a yard in New Street with a fleet of nine primrose and chocolate-liveried Mercedes Luton vans and pick-up trucks. The business had been operated by Tony and Pauline Wadham since 1973.

Southern Vectis next became embroiled in one of the most disastrous sagas of post-deregulation – that of Portsmouth City Transport Ltd, which had been formed from the city's municipal undertaking in October 1986.

The City Council had rejected a local management purchase, leading to the MD's resignation, but the delay allowed a new joint Badgerline-Southampton Citybus competitive venture to be set up, with minibuses, under the Red Admiral fleetname.

When the Portsmouth company was put on the market, a Vectis bid of £1.15m was submitted and of the ten bids received by the council, the Island one was favoured as it offered an improved and expanded service, as well as a good pension scheme for employees. However the March 1988 deadline was extended to allow the local busmen to improve their offer. In the meantime Vectis reduced their bid to £700,000 after scrutinising the Portsmouth accounts and finding the financial situation worse than expected in the 100-vehicle, 235-staff operation. Depots at Eastney and Leigh Park were not included in the sale.

The PCT problems had been exposed to rival bidders, thus reducing the company's value, but Vectis was still the successful bidder. They now stated that a workforce reduction and service cuts would be necessary but the Council refused the alternative Southern Vectis conditions which included franchising, 160 redundancies and the introduction of bus lanes. There was a hostile reaction from the City workforce which resulted in the withdrawal of the SV bid. A joint bid with the workforce was considered but rejected and by June a sale had been concluded to a joint Southampton Citybus-Portsmouth staff team who established themselves as Portsmouth Citybus – although that was far from the end of the Portsmouth saga.

At the end of 1987, when it seemed that other municipal

companies would be forced to sell, there was a proposal for involvement in a joint Bournemouth Transport (Yellow Buses) buyout in which Southern Vectis and Badgerline would have minority shareholdings. This would have intensified the rivalry with Wilts & Dorset but Bournemouth did not wish to become involved.

There was success however in the purchase of one minor and one major undertaking, within a day of each other in October 1987, to expand Solent Blue Line into a large scale operation.

The Bishops Waltham based bus routes of BS Williams Ltd, (who traded as Hants & Sussex MS) was acquired for the cost of the goodwill (£5000) and value of the fleet which included a modern Leyland Lynx and six ex London AEC Merlins and Swifts. None of the vehicles remained with SBL for long, as even the Lynx was sold to the West Riding group.

The major acquisition (for £1.15m) was the Southampton operation of Hampshire Bus (including Eastleigh and Waterside outstations) from Stagecoach Holdings of Perth. This was to include 82 buses operating in an area bounded by Fawley, Romsey, Eastleigh and Botley (with through services to Bournemouth, Salisbury, Winchester and Fareham) and the goodwill, but not garage properties. Hampshire Bus (which was a fragmentation of the old Hants & Dorset Co) retained its Winchester, Basingstoke and Andover operations, having been bought from NBC in April 1987. The Southampton (Grosvenor Square) garage continued to be used until a major service reorganisation from 3 January 1988, when some of the surplus buses returned to Hampshire Bus.

SBL operating units were established at Eastleigh, Hedge End and Hythe (in addition to that already at Southampton) with some ex Hampshire Bus work franchised to Marchwood Motorways of Totton. At the same time SBL withdrew from the Townhill Park city route.

Southern Vectis still hoped for expansion on the mainland. At the invitation of its Chairman, James Freeman, discussion opened in March 1989 with People's Provincial, the only example of an Employee Share Ownership Plan in the sale of NBC subsidiaries.. This undertaking was an amalgamation of the old established Gosport & Fareham Omnibus Co with Hants & Dorset's Fareham garage operations, and ran into SBL territory around Southampton.

Despite an initial breakdown of negotiations, talks continued during that autumn and an offer for acquisition was put to staff and shareholders. SV executive directors attended a mass meeting to discuss details but their offer was rejected by a majority of shareholders and Provincial was eventually sold to First Group, by which time it had expanded into Portsmouth.

Talks had also been held with Provincial over a possible joint approach to Stagecoach for the Portsmouth/Chichester area operation.

Still eager to gain a foothold in the Portsmouth area, SV later made an offer to Southampton Citybus for the share capital of Portsmouth Citybus, equal to a bid made by Stagecoach, but reluctantly withdrew the offer after talks. In August 1990 the Portsmouth question again arose when Stagecoach was forced to divest itself of the city routes following a Monopolies & Mergers Commission enquiry and SV made an offer, as it did again in 1994 when Transit Holdings were ready to sell the operation which had by then become Portsmouth Transit.

Another independent contender in the Bournemouth area, Poole Bay Services, made an approach to SV to be bought out in 1988, while the purchase of the 15 vehicle Stanbridge & Crichel Bus Co at Wimborne,was investigated. However, Badger Vectis had been a costly exercise and it was not desirable to compete further with Wilts & Dorset in whose territory these operators were situated.

A keen interest was maintained in the industry as a whole, particularly privatised former NBC companies.

SV also sought to diversify into tourist related businesses and from 1989 considered the purchase of the Ocean View and Cliff Tops Hotels in Shanklin and the Royal York Hotel (Ryde), as well as an oil distribution business, excursion boats in the western Solent, the Needles Hotel & Pleasure Park complex at Alum Bay and the Hythe Ferry, pier and tramway.

The most unusual potential purchase considered by SV was

The initial SBL operation was based around Southampton city services but Basil Williams then sold out the Bishops Waltham part of his Hants & Sussex business, including this ex London AEC Merlin VLW530G seen at Eastleigh. His non-standard fleet did not survive long enough to carry fleet numbers or SBL livery.

Author

Burt's Brewery in Ventnor. The 'real ale' business owned six freehold pubs and had paid a peppercorn charge for its water supply from a natural spring in the cliff. Difficulty in transferring these rights, building deterioration, liability to a family trust and then the calling-in of the Receiver in spring 1992 eventually brought a change of heart, so SV withdrew their offer. This would have been a first for a bus company although IW Tours had bought public houses at Brighstone and Nettlestone.

SV made several approaches to the IWCC to form a joint company to take on the Island's 'Yellow Bus' school fleet (in 1990/5) but fearing a monopoly the Council rejected this.

An important local purchase was made when the Seaview—Ryde–Haylands route of Seaview Services was taken over from 2 March 1992. The Seaview–Ryde route had been inaugurated on Easter Monday 1922 with a bus named *Twinkle*, owned by Newell's and driven by Charlie Nash. Until the dawning of the deregulated era, this route had been the only independent stage carriage service on the Island for many years. Latterly it had been run with ex SVOC vehicles – first a pair of Bristol REs and then a couple of VRs which were disposed of by SVOC after running the last journeys on 29 February. The takeover should have been from 1 January but the IWCC considered the tendered journeys awarded to Seaview Services could not be reassigned to SVOC and should be retendered. SVOC operated this service (12) with an open-topper during the first summer season.

Seaview Services had then recently relocated from their traditional Seafield Garage, in the centre of the village, to new premises at Faulkner Lane, Sandown (also used by SVOC as an outstation replacing Shanklin station yard), so the off service running made the service less economic and the firm wished to concentrate on coaching.

SV continued a policy of buying and selling property in the late 1980s/early 1990s. After lengthy negotiations, the former Fountain Garage site at Carvel Lane, Cowes, was sold to John Lelliott Residential early in 1991 – some 15 years after talks on Cowes Central Area Redevelopment had begun.

Latterly the process had been held up by the need for the developers to acquire former railway land in Medina BC ownership. A condition of sale was that the developer had to upgrade passenger and turning facilities by the provision of a bus turning circle at Carvel Lane (which had replaced West Hill Road as the main terminus in Cowes in the summer of 1985). The adjacent site was used for the building of a Co-op superstore.

Church Place garage, Freshwater was also sold in November 1989 and a house at 29 Melbourne Street, Newport, in April 1993. A significant purchase in April 1989, for future expansion, was the Palmer & Harvey (tobacconists) building in Orchard Street, behind Newport bus station. Added to that in May 1990 was the adjacent Bright & Minns (Island Cleaners) laundry which had access from Bowling Green Lane. The building was demolished and it had been hoped to lease the site to Medina BC for car parking but it became the parking area and office for M-Travel.

The Orchard Street building was to be let on short-term tenancy and it seemed set to become the Hollywood Nites nightclub until planning permission was refused. Subsequently it was considered for conversion to a staff rest room and paying in room which would have allowed extra shops to be built in the bus station. However this did not come about, as the closure of the bus station toilets provided the chance to relocate the Section Manager's and Inspector's offices, together with paying in room, in the western block of the bus station, and the Orchard Street warehouse and office building continued to be leased.

A flat at Fountain Court, Cowes, was purchased in September 1989 but was resold in 1994. Park Road depot, Ryde, held on a 99-year lease (expiring in 2037) with the British Rail Property Board (as successors to the Southern Railway) was purchased outright from the Railway at an auction of leasehold properties in February 1990. SVOC already owned the adjacent open parking area.

In August 1990 an accident had occurred in Newport bus station involving a schoolgirl who stepped off the pavement and came into contact with a bus (which happened to be the vintage fleet MW, No 806, moving at slow speed). The Health & Safety Executive became involved and as a result a consultant was engaged to report on safety in all the company's bus stations. Additional railings and markings were necessary at Newport and Ryde but the situation was critical at Ventnor bus station, which was on a slope. Indeed, in October 1987, a driverless VR (No 646) had run away there and collided with the shelter. As a result, after the last service departure (VR No 669) on the 22.02 service 16B to Ryde (driven by the author) on 5 January 1992, the bus station closed and services reverted to using Albert Street, with on-street bus stops, much to the chagrin of local taxi-drivers.

South Wight BC bought the site in 1995 and used it for the building of a medical centre after the company had contributed towards the rerouting of the right of way through the site.

Serious consideration was given to abandoning Newport depot in favour of a new site in 1995. The former Temperature factory at Lake was available but the repair and modernisation of the Nelson Road depot was eventually considered a cheaper option to relocation.

The proprietor of the Royal Esplanade Hotel, at Ryde, anxious to have a view of the Solent for his guests rather than a line of parked buses on the lay-by opposite his premises, had in July 1991 submitted proposals for the oft-discussed new Interchange. These would have involved resiting the railway buildings and found favour with the IWCC, who commissioned Rainey Petrie Design to submit plans, published eighteen months later. The second phase of the proposals was to be financed by the operators but the suggested Interchange was more cramped than the existing bus station so operationally unsuitable. Ryde Interchange still remains a long term project.

Southern Vectis plc (registered as a public company at the

The site of the former railway station and Fountain garage in Cowes was sold for redevelopment in 1991. Ten years later, in April 2001, Dart No 813 is seen in the turning circle at Carvel Lane, outside the Co-op. Compare this view with that of Bedford YRQ No 109 on page 146; the coach is parked just about where the Co-op building ends.

P Savage

1987 AGM having previously been titled Southern Vectis Ltd) also gave consideration to the acquisition of the Savoy Holiday Centre (on the market in 1995) and to a joint venture to purchase and develop Northwood House as a hotel and conference centre (in 1997/8, but abandoned when an expected grant was unavailable).

Before rail franchising got underway, SV had made a tentative approach to Network South East Director Chris Green in summer 1989 regarding the future of the $8^1/_4$ mile Ryde— Shanklin railway which carried two million passengers annually and employed 65 staff. It was seen as a potential tourist attraction but the SV approach to buy the route was rejected, despite support from the Island's MP and the Dept of Transport. The IWCC was concerned at not being involved, as they felt the unprofitable line could end up closed with SVOC buses replacing trains.

Subsequently a local consortium, led and managed by SV, was established to bid for the line's franchise at privatisation. The loss maker was to be turned into a successful business. Light rail operation was seen as the way forward but the planned IW Steam Railway Havenstreet–Smallbrook extension was considered to be the focal point with steam train operation on Ryde Pier, involvement with the motor ship *Southsea* on Solent cruises and the development of the rest as a bright new theme park layout all being possibilities.

By summer 1992 SV, in company with Island MP Barry Field, had met with Minister of State for Transport Roger Freeman on behalf of the consortium which included Wightlink, Hovertravel, Red Funnel and the IW Steam Railway. It seemed the Shanklin line would be one of the first to be franchised but by the time a meeting took place with the Government's franchising department in spring 1993 the Steam Railway and Red Funnel had opted out of the consortium. At that meeting SV had also expressed interest in the coastal lines between Southampton and Eastbourne via Brighton. Railtrack reacted positively but it was made clear that the Shanklin line could not be operated without subsidy.

The response from the Office for Passenger Rail Franchising was less encouraging and the Shanklin line was excluded from the first and second round of tenders. In April 1996 they indicated the Island line would be franchised with subsidy providing the difference between £800,000 income and £3m costs. The SV/Wightlink/Hovertravel consortium then prepared their pre-qualifying document for three types of bid (compliant, non-compliant and for the inclusion of steam operation), and submitted it in August 1996, but the Island Line franchise was eventually won by Stagecoach.

In advance of Deregulation Day (26 October 1986), competition on the Island had begun on 19 May when Seaview Services launched their Red Lynx service between Ryde and Sandown via Bembridge, although this incorporated their traditional Ryde to Seaview operation.

Using several coaches painted in overall red this directly competed with SVOC's service 8 and there was immediate retaliation with additional journeys worked by a special team of drivers, plus a new Ryde–Seaview & Nettlestone minibus route (12) to encroach on the independent concern's territory. In addition the Downs Circular open top route 43 was extended from Ryde to Flamingo Park during the summer of 1986. The situation continued until April 1987 when both operators reverted to their original territories, but with Seaview Services extending their Seaview–Ryde route to Haylands.

Although SVOC had registered 85% of its operation as commercial, and was awarded most of the remainder after tendering, the IWCC issued a number of Medina High School contracts to Moss Motors and Cooke's Coaches of Porchfield (who purchased a batch of ex West Midlands double deckers for the purpose) but later also put the buses to use on a Newport—Gunville route (subsequently started back from Ryde). This operation (trading as Island Travel) began early in 1987 but Mr Cooke's licence was revoked by the Traffic Commissioners in June 1987 because of financial problems. The situation had not been helped by a bad accident involving a school bus near Wroxall. SVOC regained one of the Medina contracts as a result.

In the meantime two other operators had emerged – John Gange, of Cowes, running a minibus between Ryde, Cowes and

Gurnard from early October 1986 and Grand Hotel running hourly between Sandown and Shanklin, with an ex Barton coach.

SVOC reacted again by running extra journeys on existing routes and banned Gange's from using Ryde and Newport bus stations. However, owners John and Julia Gange took the bus station issue to the Office of Fair Trading contending that the 1985 Transport Act decreed that no operator should be in sole control of a bus station as that would allow them an unfair advantage. SVOC argued that their stands were fully utilised but the OFT ruled in February 1988 that they were "pursuing an anti-competitive practice", although they could levy a fair charge. It was a victory for Gange's and a test case having countrywide implications for large operators.

At a subsequent Traffic Commissioners' inquiry, Gange's accused SVOC of putting on unregistered services ahead of him and causing harassment. Indeed SVOC ran a vehicle – nicknamed the 'Gange-buster' by staff – regularly on a 1D service, in a manner not dissimilar to that used by Frank Dodson sixty years before! However when SVOC presented their evidence they accused Gange of altering his timings to gain an advantage, so the Traffic Commissioner told both sides to set aside their differences and put the public first. Eventually, the Gange service, truncated to run between Newport and Cowes, was given up in March 1989 as it was no longer viable.

Although Island Travel (Cooke) had ceased operating there was a threat in July 1987 that Islandlink (responsible for Cooke's maintenance) would start running a bus service as they had impounded the buses in lieu of debts. Grand Hotel ceased their bus service in September 1987 but Moss Motors had started a summer Newport market day service (extended to Carisbrooke Castle) from Sandown and Bembridge which continued until 1991. Regarded as a more serious threat was their peak season Sandown to Blackgang route in 1988 using 'Blue Ferret' branded buses, even though they were still in the red and cream livery of their previous Surrey owner. SVOC counter registered additional journeys on the Blackgang route. Moss also ran from Bembridge (Warner's) to Shanklin, Sandown to Brickfields via Bembridge & Ryde and from Sandown to Ventnor & Whitwell but with a minimal number of journeys that caused SVOC no real concern.

The next competitive route was a Shanklin–Newport (via Arreton Valley) minibus operation commenced in the summer of 1989 by Wiltax and funded by the Rural Development Commission with County backing. SVOC objected on the grounds that public funds should not be used for competing services and counter registered a near identical 99 route from 14 August 1989. This became the preserve of the restored vintage fleet MW saloon (No 806) until the route was withdrawn in April, 1992.

In the spring of 1991, a Sandown–Shanklin minibus service was introduced by Shanklin Coaches and quickly shadowed by an additional SVOC service 2 working for a month or more.

Although in the 1992 season there was slight competition at Yarmouth in the running of a 'Best of the West' Classic Tour by Derek Gawn, the real West Wight clash came in 1993 when Wightline Coaches started to complete on SVOC's important open-top service 42 between Yarmouth and Alum Bay. The Newport based operation had been set up by two former coachmen, Derek Croucher and Mick Ryan, who started running excursions similar to those of SV Coaches and then bought three elderly Leyland PD3 half-cab open-toppers from Brighton Borough Transport.

Although SVOC had the advantage in continuing above Alum Bay to the Needles Battery, the fierce competition attracted press publicity and the IWCC, endeavouring to remain impartial, insisted that the Yarmouth Interchange office should be shared by both operators. The council even offered to refund SVOC's contribution towards the construction costs.

The National Trust, who control operation along the cliff-top road to the Battery, put the working out to tender for 1994 and SVOC was successful. The Wightline service did not resume in that year after the open toppers had been left in all weathers at Alum Bay through the winter. All three were eventually sold to a London tour operator and Wightline continued for a while with their coach operation.

Some parts of the network had always been less remunerative and the Newport Town Services were franchised out on the same basis as had been successfully employed at Solent Blue Line. Services 5b and 9 were passed on 29 April 1991 to Redbeam Ltd (t/a M Travel), a new operation by local businessman Keith Merrett, and marketed as 'The Cross Town Shuttle' which ran on a hail and ride basis. Several redundant 16 seat Transits were supplied by SVOC and ran from a base at Dodnor Industrial Estate but later moved to the former laundry site behind Newport bus station and an office established fronting Bowling Green Lane.

Their scarlet and cream painted fleet expanded and in 1993 M-Travel was awarded the Ventnor & District town bus (service 31) operation, followed by the evening Newport–Blackgang—Ventnor service from 1996. A novel addition was the 'Ventnor Buggy' town tour, worked by a Transit converted to open top, but it lasted only a season. M-Travel suffered an arson attack, totally destroying three buses, at their yard in October 1997 but maintained the service with Ivecos loaned by SVOC.The Cowes–Gurnard route had also been franchised to them, but the business crashed abruptly on 26 November 1999 with the loss of nine jobs and leaving passengers stranded. SVOC resumed partial operation of the services.

For the summers of 1998/9, the Sandown/ Shanklin open top route, the preserve of the unusual 'Shanklin's Pony' open-top Bristol RE single-decker, was franchised to the Traditional Motor Bus Co together with three vehicles. The route was further franchised in 2000 to the Village Bus Co, operated by two of the three Traditional directors. By now Traditional had branched out into coach work as well, trading as Fountain Coaches. Newbus (t/a Westbrook Travel) were sub-contracted to work the route (now renumbered from 44 to 43) and operated as a premium fare tour in 2001, before it was returned to the SVOC fold in the subsequent season to be marketed with the remaining open top routes.

In the meantime Traditional had also been granted the franchise for the Ventnor local bus and Ryde Town service 10 but their involvement with Wightlink in a Newport–Ryde Pier Head cut price catamaran link 'Shuttle' from January 2000 soon resulted in the termination of agreement with SVOC on all routes and they formulated plans to compete on service 44.

As Fountain Coaches, Traditional now took on the Newport Town Service but they also crashed in September 2000 with financial difficulties (after the Wightlink Shuttle had abruptly ceased). After a period in which SVOC and the IWC's Wightbus jointly participated in the town operation, another Newport operator, Alpha Travel (with Capitol Circle fleetnames) took over for four months but the complicated franchising saga ended when SVOC resumed the routes themselves (as service 38/39 now serving Sainsbury's) in May 2001.

Another operator, Brian Isaacson, who traded as Bill's Taxis, had operated a franchised evening service on route 8 (Ryde—Seaview) in 1996 and later took on the Cowes/Gurnard routes on a similar basis for a while.

The last vehicles purchased by the old regime had been the Ford Granada taxi and hire car for the coaching unit (Fountain), although both operations were later franchised to their drivers.

In 1987 ten Robin Hood bodied Iveco 23 seaters were the first privatised era purchases (split between SVOC and SBL) and these permitted the conversion, in September, of route 4 (Ryde—East Cowes) which was branded *Medina Nipper* and crossed the river on the Floating Bridge to Cowes before continuing to Gurnard. The month long winter overhaul of the bridge caused disruption but use of the new service was disappointing, so it was cut back from October 1991. Similar batches of small Ivecos followed for both fleets giving a total of 27 by 1992. Several of the early examples sustained bad accidents, attributed to steering design defects, including No 272 which careered into the Busy Bee Fish & Chip shop in George Street, Ryde.

The first full size vehicles ordered for five years arrived for the 1989 season – three for SVOC and four for SBL – and by 1991 there were 28 in the combined fleets (and the 1990 SBL order had been cancelled in favour of eight somewhat unsatisfactory Mercedes midibuses). The double-deckers were Leyland Olympians with Cummins engines and fully automatic ZF gearboxes. The Leyland bodies, built at Workington in the former Leyland National factory, were disappointing and within a short time defects including water ingress had to be remedied. They also had various mechanical problems so in November 1991 Volvo Bus (who owned Leyland) agreed to supply a new vehicle built to SVOC specification for a free trial in May 1992. There would have been the option to purchase after an agreed period of time but in December Volvo announced the Leyland Workington factory would close.

Looking for an alternative bodybuilder SV authorised purchase of a single Alexander bodied Olympian but Alexander pulled out of the Volvo contract so enquiries were pursued with Northern Counties of Wigan who became subsequent suppliers.

Nine Leyland-badged Olympians were ordered for the 1993 season in a revised cream/holly green livery for the new SVOC *Island Explorer* 7/7A routes combining existing services into a 4-hour 'Round the Island' circuit which phased out the traditional Island coach tours.

The April *Explorer* launch, by comedy actor Windsor Davies, had to go ahead without the new buses, as delivery was two months late. When they arrived, more displaced Bristol VRs were cascaded from SVOC to SBL who had the 1994 new deliveries – four Volvo B10B single-deckers and four Iveco midibuses. Subsequently SBL has received a large batch of Iveco 59.12 midibuses, more Olympians, batches of Dennis Tridents, Volvo B7TLs and Transbus Darts plus a few secondhand purchases, totally transforming the original fleet that consisted mostly of Bristol VRs and Leyland Nationals.

SVOC received seven Northern Counties bodied Olympians in 1995, introducing a new logo and parchment and holly green livery which had already been applied to a few repaints in previous months and replaced the post-privatisation emerald green and greensand cream. The *Explorer* route was revamped in 1998 with the last new Olympians – a batch of eight in a mid and light blue livery including distinctive vinyls.

The previous deliveries (in 1996/7) had been eight Iveco midibuses and a hard worked batch of UVG bodied Dennis Darts, while the most recent new SVOC buses are low floor – a Transbus Dart and seven Volvo B7TLs, with Plaxton President bodies.

Earlier deliveries saw the demise of the 'Vintage Fleet' of 1950s and 1960s buses that had been returned to regular service since 1987. They had first worked Ryde–Cowes 'rounders', a Ryde–Blackgang service 43, followed by an extended 8 Circular (Ryde– Bembridge–Shanklin—Havenstreet–Ryde), the 8/8a between Seaview, Ryde, Robin Hill, Shanklin and Sandown Zoo and, in their final season (1996) the 11/12 from Ryde to Alum Bay. Latterly the buses were becoming more difficult to put through their annual inspections, availability of spares was a problem and an incident in Ryde involving a schoolboy who fell down the stairs of No 565 into the road led to a decision that they would be withdrawn and placed on loan to the new IW Bus Museum, which had opened in 1997 at Newport Quay, Later, coach No 301, MW No 806 and FLF No 611 were sold to the Museum.

The three open-top Lodekkas (two of which had been reacquired) continued on service 42, which had been extended on the tortuous climb from Alum Bay to the Needles Battery from 1988, for a few more years but they too were replaced by VR conversions and sold in 2002 to Rexquote for use over Exmoor.

Another major investment for SVOC was the introduction of Wayfarer III electronic ticket machines from St Valentine's Day 1993. The company had long been the last large operator to use manual Setright ticket machines although many of them only dated from the late 1970s, having replaced short-range models dating back to the Setright introduction in 1951. A total of 576 machines had been purchased during that time and latterly they could issue tickets to a value of £19.95.

The company purchased two Ford Granadas for use as a taxi and hire car in 1987 and placed them under the control of Fountain Coaches. Les Baldwin (Coaching Manager), Gary Batchelor (MD) and Alan Peeling take delivery from Premier Motors at Newport.

SVOC

Wayfarer and Almex electronic machines had in fact been used experimentally in September 1991 on the East Cowes-allocated bus (No 680) used by regular driver Arthur Joy in a bid to find the best replacement. With such a high volume of 'on bus' rover ticket issues, SVOC needed a validator machine that could both read and issue these magnetic cards.

Staff training was held and on the night of the changeover every bus had to be adapted, depot readers brought into use and modules issued to all staff, although conductors retained the old machines until portable Wayfarers were introduced later in 1993. Initial teething troubles with validators were largely due to severe vibration on the Island's 'different' road surfaces.

One of the benefits of the new ticketing was the ability to produce a picture of travel patterns which could assist in subsidy provision and the Council also purchased computerware to obtain the data. Hand-written waybills were also discontinued and duty cards now provided for the first time.

At privatisation, the coaching fleet had been almost halved in ten years. Three high specification 62-seat Leyland Olympian/ECW double-deck coaches costing £85,000 each had been due for May 1986 delivery to work Island coach tours. However delivery was so late the vehicles were not accepted and instead were supplied to Alder Valley (North). SVOC then decided to undertake a thorough rebuild of its two newest Olympian buses (701/2) to convert them to 64 seat soft trimmed high specification coaches for both Island and mainland work. The work was spread over two years and they entered service, with 'cherished' registrations, in 1987/8. A new metallic silver livery had been introduced in 1986 and the double-deckers had a variation of that with blue relief and promotion for ferry operator Wightlink. Older coaches were repainted grey, except for vehicles to be used on *National Holidays* work which carried the appropriate white 'corporate' livery.

In 1987 the coach fleet was almost equally divided between lightweight Bedfords, up to nine years old and the heavyweight contingent of two Bristol REs, four Leopards and eight Plaxton Paramount bodied Leyland Tigers (of 1983–6), for mainland work. The West Wight acquisition brought another four lightweight coaches into the fleet and two secondhand Tigers and a Leopard were also bought in 1987.

The company had leased four ex Shearings Volvos and two ex Hills (Tredegar) Tigers from a dealer to set up a franchised coach operation, Blue Line Coach Hire, also trading as Weypac Tours, in association with Solent Blue Line at Southampton. This was short-lived and the coaches returned to the Island upon cessation in spring 1988. All six vehicles joined the SVOC fleet.

Two new Tigers also joined the fleet in 1988 for mainland tours, plus four Leopards (of which only one was used) acquired secondhand from the Berks Bucks Bus Co in the following year. The Coaching Unit still needed more mainland *National Holidays* work but the most profitable area of operation by 1989 was the *Wightrider* mainland tour programme, Round the Island and continental work. By 1990, *National Holidays* work had decreased and excursion work was faring less well in a recession year.

The old established Sandown firm of Moss Motors was for sale in 1990 and again in 1991, at which time SVOC made an offer for the goodwill plus the top five coaches but the shareholders decided to carry on. In the meantime January 1991 saw the retirement of Coaching Manager, Les Baldwin, MBE, after 52 years in the industry, having begun his career as a Fountain Garage apprentice. He was succeeded by his nephew, David Baldwin, but for 1991 the coach fleet was reduced to 16 instead of 30, while the full time drivers' establishment was reduced from ten to seven, with altered conditions of service. An amalgamation with Seaview Services had been considered at the end of 1990 and proprietor Albert Robinson would have run the combined coaching unit operation as a branch of the newly formed SV Leisure & Retail Division under MD Geoff Browne, who had responsibility for travel offices.

Another Island coach operator, Neill's Mini Coaches of East Cowes, was declared bankrupt in July 1992 and SVOC took over their order book and contracts.

It was decided a decision would have to be made on the

future of coaching after the 1992 season although there was a reluctance to end this operation. A new coaching manager, Adrian Banczk, was appointed in November 1993 but when he was made redundant two years later Keith Merrett, who ran the franchised Newport Town Minibuses, took over on a year's contract to assist on the tours programme. In early 1997, Geoff Browne (Leisure & Retail MD) took early retirement and Retail Manager Shirley Langridge departed to another coach operator. A new L&R MD, Gerry McKenna, was appointed but upon his departure in June 1998 coaching (as well as retail and the Vikki Osborne organisation) was placed directly under the control of SVOC MD Alan White.

The problems of poor seasons and a changing market not only affected the SV operation – by now marketed as Southern Vectis Coaches – but also many NBC subsidiaries that abandoned coaching. In the Island, Moss Motors of Sandown, established by Major Moss in 1922, finally sold their trading name and existing business to SVOC in January 1994, including a six month lease on their Sandown High Street property, which became a Travel Office. Moss owned two garages in Sandown and other property but this, and the fleet of immaculate two-tone blue/white coaches, were sold separately. Their newest coach, a Leyland Tiger, was considered by SVOC for acquisition but was then found to be nonstandard.

The disappearance of Moss did have a beneficial effect on the Coaching Unit, particularly on Island tours, but, with a huge increase in car ferry traffic, that traditional market was no longer in such demand. Extended tours were not without their problems in 1994 and a serious engine failure on a coach on the mainland eroded the profit.

In a bid to upgrade the fleet two quality Setra coaches were bought in 1991/2 but spares were found to be prohibitively expensive and they were replaced by three modern, but secondhand, Volvo/Plaxton vehicles in 1996/7. In the autumn of 1994, the Coaching Unit had tendered unsuccessfully for the

contract to run inter-terminal and staff buses at Heathrow Airport. Some of the coaching fleet was painted in a new white livery with vinyls of a stereotypical scene (featuring church, hill and a sun) not dissimilar to that used by French operator, Cariane.

By 1996 it was again planned to work with Seaview Services, the Island's other major coach operator, in a bid to overturn the loss. The unit, with clerical staff and fitters, was thus moved to the relatively modern Seaview Services garage in Sandown, which was already used as an outstation. By the following year, broad agreement had been reached with mainland operator Marchwood Motorways of Totton to franchise the entire SV Coaching operation. However at the same time, discussions were underway to franchise the Solent Blue Line city work, which involved acquiring a fleet of Dennis Darts, so they did not wish to take on both operations.

Ten coaches were sold in May 1997, some to Seaview Services who took on part of the business. Two years later, in May 1999, it was decided to sell the remaining fleet, involving seven staff redundancies, and to 'outsource' the business to Kardan Travel of Newport. Southern Vectis Coaches remain with a clerical department to organise and promote a programme of British and European extended tours, as well as mainland day excursions, but the actual coaching work is sub contracted to Kardan.

The Leisure & Retail Division also had responsibility for the Post Offices which Southern Vectis took over from 1992 following discussion with Post Office Counters. The first was at Cowes – reopened in June in the Travel Office at 32 High Street and replacing a former Crown Office further along the High Street. Sandown followed in September but on this occasion the existing post office in Beachfield Road was utilised with the company Travel Office at 32–34 High Street (opened from Summer 1990) being transferred in November.

By this time, talks had also been held with South Wight BC regarding the incorporation of Tourist Information Centres into

The re-introduction of a 'Vintage Fleet' in 1987 created much enthusast interest in SVOC although regular passengers were often less impressed. The busy Ryde–Cowes 1a was the route initially chosen and required four buses. Lodekka No 565, previously on training duties, is seen working along Queens Road, Ryde. The buses were eventually moved to quieter routes but operated for almost ten years.

Author

Travel Shops but the idea was not progressed. In August 1993, SV was successful in bidding for the Shanklin (Regent Street) Post Office franchise, which was taken over in November, replacing the SVOC King's Corner Office at 49 Regent Street. The lease was given up on the former Travel Office, flat above and adjacent property in March 1994. The final Post Office franchise obtained was at Freshwater which was opened, incorporating a new Travel Shop, early in 1994 in the School Green Road premises shared with the Royal Mail operation. SV was offered the franchise of the Southsea Post Office but that was declined.

The company was also interested in the government plan to privatise the Royal Mail and prepared to make a local approach. Although the volume of business increased, within a few years there was concern at the viability of the post offices and in November 1997 negotiations opened with the Portsea Island Co-op for their transfer. They took over Cowes and Shanklin offices in 1998 while Freshwater went to private enterprise in November 1999. The Travel Offices at Sandown and Ventnor were closed just before the 1999 season.

The other important arm of the Leisure Division was the package holiday facility, still marketed as Vikki Osborne Breakaway Holidays. This had always fluctuated according to the fortunes of the Island's holiday industry and in 1987, following a poor season throughout the south, was considered for sale to Sealink who ran a similar scheme. At this time the organisation had been split into three with Vikki Osborne (IW) Holidays Ltd dealing with the domestic business. Also established had been Vikki Osborne (UK) Ltd, a joint venture with Badgerline for coach-breaks to the South Coast or IOW, and Golden Sovereign Holidays, a joint venture with the Royal York Hotel to bring passengers to their Ryde hotel. There was also an associated Club Holidays Ltd business established to bring groups such as British Legion Clubs to the Royal York but a serious loss resulted in the winding up of the venture in

1989. Badgerline Holdings withdrew their involvement in the UK operation, thereby terminating the experiment and Golden Sovereign Holidays was also eventually terminated. By 1998 Vikki Osborne Holidays had expanded to include Isle of Man business and offered to take over the Manx Government's package holiday scheme. However in late 1999 it was decided to sell the Vikki Osborne organisation to Keith Merrett (of M-Travel) and it vacated its Newport bus station offices for premises in Pyle Street, Newport, but sadly crashed and was wound up in 2002.

One project initiated by SV and deserving greater success than it actually received was the Great Britain Bus Timetable. Stuart Linn, with his interest in timetables and scheduling, had approached Westbrook Travel owner Peter White in December 1993 about editing an ambitious publication that would list all principal bus services throughout mainland Britian. A pre-production issue, published in January 1995, contained 3300 tables with information from 400 sources. In five years there were 17 more issues produced with support from major bus groups including, from 1998, *National Express*, which enabled the inclusion of coach services.

Wider distribution to libraries, tourist information centres and railway stations was now possible and the GBBTT was distributed by major booksellers. In addition, a series of 'Getting Around' derivative books – covering Wales, the Highlands, Lake District, Rural Yorkshire and Norfolk/Suffolk – were produced in partnership with local authorities and tourist boards. Timetable production ceased when the major groups withdrew funding as electronic systems were seen to be the future direction.

By 1998 the timetable had been developed into an electronic system – initially titled TBC2 but then uniquely named Xephos. The first practical trials for outside customers were at Swansea and York and, as an industry initiative, Xephos won support from the Confederation of Passenger Transport. The multi-mode system produces answers to place-

Two Olympians had a comprehensive rebuild to convert them to luxury coaches. Number 701 (later 101) received a silver and blue livery and encouraged tourists to the 'Round The Island Tour' before this was replaced by the *Explorer* bus service. It is seen here on Ryde Esplanade and was later sold to Southend Transport. As A110 FDL it can now be found in north Cornwall working for Western Greyhound.

Author

to-place bus, rail or coach enquiries in seconds with faster results than any rival.

The government had demanded an information system to be in place by 2000. Xephos was launched at the Coach & Bus 99 exhibition. By now, 15000 key bus stops were included and the system could be customised to precise local requirements with town centre maps or route options. It was adopted commercially by some authorities, the new regional travel enquiry lines standardised on other equipment. The SV board decided no more finance could be allocated to the project and it was sold off in 2003. However the Xephos system is still kept updated for its clientele.

At the end of 1994, SV proposed the establishment of a national telephone enquiry bureau at Newport bus station to deal with rail and bus enquiries, using an 0891 phone number. It was anticipated that if 10% of the travel enquiry market could be achieved, the bureau would require a staff of 60 but, in the event, the maximum number was 16. The TBC Hotline, as it was designated, became operational on 1 March 1995 and a SVOC bus, adorned with TBC posters, was sent to London for the launch. By April 1998 the Train Bus & Coach Hotline was set to be franchised to a company with necessary skills to improve the business while SV provided the back up service. It was relocated to Newstel in Glasgow although a bus enquiry line was maintained at Newport.

The company was keen to establish itself as a consultancy to sell its management services and expertise, especially in Europe and in 1989 it submitted a proposal for minibus operation in the French city of Brest. It became aligned with Via Transtec, a French group who were invited to the UK to inspect urban bus operation. A successful meeting followed in which SV proposed French minibus schemes.

SV next turned its agency expertise to East Germany by putting together a package for marketing and ticketing; an early success was a feasibility study for network changes at Auerbach Kreis. Following a visit to Holland and Germany in late 1991 to study continental transport systems, a German group visited the Island in February 1992 with a 60-foot, articulated, dual-mode Mercedes from Essen. Capable of operating as a trolleybus under town centre wiring, this was tested in diesel mode around Newport (and even successfully negotiated the blind corner to Carisbrooke Castle).

The Polish city of Kalisz provided the first opportunity and, following a strategic review of the bus company early in 1994, SV provided the expertise to update the undertaking in return for a 20% equity stake. An agreement signed with the City Council in June 1994 included the introduction of economies and new working practices to make Kalisz Transit Lines profitable. SV hoped that it would provide a presence in Poland ready for future opportunities as three more towns, including Chelm, expressed interest. Having begun with two gas buses in May 1945 on a Railway Station–Kilinski Plaza route, the municipal system grew to 51 buses on 15 'lines' by the time the controlling company was reformed in 1963. National economic changes caused a passenger decline by

1989, as well as the loss of several routes to competition.

At the time SV became involved with Kalisz Bus Lines Co (the new joint company) 74 buses were operated. Much of the Kalisz project was undertaken by Ken Pond, the SBL MD. To celebrate the 50th anniversary of the Kalisz undertaking, a SVOC Volvo double-decker (No 750), suitably adorned with a Polish inscription, was driven across Europe to take part and was mobbed by eager passengers.

With its understanding of the French bus industry and experience in urban minibus operation, SV was eager to obtain concessions in French towns and in 1995 had a Renault bodied as a prototype demonstrator to be shown to various undertakings. A stake was obtained in the Chelm (Poland) operation but there was less success at Itzehoe (Germany), Agen, Villefranche and Chateaullerault (France). An alliance was formed with Cariane, the state owned French operator and SV was successful in providing its expertise in the French town of Louviers. Following a network revamp, SVOC sent a Lodekka on a publicity visit in October 2001.

The Xephos journey planner system has found a market in France as Connex France invested in the system for new call centres at Beauvais and St Etienne.

Brian Hancock, who had been SVOC CE some twenty years earlier, before achieving eventual promotion to NBC as Group Executive Engineer, returned to SVOC in February 1989 on a six month contract while Alan Peeling was seconded to Solent Blue Line to sort out mainland engineering problems. Alan Peeling subsequently left the company and Brian Hancock was designated Group Chief Engineer with overall responsibility for a combined fleet of 230 vehicles from October 1989 until February 1993. From the beginning of 1993, Alan White, whose engineering background included Yorkshire Traction, Cumberland, West Riding Leicester City Bus and a period abroad, was appointed as SVOC MD, combining both traffic and engineering functions.

At the 1993 AGM Chairman Alford Collins stood down, although he continued as a non-executive director for another year. Gary Batchelor became Chairman of the plc from 1993 until 1997, when he retired and was succeeded by Jack Barr, a non-executive director since January 1994. He had a shipbuilding industry background with FBM Marine and as Sales Director of Vickers at Southampton and served as Chairman for two years until 1999. Mike Killingley, the present occupant of the post, then took over, having previously been senior partner at KPMG Peat Marwick, the Southampton based accountants used by the company. Mel Williams, former Wightlink MD, had served as a director for two years, from 1995, while Dick Dabell, one of the leading business figures in Island tourism, having run Blackgang Chine for fifty years, retired from the directorate in 1996. Kate Boyes, company Secretary, was appointed to the board in 1997 as was Tony Holmes, senior partner in Roach, Pittis, the company's Newport solicitors. Ironically, Tony Holmes, together with his business partner Tony Bradshaw, had briefly been directors in 1986 as a formality in the setting up of the new concern prior

Eastbound buses out of Newport bus station no longer have to negotiate the High Street traffic congestion on their way through the notorious Coppins Bridge bottleneck. The Plaxton (Transbus)-bodied Dart, No 300, turns on to 'the Red Carpet' bus lane in South Street in January 2004.

Author

to handing over to the SVOC team to make the privatisation purchase. A more recent directorate appointment, in December 2002, was that of Brian Cox, formerly well known in the Stagecoach Group.

Several long serving employees retired in the early 1990s including Gerald Kent, latterly Coaching Engineering Manager but he had spent most of his 47 year career at Shanklin; John Pullinger (Senior Coachbuilder) whose 40 years had included open-top conversions of the K5Gs and the five LAs and Alec Morris who commenced as a Shanklin conductor in 1949 and became Depot Clerk and then Section Assistant. Bob Downer, who had also been at Shanklin earlier in his career, retired from the post of Section Manager (previously designated Operating Superintendent) early in 1994 after 43 years, while David Cham took early retirement from heading the Traffic Office (latterly designated Commercial Manager) having started and finished a lengthy career with SVOC, although promoted to West Yorkshire and Devon General in the interim. Another long serving member of staff, Chris Squibb who is currently Engineering Manager at Nelson Road, became the third SVOC recipient of the MBE medal, awarded in the 2002 New Year Honours List for services to the bus industry.

Steve Mills, who came to the Island in 1993 from Midland Fox to take over as Operations Manager encompassed the former Section Manager's duties. He returned to the mainland and a new Commercial Manager, Phil Stockley, was appointed to be based at Head Office. Day to day operational duties were then placed under the jurisdiction of a Chief Inspector (Jeremy Rolf), located at Ryde. Phil Stockley had joined SVOC from Buffalo of Flitwick as a management trainee but departed on promotion for Stagecoach Cheltenham & Gloucester in August 1999, although he returned to the SV Group in Spring 2004 as MD of Solent Blue Line succeeding Malcolm Venn.

The next Commercial Manager, appointed from October 1999, was Eric McQuillan from First Eastern Counties although he had previously run Flying Banana, a minibus operation in Great Yarmouth and in fact returned to Norfolk to set up another local bus business. IWC councillor and former Council Leader Marc Morgan-Huws, who had previously operated the Traditional Bus Co, was the next appointment (in May 2000) as Commercial Manager, although during his tenure the post was retitled Operations Manager. He moved to Solent Blue Line in 2003 and was succeeded by Mick Poole.

Although the board was inclined towards non-bus avenues of business, the purchase in April 1995 of 65% of the shares in Knowpower Ltd (renamed Vikoma International Ltd), a world leader in the environmental protection business, came as some surprise to shareholders and staff. The new company, based at Prospect Road, Cowes was part of the Christian Salvesen group (the parent company based in Edinburgh) and were designers and manufacturers of oil pollution control systems, and employed a workforce of 117. Their market covered 120 countries with Japan and Russia being major customers. The firm had originally been created by BP in 1967 and was purchased from them in 1982 to continue the design and building of booms and skimmers, to be employed on oil spills from the Shetland Isles to the Middle East.

Vikoma MD Graham Norman was appointed to the SV Board, although ill-health brought about his resignation in March 1996 when he was succeeded by Albert Brown of Park Brown International Ltd. SV purchased Mr Norman's shareholding, giving them a 77% stake in the business. Albert Brown remained on the SV Board until 1998, latterly as Group Business Development Director.

One part of Vikoma, Branch Hydraulics, was quickly sold on to Dowco Investments Ltd in May 1996. However a further purchase added to Vikoma in April 1996 was lsland-based Air Vehicles Ltd (AVL), manufacturer of high specification fast ferry seats, although the firm was in serious financial difficulties and was eventually 'traded-down' with the loss of twelve jobs at the end of 1997 on completion of an FBM Marine order to equip Hong Kong vessels. The seat drawings were sold to a Folkestone marine company.

Vikoma, which suffered a setback in January 1997 when fire destroyed the Boom Shop at its Cowes factory, needed new premises to expand and sites at the St Cross (Newport) development and Three Gates Road (Cowes), as well as another factory in Prospect Road, Cowes, were investigated. Serious consideration was given to setting up on the mainland, possibly to an assisted area status location, although a site at Hamble was inspected. Late in 1998, Vikoma's commercial section was relocated in new office premises at Southampton's Town Quay. SV bought the remaining 23% of Vikoma shares from Christian Salvesen and also acquired the assets of an air pollution control company, GBE Environmental.

In May 1999 Vikoma acquired the fifty year old Conder Products company based in Eastleigh. It principally produced surface water inceptor tanks and oil/water separators while a subsidiary, Conder Sewage Technology, produced waste water treatment plants. Conder Products Ltd became a wholly owned Vikoma subsidiary and in October 2000 acquired the business and assets of close rival Fibre Reinforced Products Ltd, based in Peterlee, Co Durham. In addition to its pollution control products, FRP had an electrical composites division for the manufacture of high voltage insulator material for the electrical engineering industry. In November 2000 Conder's tank and sewage plant manufacturing was relocated to Peterlee from Hampshire and Devon.

Although Vikoma had at times been highly profitable for the group, economic crises in Russia and the Far East had caused business fluctuations so that a single group owning both transport and environmental concerns lacked industrial logic. As a result Conder and Vikoma were, in December 2000, placed into a new group trading in its own right as Conder

Environmental plc, following the demerger of the environmental division. Vikoma Chairman Gordon Tourlamain and MD Glyn Humphries, who had been SV directors since 1997/9 respectively, moved to Conder Environmental at the demerger.

With the decreasing bus fleet, SV had spare workshop capacity and after privatisation branched out into a commercial engineering organisation within Central Works. It had been accepted as a vehicle testing station and was vetted by Volvo as a potential coach and truck servicing facility and spares dealership, this being granted in summer 1987. From August 1990, Southern Vectis Commercials Ltd, as it had now become, was appointed an official Iveco Ford dealer. This gave even greater potential for the servicing of vehicles and supply of parts as it was a common make of van or minibus on the Island. They hoped to obtain maintenance work from the County or Borough Councils which would entail double shift working.

The Wadham Rentals hire business was placed under the jurisdiction of Commercials and in May 1990 four new DAF vans in a new white livery (with green fleetnames) and two Ford cars replaced most of the existing fleet but it was then franchised and later (in January 1994) sold to M-Carriers. In 1993 the servicing of 24 tractor units and 30 trailers for Vectis Transport was taken on with one tractor unit being retained at Newport Depot as shunter for trailers being manoeuvred.

In June 1996, SV Commercials sought authority as an HGV Testing Centre and Tacho Centre, following which it took over the Island Group 90 vehicle maintenance arm of the IWC including six fitters, a supervisor and a clerk. This meant servicing of the Yellow Bus school fleet and ancilliary council vehicles, but coinciding with an update of the school bus fleet which reduced the maintenance requirement. Closure of the Islandlink commercial garage brought more business to SVC from early 1993 and within a few years 80% of the work undertaken in Central Works was commercial with only a 20% involvement with buses.

SVOC had long pressed the Council to provide better bus

Having bought the Leyland/Volvo Olympian since 1982 Southern Vectis then purchased its natural successor, the Volvo B7TL. A batch of seven with Plaxton President bodies arrived in 2002 and No 103 is pictured here at Freshwater Bay, on a journey from Ryde/Newport, in April 2004. These are the only fully accessible double-deckers in the fleet.

P Savage

Route Rouge livery was eventually applied to all of the 1989/90 Leyland Olympians. Number 712 is pictured here climbing away from the Cowes terminus at Carvel Lane, at the beginning of its run to Newport, Shanklin and Sandown. En route this journey will call at the new Cowes Park & Ride site at Somerton.

P Savage

priority, especially in Newport where the closure of St Thomas's Square to traffic had created a time-consuming diversion to the bus station through the Coppins Bridge bottleneck. A three month trial bus lane (introduced October 1989) through Newport High Street between The Square and Coppins Bridge had alienated traders because of decreased takings and the loss of car parking spaces so was ended.

Following the SV studies of European transport, consultant Colin Buchanan was asked to produce a report entitled *Wight's Transport – The Way Ahead* outlining suggested bus priority measures for the Island. This document was handed to the IWCC Leader and released to the press in February 1992. Its main theme was the idea of a series of Urban Green Routes with streets designed for pedestrians, cyclists and buses. The IWCC allocated capital for bus lanes and bus activated traffic lights and launched a major survey to establish existing traffic patterns in Newport and establish the Report's impact.

In 1999, SVOC came up with a deal for Island firms allowing bulk ticket discounts of up to 50% for their staff to use the buses for work travel, but, sadly, no local firm took up the offer. Again in 2003, it submitted a Universal Green Travel Plan, providing for companies to contribute 1.25% of their wage bills in return for free bus travel for their employees. There was some take-up but large employers such as the IWC or Healthcare NHS Trust did not participate.

SVOC continued to work with the council to change the Newport traffic pattern. An important factor in speeding services through Newport was introduced experimentally from 24 November 2003 when a bus priority contraflow through St James's Square into South Street was introduced for an eighteen month period as part of the Newport Town Centre Management Scheme. The benefit of the 'Red Carpet' (as it was quickly dubbed because of the coloured bus lane tarmac) was the partial avoidance of the notorious Coppins Bridge which caused lost time and wasted fuel. Eastbound buses could

now leave the Bus Station via South Street, against the flow, although this eliminated the busy Guildhall stop.

The *Explorer* route had its blue liveried buses and in 2000 it was decided to phase out green liveries, except for open-toppers which had received the same prewar style apple green as had been used to restore K5G CDL 899 for its 60th birthday. Overall red was chosen for buses working the north–south Cowes—Sandown/Ventnor routes, marketed as *Route Rouge*. These had received a mid-life refurbishment at Southampton, as had the earliest Olympians some years beforehand. An experimental yellow and green livery was chosen for the *Ryde Runner* service (applied to two ex London United Darts), but a dark blue later became standard for single-deckers and midibuses.

January 2001 saw a major service revision with Ryde town services replaced by a diversion of trunk routes 1, 7 and 8 through the suburbs. The *Explorer* no longer ran via Havenstreet, where the service was reduced to a rural midibus route (Ryde–Newport, extended to Gurnard & Cowes) and the Council then inexplicably reduced the height limit on Havenstreet railway bridge to prevent double-deck operation, thereby reducing the road to an overgrown, and highly dangerous, country lane. A further livery change occurred for 2003 when the open-top fleet (except for the K5G) was painted in an eye catching orange. The routes were now marketed as tours with a new service 41 out of Ryde being added to the network. The latter, using the vintage K5G, ran a shorter version of the Downs Tour of another operator.

SV's agency work continues in Europe and with its 'Quality Networks' concept, it has won recent contracts in Essex, Hampshire, and with Ceridigion CC to produce a study of that North Wales transport operation. Southern Vectis has certainly kept in business and independent, by diversification and involvement in a variety of ventures – probably more than any other bus company.

The road ahead –
Southern Vectis in the 21st century

More than ever before, the service pattern now revolves around passenger flows through the ports of Ryde, Cowes or Yarmouth. The basic core network consists of the *Explorer* 'Round the Island' routes (7 group, in mid blue livery), the *Route Rouge* (red-liveried routes 2/3/3b) running north to south from Cowes via Newport to the South Wight resorts and the service 1 corridor, employing dark blue single-deckers, between Cowes, Ryde, Bembridge and Sandown. Open-top services from Sandown/Shanklin, Yarmouth or Ryde, re-marketed as premium fare tours with pre-recorded commentaries (by Company Secretary Kate Boyes) are now an increasingly important part of the seasonal network.

SVOC no longer has a complete monopoly of Island bus operations but the routes that others operate are those that it would not find remunerative. The IW Council provide a number of rural or 'shopper' buses between school times with its fleet of 'Wight Bus' midibuses, while there is also a rural Community Council route serving Ryde, Havenstreet and Wootton.

Despite the negative effects of large car ferries on Island public transport, SVOC still enjoys a heavy influx of tourists patronising its services to reach the wealth of Isle of Wight attractions. It has an advantage in that mainland operators (Stagecoach, Wightlink, Hovertravel and Red Funnel) issue a wide range of tickets which include SVOC travel.

Rover tickets are a vital part of SVOC's commercial policy and these allow economic travel for a day, two days, week or 28 days on buses and Island Line trains. The range has been expanded in recent years, having first been introduced after the 1966 rail closures.

SVOC publicity is second to none for the visiting tourist. In addition to a twice-yearly timetable, complete with Besley cartoon cover in the summer edition, there are 500 bus stop timetable boards around the Island with all bus stop flags named by location, although a few in isolated locations have purely fictitious names, such as 'Back of Beyond' or 'The Way West', to amuse passing passengers!

Road staff continue to act as the company's ambassadors, patiently answering tourist enquiries with good humour. In addition to the permanent visitor attractions such as Osborne House or Carisbrooke Castle, the Island hosts a succession of crowd-pulling events. These include spectacular carnivals in all major towns (although this means the closure of roads for the processions to proceed, causing disruption to bus services for the duration) and an annual two-day Garlic Festival, near Newchurch, served by a special service 77 from Ryde or Shanklin.

During Cowes Week, visitors use the buses en route to Cowes to view the yacht races while the Friday night finale – Cowes Fireworks – has long been one of SVOC's major crowd moving activities when even the Group Managing Director can be seen driving a bus! From 2002 there has been a Pop Festival revival with a rock concert held just outside Newport over a June weekend. Performers at the 2003 event included Bryan Adams and The Darkness while planned for 2004 are The Who

An important part of the Southern Vectis network is the seasonal open-top service from Yarmouth to Alum Bay and the Needles. For the 2004 season Olympians Nos 742 and 743 have been converted to open-top and painted in the striking orange and yellow tours livery. These vehicles, along with the Bristol VRTs used at Ryde and Sandown/Shanklin, are fitted with public address systems for pre-recorded commentaries (by company Secretary, Kate Boyes).

P Savage

(performers at the 1970 festival) and Manic Street Preachers. For SVOC this means another regular crowd moving event, although on nothing like the scale of the original festivals.

Heavy industry either side of the River Medina at Cowes, together with the need for workers buses, is almost consigned to history although GKN (successors to Saunders-Roe) still has a 400-strong workforce. There are still plenty of commuters travelling by bus from all parts of the Island to Newport, the commercial centre. In addition, High Schools at Ryde, Sandown, Carisbrooke and Medina provide plenty of year-round traffic to justify a continuing need for double deckers in the fleet.

The company is faced with plenty of operational problems such as narrow roads, parked cars and areas prone to flooding. Congestion of towns, especially Newport, is the major one and SV management continue to press for bus priority schemes such as the South Street 'Red Carpet'. As long ago as 1985, the then GM Gary Batchelor had addressed Newport's Chamber of Commerce on the need for Park & Ride from the town's outskirts, suggesting a site off Staplers Road, and since then the situation at the notorious Coppins Bridge roundabout has become much worse. A council bye-law, introduced in early 2003, to create bus stop clearways by banning car parking in bus lanes, was a beneficial measure.

Road closures, sometimes requiring lengthy diversions and the provision of shuttle services, occur frequently for highways work. At several places, especially on the Military Road west of Compton Bay, major cliff falls have resulted in prolonged closures for remedial action but at some future stage the closure may be permanent. A massive landslide in the Undercliff early in 2001, although repaired for light traffic, has probably finished bus operation along the lower Ventnor to Niton road for good, and there are other locations, such as Bouldnor and Upper Bonchurch, where future problems are likely.

Staffing is a problem for the company, as it is for most bus operators, despite frequent recruitment campaigns. No longer is the bus industry a lifetime career and few will clock up the commendable length of service achieved by many in the past.

Retired staff are catered for by an Old Pals' Association, established in 1980 by retired Inspector Maurie Cooper, which meets monthly to bring former personnel together.

The Island is basically a rural area, as reflected in its farescales, and the problem of low usage in winter, off peak, evenings and Sundays requires intervention from the local authority with a subsidy of about £250,000 per year to maintain socially essential journeys. 25% of the total population (132,719 at the 2001 census) is retired so there are many enjoying concessionary fares. By comparison, the 1961 census figure was 95,752. Island towns continue to expand with new housing developments, such as those planned around Newport, providing an ongoing need for local buses.

A Transport Interchange at Ryde Esplanade, discussed for nearly twenty years, will no doubt reach fruition one day while the skyline around the present Newport bus station may well be changed by current planning proposals. The complete midibus fleet is scheduled for replacement by marginally larger vehicles early in 2005 and the name of Southern Vectis will continue to serve the Island well into the 21st century. On the mainland, Musterphantom Ltd, operating the Solent Blue Line buses in Southampton, also continues to be an important part of the Group's operation.

Many privatised bus companies have changed hands but Southern Vectis, carrying almost six million passengers per year and, with a prime duty to its shareholders, remains staunchly independent.

This overview of Ryde bus station and Esplanade railway station, taken in April 2004 from the footbridge linking the Esplanade to the hovercraft terminal, shows the basic facilities on offer by 21st century standards. The *Island Line* class 483 unit of converted 1938 London Underground stock is departing for Shanklin and will shortly enter Ryde Tunnel. Bristol VR No 681 awaits its next departure on *The Downs Tour* while an *Explorer* Olympian loads for Newport and the West Wight.

P Savage

Single-deckers

At the 1929 formation, Southern Vectis inherited fifteen elderly Daimlers of the Y or CK type. Most of these had been bought by the Vectis Bus Co as reconditioned chassis that had started life as lorries in the First World War. The oldest was No 8 (DL 2448), one of a trio that had started Dodson's operations in 1921, and which is seen in the grounds of Somerton Garage. Some survived long enough to be repainted green, the last Daimlers being withdrawn in 1933. Dodson's family firm built the bodywork.

RH Davies/SVOC

Apart from some low capacity 'chasers', the best ex Vectis Bus Co vehicles were thirteen ADC 416s, all with Dodson bodies. Number 33 (DL 5581) bumps its way over the unmade road from Somerton Garage. Brickwood's Sunshine Ales were brewed in Portsmouth but available at many local hostelries.

RHD/SVOC

This side-on view of another ADC, by now repainted into Southern Vectis green, shows the dual doorway and steep steps into the saloon; passengers had to be fit to clamber aboard! Seen at Somerton Garage, this vehicle was sold nearby to Jolliffe's yard, with the rest of the batch, in 1935 and many were resold to fairground showmen on the mainland.

RHD/SVOC

Opposite top: SVOC initially made new purchases from AEC – these were a number of Reliances plus this AEC Regal with Dodson 32 seat body. It was built to an advanced design and was exhibited at the 1931 Commercial Motor Show. Numbered 70 (DL 7811), later renumbered 216 and converted to oil engine, it was nicknamed *The Silver Ghost*. Requisitioned by the War Dept in 1941, it never returned to the Island but was sold on elsewhere and ran until 1958.

RHD/SVOC

Below: The bus services of the IW Tourist Co of Ryde passed to SVOC in June 1930 along with five vehicles, all of Dennis manufacture. DL 4468, an E type with local Margham bodywork, became SV No 63 and was rebuilt as a lorry (qv). (See also page 152.)

RHD/SVOC

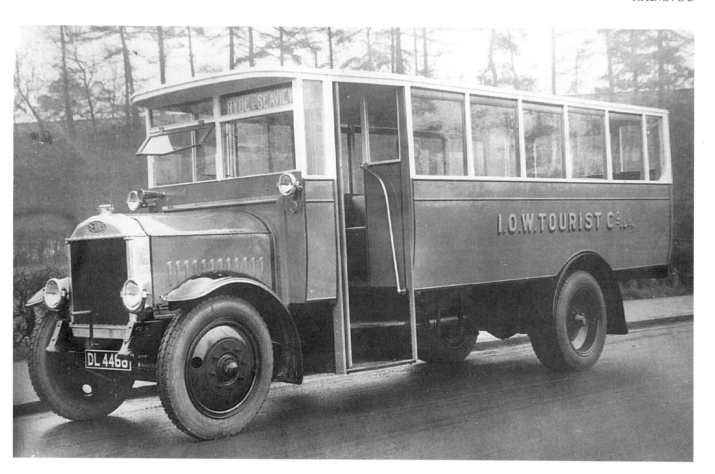

Opposite bottom: In 1932/3, six Tilling-Stevens buses were purchased. Bodied by Brush of Loughborough. Number 103 (DL 8436) is seen with driver George Hyde prior to delivery. By this time the old Vectis red/ blue/ white livery had given way to apple green and cream in Southdown style. These buses were also requisitioned for the War Dept but do not seem to have survived the war.

RHD/SVOC

Opposite top: A later acquisition was the firm of Colsons with its route between Newport and Carisbrooke, bought out in March 1939. The oldest vehicle was this Dennis 30 cwt., built in 1929 and seen in St James's Square, but it was soon disposed of. A couple more modern Colson vehicles, both Bedfords, were used as one man buses until 1954.

A Norris/SVOC

Opposite bottom: One man operation is nothing new! After the Dennis Aces were delivered in 1934, SVOC established the Coastal Service from Ryde to Alum Bay via the Military Road. It also called at Ryde Airport to connect with air services bringing visitors from Portsmouth, Southampton or Croydon. Number 405 (DL 9015), which still survives, is followed by another of the batch as it prepares to turn inland at Brook Chine, as the western end of the Military Road had still not been completed.

RHD/SVOC

Above: Between 1934 and 1936, the Company passed into its Dennis phase. A number of IOW operators purchased this make as they were built not far away at Guildford. Batches of ten Lancets and six Ace 20-seaters were followed by another 15 Lancets and a pair of Aces, plus the Lance double-deckers of 1936. Lancet No 521 (DL 9711) of the 1935 delivery had a body by Harrington of Hove and is seen in the swirling mists of St Catherine's Hill, near Blackgang, on the new road built to replace the old coastal route swept away in a cliff fall.

Bus & Coach/SVOC

Opposite: Number 512 (DL 9702) was a Harrington bodied Dennis Lancet which was taken to Carisbrooke Castle for an official photograph when new in 1935. That Norman fortress with its associations with Charles I is still used as a backdrop for photographing a line-up of new vehicles for the fleet but the bus left the Island in 1952 when it was sold to Sparshatt's, the Portsmouth commercial vehicle dealer and garage that was also the Dennis agent for the Island. It was resold to Waterlooville contractor Faulkner who used it as a site hut for roadworks on the Fareham Road at Portchester until 1959.

RHD/SVOC

Above: Some of the Lancets were requisitioned in 1941 but in two years became so down at heel they had to be rebodied. In wartime, this was no easy task but six buses received utility ECW bodies in 1944. These were built at Irthlingborough (Northants) as the vulnerable Lowestoft works had been vacated in wartime. Number 516 (DL 9706) was one of these, and still exists as a preservation project after use by Cheek, a local contractor, as a site hut.

Author

Opposite top: A need for a couple more 20-seater buses brought a pair of ECW bodied Dennis Falcons into the fleet in 1939. They worked the Newport town services as well as in the West Wight and lasted as buses until 1954. After serving as chicken houses at Great Thorness Farm, they were rescued in the hope of restoring one of them but they had decayed too far. Number 200 (CDL 900) is seen in post-war years.

JH Aston/SVOC

Opposite bottom: As part of the Tilling & BAT group, SVOC could now buy Bristol vehicles and from 1937 that became the standard. A pair of J type saloons, in Southdown style colours, were bodied by Eastern Coachworks where No 801 (BDL 103) was photographed before delivery.

RHD colln/SVOC

Above: A large batch of L type Bristol single-deckers was bought in 1938–40, bodied by Beadle (of Dartford), Harrington, ECW or, in the case of No 823 (CDL 614), seen at Newport depot, and No 824, by the local firm of Margham, who were contracted to undertake all SVOC body repairs and repaints. The 27 L5G saloons carried huge loads in wartime, some as standee conversions known as 'cattle trucks', yet soldiered on until 1954–7. They were replaced largely by secondhand double-deckers of similar age, but providing greater capacity to shift holiday crowds.

RHD/SVOC

Opposite top: One of the Beadle bodied batch, No 805 (BDL 853) was positioned in York Avenue, East Cowes, and elsewhere, to prove to the council that there was a need to remove overhanging trees, particularly with the increasing use of double-deckers.

RHD/SVOC

Opposite bottom: After the War, the Bristol L5G, with standard ECW 35 seat body, was again purchased. The Company was fortunate to obtain three in 1946, of which No 831 (EDL 16) is seen on service 1 at Cowes (Medina Road), adjacent to Shepard's Wharf and the chain ferry. This was once a busy peak-hour terminal serving the shipyards on both sides of the River Medina, but today that traffic has virtually disappeared.

RHD/SVOC

Above: These three saloons were selected for rebodying in 1961/2, being given full-front bus bodies by ECW in the style of the lightweight SC model produced by Bristol at that time for rural operations but to which SVOC was never tempted. Number 829 (EDL 14) is seen in Central Works at Newport. They were not ideal for one-man working as the driver was not close enough to check tickets and he had to twist his back to conduct a transaction. Visibility was not good and when the service 3 reached Knight's Cross from Havenstreet, the driver had to ask a passenger if any traffic was sighted coming from the left!

RHD/SVOC

Opposite top: Later single-deck purchases (in 1950–2) were of the longer LL5G type, this time seating 39 in the half-cab ECW bodywork. This design of rear-entrance bus quickly became dated, especially as there was an economic need to introduce one-man working. While Hants & Dorset undertook rebuilding of their similar vehicles by making them forward entrance and full front (for OMO), SVOC just sold theirs after a 12–14 year life span. Number 839 (HDL 283) is seen on Ryde Esplanade on the cross-town 7 route, with the office and paying in room at No 20 Esplanade visible beneath the furthest bow window.

RHD/SVOC

Opposite bottom: Acquisition of Wavell's Enterprise Bus Service brought a mixed selection of vehicles into the SVOC fleet. One of them was Dennis Lancet No 526 (AJH 870), which had started life as a Thurgood-bodied coach with Berkhampstead & District and passed briefly into London Transport hands. After use by Criterion Coaches of East London it was rebodied as a bus and came to the Island. Although it survived for three years with SVOC, it was a most unpopular vehicle which spent much of its time in Newport depot. It would emerge to work a teatime service to Sandown via Newchurch and back before being 'turned in' for some defect or other!

RHD/SVOC

Above: The longest surviving ex Enterprise bus was No 207 (GDL 226), a Bedford OB with Duple bus body, which eventually became a useful addition to the one man fleet. It is seen entering Newport depot but spent some years on the Shanklin allocation. After sale it was exported to Cyprus, with a number of other SVOC OBs. It was put to good use there but eventually dumped in a yard near Larnaca Airport where it remained, covered in vegetation and inhabited by snakes, with a veritable treasure trove of old British buses, until a devastating fire destroyed them all.

RHD/SVOC

Opposite top: Most of the Bedford OB coaches new to SVOC were downgraded to buses for one-man operation on Newport or Shanklin town services or lightly-loaded rural routes serving villages such as Alverstone, Havenstreet or Merstone. Nos 211/2 (EDL 640/1) are in Tilling green bus livery but have fleetnames painted out as they were, in April 1959, about to leave Newport depot for the last time, sold to a mainland dealer.

RHD/SVOC

Opposite bottom: Surprisingly, SVOC bought only one Bristol LS5G/ECW bus – No 844 (JDL 43) – seen in the former Shanklin Bus Station. Most Tilling companies bought quite a few of this underfloor engined type, although SVOC did have the coach version. Number 844 was initially based at Shanklin, during which time it was involved in a fatal accident with a motorbike on Cowleaze Hill, before moving to Newport where, appropriately, it regularly performed service 43 across the Downs to Sandown; Knighton Shute would have severely tested its hill climbing ability. After sale it worked for a Dorset operator who ran a service into Salisbury from villages in the Nadder Valley.

RHD/SVOC

Above: When they reached post-middle age, several of the LS coaches were downgraded to bus status by modification to seats, cab and doors, and repainting in Tilling green livery. The former No 303 became No 853 (JDL 44) and is seen in Ryde depot yard with the orchard, purchased for possible extension, in the background. A number of the later LS coaches passed to Hants & Dorset who also had them rebuilt as buses in a similar manner.

RHD/SVOC

The next type purchased was the Bristol SUL4A which featured the unusual combination of Albion engine and David Brown gearbox. SVOC bought eight of the model, intended for lightly loaded rural routes. Number 845 (458 ADL), followed by another, is seen at the Portsmouth car ferry terminal while on delivery form Lowestoft in May 1963. Drivers Hector Hemming and 'Dick' Whittington have collected them, as was the prerogative of senior staff. Note that both men are smartly turned out in collar and tie, the custom at that time even in 'civilian' attire. Hector had driven a steam lorry before joining SVOC! The second view shows No 850 (463 ADL) in Fort Street, Sandown, on service 43 via the Downs, one of their regular haunts. The building in the background made way for the Wight City leisure complex. *RHD/SVOC (top)   Author (bottom)*

Two Bristol MW coaches were bought in 1958 but it was 1965 before the bus version entered the fleet. Seven of them were bought but they were already outdated at the outset as semi-automatic transmission was replacing the crash gearbox by then. Number 801 (EDL 234C), numerically the first, is seen at Carisbrooke school site during a local driving competition trial. They had a relatively short life with SVOC but one bus, No 806 (FDL 927D), seen ascending Carter Road, Shanklin, was bought back out of preservation for the company's revived 'Vintage Fleet' and ran on a Shanklin to Newport service (99) in competition with local operator Wiltax. It eventually passed to the IW Bus Museum.

RHD/SVOC

SVOC

Opposite top: The semi-automatic gearbox made life considerably easier for drivers – although bad gear changing by some staff led to problems for the engineering department. The Bristol RESLs were the first SVOC vehicles to be so equipped and three small batches were acquired in the late 'sixties. Number 814 (NDL 766G), also seen in the Safe Driving competition but at Coppins Bridge car park, was sold with the remainder in 1981 as a result of better vehicle utilisation. The type was somewhat underpowered and timekeeping on the Shanklin–Ventnor rail replacement route could be a problem.

RHD/SVOC

Above: Bristol RE No 864 (TDL 564K), seen at Chine Avenue, Shanklin, created great interest when it was rebuilt to open-top form as 'Shanklin's Pony' in a bright yellow and blue colour scheme. This initially ran between Shanklin's Esplanade and railway station but later ran through to Sandown. The author was the first driver to work the bus in normal service after its conversion and became its regular driver for a number of seasons. There was considerable flexing in the body and the company's engineer concluded at least one extra bay should have been retained to overcome the problem.

SVOC

Opposite: Later vehicles of the Bristol RE type were far more successful and the nine buses of the longer (36 foot) RELL6G model (Nos 861–9) bought in 1971–3 served the company well. The lack of power steering proved unpopular in later years but they were rugged and reliable and performed on nearly all the company's routes at some time. Number 865 (TDL 565K) is seen on a 19B journey from Newport entering Ventnor bus station, now built over.

Author

Opposite top: Southern Vectis never really wanted the Leyland National because they were too large for the Island's narrow roads but was obliged to take delivery of 19 of them as they were allocated by NBC. Number 887 (ODL 887R) driven by Merv Jones, and on the *Rydabus* town network which had a 10p flat fare, sets down at the Commodore in Ryde while on service 6 from Elmfield. Some of the Nationals saw less than ten years' use but Halton Borough Council made good use of many of them and one of those is awaiting restoration for the Bus Museum.

SVOC

Opposite bottom: One of the first batch of Nationals, No 874 (XDL 798L), which was not equipped with the anti-roll bar of later models, is seen in Newport's East Street in 1982, working in from East Cowes. At closer examination the scene is different from today for only the northern part of the roundabout had been completed. The bus would thus have passed across the stone river bridge; the background also shows the town's gasholder, no longer part of the skyline.

Author

The small capacity SU was superseded by the LHS model, another Bristol/ECW combination supplied to just a few operators. The first ones were actually bodied by Marshall but subsequent buses, such as No 838 (HDL 414N), seen emerging from the narrow exit from Cowes Pontoon, all came from Lowestoft. In fact the company received three of the final build of the type in 1981. These were dual purpose and were intended to be used as coach feeders as well as buses.

SVOC

Southern Vectis newest single-decker is No 300 (HW52 EPX), a Dennis Dart SLF with Plaxton Mini Pointer bodywork. Number 300 is also the only low floor single-decker in the fleet. It is pictured here at Fountain Quay, Cowes awaiting an arrival of Red Funnel's *Red Jet* service from Southampton. Beyond the archway in the background, through which No 300 will just have squeezed, can be glimpsed the SV Travel Office, also seen on page 46. Behind the bus is The Arcade, which at various times housed the offices of Fowler's Royal Blue, Vectis Bus Co, Bernard Groves and Fountain Coaches. At the same location as the Bristol LHS overleaf one of the latest additions to the Southern Vectis fleet is seen. Dennis Dart No 818 was acquired in 2003 from a dealer but had been new to London Buses Ltd, later Metroline.
P Savage

Minibuses

As with most NBC constituents, Southern Vectis received an allocation of Ford Transits in 1985. An initial batch of three converted the Ryde–Binstead route under the Wanderer brand name, followed by more at Ryde, with 'Hydrobus' based at Cowes and 'Medinalinx' at Newport. Ryde-based No 258 (B258 MDL), in blue livery, descends Well Street en route to Elmfield and Tesco. Behind the bus was the entrance to a former dairy that became the depot of Casey, the first operator to sell out to Southern Vectis in 1929. *Author*

An interesting aspect of the minibus operation was the network of services along Ryde Pier to the Pier Head. Local services 6 (Elmfield) and 10 (Binstead) ran a frequent service connecting with the Portsmouth ferry, as did the 81 limited stop from Newport. Number 263 (C263 SDL), in Medinalinx peach livery, is on the latter, while the other vehicle is a longer 18-seater on loan from West Yorkshire Road Car (C87 AUB). This was painted dark blue and white and acquired the nickname 'The Ambulance' in the six weeks from December 1985 that it ran on the Island. SVOC took delivery of two similar Transits in 1986. The covered shelter at the Pier Head was later dismantled to provide a larger car park area while the wooden ticket collectors' hut was moved to the IW Steam Railway at Wootton. *Author*

The extension of minibus operation encompassed the East Cowes and Gurnard services and required 23-seaters. Ivecos, bodied by either Robin Hood or Phoenix, were provided in 1987/9/90. Solent Blue Line also had several of the batch. Number 287 (F287 SDL), painted in two shades of red and white, is seen at Cowes Pontoon awaiting the Red Funnel hydrofoil from Southampton   *Author*

One of the Ivecos, No 285, received a black overall advert for Northwood Garage which made the vehicle dangerously inconspicuous and gave it the name 'The Black Maria'. The Newport Marks & Spencer store had just opened and the bus is on a free bus service to promote the new shop, built in 1994 on the site of the Gould, Hibberd & Randall soft drinks distribution depot.   *Author*

Double-deckers

Although double-deckers had run on the Isle of Wight as early as 1905, the first in the SVOC fleet were six Eastern Counties bodied Dennis Lances delivered in 1936. They wore the Southdown style apple green and cream livery introduced by manager Walter Budd, as shown in these maker's photographs of No 603 (ADL 503), taken near the factory in Lowestoft, Suffolk and had well appointed interiors with polished woodwork and green leather seats.

SVOC

The body styling was quite advanced for its time – especially compared with that on bodies built by Eastern Coach Works, successors to Eastern Counties, a few years later. This prewar view shows No 605 (ADL 505) waiting for custom in St James's Square, Newport, adjacent to Wadham's Furniture Store which only ceased trading in the last decade. 'Push on' handbrakes proved confusing to drivers as the buses reached old age for the majority by then had 'pull on' handbrakes.

RHD/SVOC

Another pair of double-deckers was obtained in 1939/40 – Bristol K type with five cylinder Gardner engines and ECW 56-seat bodies. Number 702 (CDL 899) arrived (via the Lymington–Yarmouth ferry) in July, 1939 while the sister No 703 came in January 1940. Both of these were converted to open top and remarkably still survive today. Number 702, seen here at Gurnard, is still in regular use (as No 502) with the Company while No 703 is preserved. Both these buses would work the last departure from Newport to the West Wight in wartime, conveying off duty military personnel stationed at coastal defence establishments and stories are told of the buses racing each other along the Forest Road, urged on by their passengers.

RHD/SVOC

Opposite: From 1937, when two G type double-deckers arrived, together with a pair of corresponding J type saloons, Southern Vectis standardised on Bristol chassis, built at the Brislington Works in that city. Number 700 (BDL 100) leads a line-up of buses in post-war years at the Newport (St James's Square) terminal. The wide road allowed bus loading on either side while still allowing plenty of space for passing traffic. Almost all of the background buildings still stand today, although shops will have changed ownership many times. Note how the smaller windows (six-bay construction) gives a dated appearance compared with the Dennis Lances.

RHD/SVOC

Above: The island was a busy place in wartime, despite the lack of tourists, as workers' services ran to the Cowes and East Cowes shipyards from all over the island. Southern Vectis was fortunate to be allocated four Bristol K type utilities in 1944/5. Number 704 (DDL 688) was the first of these, delivered in drab brown primer and was followed by three more of slightly less austere specifications. Bodywork was of angular cornered steel over a framework of 'green' unseasoned timber so rotted quickly. The company was fortunate in obtaining Bristol manufacture vehicles, albeit with six cylinder AEC engines, whereas many operators had to make do with nonstandard Guy Arabs or Daimlers. Number 704 is at Ryde Esplanade, with the ornate canopy of the WH Smith bookshop behind and the SVOC offices visible to the right.

RHD/SVOC

Opposite: Re-engined with a five cylinder Gardner and rebodied as a standard 55 seat Eastern Coachworks lowbridge, No 704 (DDL 688) appeared similar to the large batch of post-war K types from 1953. It is seen further along the Esplanade bound for Seaview (displaying full screens) alongside the concrete shelters and plane trees.

RHD/SVOC

Opposite bottom: From 1946, for a period of seven years, the Company took the standard Tilling Group Bristol/Eastern Coachworks 'Lowbridge' double-decker for its intake of the new vehicles. These provided useful extra capacity for the predominantly single-deck fleet at a time when the Island was experiencing a huge influx of tourists. This official ECW photograph (by Boughtons of Lowestoft, who photographed all new batches of their vehicles) shows the low height effect that enabled these buses to pass beneath the low railway bridges that obstructed several trunk routes in those days.

SVOC

Above: The first batches of 'LBs', as they were known in Company circles, featured three-piece screen boxes. Nos 713 (EDL 17) and 716 (EDL 20) are seen leaving the Fishbourne–Portsmouth Car Ferry in June 1963 while en route to Clacton-on-Sea to help out on hire to Eastern National who used them in their last summer. They returned to the island but were sold a few months later to a Macclesfield dealer.

RHD/SVOC

Opposite: Larger two-piece screenboxes were fitted to subsequent K types including No 738 (GDL 711), built in 1951. It is seen in Ryde depot yard with the iron-clad chapel, which later became a furniture repository before being destroyed in a spectacular fire, to the right.

RHD/SVOC

Opposite bottom: From 1950, new regulations allowed two axle buses to be one foot longer. Number 750 (HDL 264), with chassis type designated KS5G, is seen in Fort Street, Sandown, near to the Company's bus park in 1965. Note the pebble covered walls fronting the houses on the right – a feature of late Victorian Sandown.

Author

Above In addition to new purchases, SVOC had managed to buy three secondhand Leyland TD1s in 1945/6, including No 708 (TF 6821) which had originally been a demonstrator and then passed to Cardiff Corporation. It is seen in Pyle Street, Newport, about to turn into 'The Square' after being re-engined and rebodied (by ECW) in 1949. Some of the background buildings gave way to the building of the International (later Somerfield) Supermarket.

AB Cross

Above: The takeover of Enterprise and its Newport to Sandown routes brought a pair of Guy Arabs with Strachan lowbridge bodies showing an even greater degree of austerity. New to Reading Corporation in 1942, No 900 (BRD 754) had just been repainted green when photographed on a wet day in 'The Square' at Newport. The space above the screen box is used for an advert just as in Reading.

AB Cross

Opposite top: Still desperate for vehicles to meet the post-war tourist demand, the company hired six elderly Leyland TD1s from Wilts & Dorset (which stayed for nearly two years) in 1950/1 and which were repainted from red to green for Island service. All had originated with Southdown but had moved west just before the war to convey construction workers building military installations on Salisbury Plain. Number 745 (UF 7396) with 1944 built Brush utility, is seen at Newport depot. *AB Cross*

Below: To increase capacity, a batch of 15 prewar Bristol K type double-deckers were bought from Bristol Tramways and Hants & Dorset to replace single decks of similar age. Number 787 (GAE 498), ex Bristol, waits at Gunville (Crescent) before working back on the local service into Newport. They were only a stop-gap purchase and all had been sold within five years after seeing seasonal use.

RHD/SVOC

Another of the batch, No 786 (GAE 493), went to a Hampshire showman after sale and returned to former territory with a visiting fair. Seen in St James's Square, Newport, this bus went for scrap at Fareham in 1963.

RHD/SVOC

Opposite top: The most popular conventional buses were the 74 rear entrance Bristol Lodekkas (designated LA by the Company) which entered service between 1954 and 1962. Many were for railway replacement and equipped with large luggage racks at the rear of the lower saloon. No 517 (KDL 413) of 1954 and No 551 (ODL 11) of 1957 reach the traffic lights at the bottom of Arthur's Hill, Shanklin. Both have originated at Ryde, having operated Ser 16 via Brading and Ser 8 via Bembridge respectively.

RHD/SVOC

Opposite bottom: The Lodekka combined a conventional upper deck seating layout with low height (13'5") allowing operation under the two railway bridges either side of Sandown. Number 566 (TDL 999), an FS type, descends Lake Hill while on the busy service 16 from Ryde to Blackgang. Note the inscription painted on the bridge ironwork – TOO LOW FOR HIGHBRIDGE BUSES.

Author

Above: One of the 1957 LD-type Lodekkas manoeuvres through a near deserted Shanklin Old Village. Today the background remains unaltered, but buses frequently encounter confrontation with speeding oncoming traffic.

SVOC

Opposite top: Some of the 'LA' 60-seaters lasted well into National Bus days but clocked up a relatively low milage as they were delicensed every winter. LD-type No 552 waits on the 1A stand in Ryde Bus Station. It appears a previous reversing manoeuvre off the stand has resulted in a collision, judging by the damaged corner panel.

SVOC

Opposite bottom: Although fitted with 5-speed gearboxes, the 23 front-entrance 70 seat FLF Lodekkas did not have the same appeal as the nimbler rear loader 60 seaters. Number 600 (BDL 576B) is seen when new in 1964 outside Newport depot.

SVOC

Above: The need for seasonal crew operation ensured a good innings for the SVOC FLFs, which ran until 1983 between Ryde and Cowes; many mainland operators had dispensed with similar vehicles because of the need to introduce one man working. Number 607 (BDL 583B), by now in NBC leaf green, prepares to pull away from the Chapel Corner stop at Parkhurst. One FLF, No 611, returned in 1986 as part of the 'Vintage Fleet'.

Author

Opposite: The rugged Gardner engines and low mileage figures made the Lodekkas from the Island attractive second-hand purchases and many are still in use in Europe and America. Number 559 (PDL 519) made 20 transcontinental journeys to Afghanistan, conveying young people on cut price treks with Top Deck Travel, before returning to the Island as an exhibit in the Bus Museum. The worse mishap it encountered was being rammed at the rear end by a lorry, necessitating a rebuild.

B Bradbury/SVOC

Above: Eventually Southern Vectis had to introduce wholesale one man operation and by then the Bristol VRT had become the standard rear engined high capacity bus. The earlier examples, including No 624 (SDL 634J), seen creeping off the Sealink car ferry *Camber Queen* at Fishbourne, were initially crew-worked and were fitted with a 'stair gate' enabling one-man operation with the top deck closed off.

RHD/SVOC

Opposite top: Whilst the earliest VRTs featured the somewhat dated-looking flat windscreen, the 1972 delivery of four buses for the company included the first built by Eastern Coach Works with the 'BET style' curved windscreen. Number 630 (XDL 377L), which had appeared in the Commercial Vehicle Show and was one of a handful of NBC vehicles trimmed in a special 'mirror N' symbol blue moquette, is seen in East Cowes when new.

RHD/SVOC

Opposite bottom: Number 641 (NDL 641M), a VRT/2 new in 1973, negotiates the now pedestrianised St Thomas' Square en route for Newport Bus Station. Behind the bus is the Army & Navy department store, since demolished, but once known as Emor Corner as it was owned by Edward Morris. The closure of this link cost the company fuel and time as all the buses from Cowes had to negotiate the notorious Coppins Bridge Roundabout; the opening of the South Street bus lane in November 2003 was designed to solve this problem.

Author

Above: Some 70 new and 13 second-hand Bristol VRTs entered service with Southern Vectis on the Island. The new purchases were made 1969 and 1981 and later Series 3 models included No 680 (FDL 680V) which received the emerald green livery and was a transfer to Solent Blue Line. It is seen ascending Shanklin High Street in March 1994 on a Shanklin to Wroxall shuttle service necessitated by a road closure at Upper Ventnor due to subsidence. Fields the outfitters have since closed their Shanklin branch.

Author

Three batches of semi-automatic Leyland Olympians with bodies built by Eastern Coachworks were delivered in 1982–4. The first was No 686 (RDL 686X), seen in NBC leaf green livery, on the old Yarmouth Swing Bridge at the start of the seasonal service 46 coastal route. The bridge, dating from the 1860s, was single carriageway controlled by traffic lights, at one time the only set on the entire Island. The NBC livery gave way to the post-privatisation emerald green and greensand devised by Engineering Director Alan Peeling. Olympian No 696 (WDL 696Y), of the 1983 batch, waits for time at Whitecliff Bay. At this time the 'Round the Island' route ran via Bembridge.

Author

1989, the Company's 60th anniversary, saw the arrival of the first 'new generation' automatic double-deckers, which featured coach-style seating and carpeted ceiling panels. The first example at Ryde depot, No 712 (F712 SDL), is seen at St Helens (Vine) on the return working of a Tesco service. Originally this Leyland Olympian, with Leyland body constructed at Workington, was allocated registration F703 RDL, until it was realised there was a fleet number 703 at Solent Blue Line! Below, No 713 (G713 WDL), of the 1990 delivery, descends from St Catherine's Hill to Blackgang Chine at the end of service 16 from Ryde. The roundabout and new approach road was put in place when the original road became threatened by rapid coastal erosion.

Author

Although at one time the road through Newport Town Centre was regularly served by buses, traffic schemes now largely take services round the perimeter to reach the Bus Station. Because Trafalgar Road was closed for resurfacing, No 736 (K736 ODL) passes through Castlehold, at the west end of the High Street. The Fox estate agency on the right was once Wray's, the Island's famous grocer, while the St Crispin public house adjacent had temporarily closed.

Author

Volvo B7TL No 102 met with an unfortunate mishap in June 2003 when only about nine months old. It was involved in an incident with some scaffolding around a building in Union Street, Ryde. The bodywork was distorted as a result and the bus had to return to Transbus for repair. The driver was cleared of any blame.

R Johnson

Open-top

In the mid-fifties the Island joined the growing number of locations running open-top services when it acquired four AEC Regents from Brighton, Hove & District. Only two of these entered service with SVOC, including No 901 (GW 6276), seen in Trafalgar Road, Newport, as they were already quite elderly. The original archaic open staircase Tilling bodies had been totally reconstructed by BH&D at the end of the war. They worked service 11 duplicates between Sandown and Ventnor before a dedicated open-top route was established for the 1957 season.

RHD/SVOC

Opposite top: The popularity of open-toppers increased and two of the oldest double-deckers, Nos 702/3, were converted in the Nelson Road bodyshop in 1958/9. Number 702 (CDL 899) has just departed Sandown Zoo and is passing Sandham Grounds on service 44. Distinctive red background destination blinds were a feature of SVOC open-toppers.

Author

Opposite bottom: For a time from the mid 80s, CDL 899, by now renumbered 502, carried a mid blue, peppermint green and white livery. It worked a Downs service (43) from Ryde in 1984 and is seen at Downend. The cottage in the background has since been demolished but the 65 year old bus is the oldest vehicle still running for its original owner and it revived the service 43 in 2003.

Author

Above: Some ten secondhand Bristol K5G open-toppers arrived between 1960 and 1964 from Brighton, Hove & District, Bristol Omnibus and Hants & Dorset. These replaced the AECs and allowed some expansion, which included a short-lived operation at Ryde. Number 907 (GHT 124), new to Bristol Tramways but bought from Brighton, is seen on Ryde Esplanade ready to work to Seaview.

RHD/SVOC

Of the Hants & Dorset acquisitions, No 908 (FLJ 538) was the oldest with the chassis dating from 1940. It had been fitted with a convertible body but lost its roof in a low bridge accident at Fareham. It spent most of its time working between Yarmouth and Alum Bay. Long serving conductress Beryl Wadham is seen collecting top deck fares at Bridge Road, Yarmouth; headscarves were *de rigeur* for conductresses on the open-toppers! The bus survives, disused, in Holland.

RHD/SVOC

A 'one-off' purchase in 1976 was an Alder Valley Bristol FLF that had lost its roof in a bridge strike at Bracknell. Despite conversion and painting in silver and blue for the Queen's Silver Jubilee, it was never popular with drivers and served for only two seasons at Shanklin. Number OT6 (BRX 142B) is seen posed beside Ryde Canoe Lake.

SVOC

The open-top fleet was updated in the 1970s by the conversion of five Lodekkas in the company's bodyshop. Four of these only served for a few years before sale although two were subsequently repurchased. Number 501/ex OT2 (MDL 952) in blue/green/white served the company for forty-six years and is seen departing Alum Bay for the Needles Battery. The Lodekkas were replaced in 2001 and Bristol VR No 681 (ODL 447) is seen here negotiating one of the two hairpin bends along the cliff top road on the climb from the Needles Park at Alum Bay up to the Battery   *Author/P Savage*

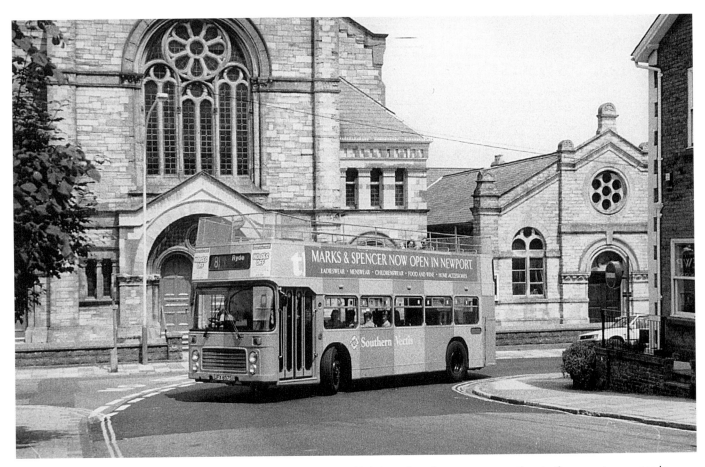

The hardest worked open-tops have been the convertible VRTs which introduced one-man operation to the open-top routes in 1979, as part of a six vehicle exchange with Hants & Dorset. Two still remain although they have now been rebuilt as permanent open-tops with a front canopy. Number 505 (UFX 857S), now working for Solent Blue Line on the *New Forest Tour*, is seen passing Garfield Road Church in Ryde when adorned in the startling lime green/purple 'Battenburg' livery while No 503 (XDL 872) is pictured climbing from Shanklin Esplanade in April 2004. The stunning orange livery with yellow sun motif was first applied for the 2003 season.

Author/P Savage

Coaches

After the purchase of three Bedford WTBs in 1939,the similar OB type with Duple 29-seat body, became the standard coach for local day or part day excursions. They were ideal for the narrow lanes, of which the Island has a many, and so 16 OBs were purchased in the period 1947–50. Most performed years of further service as one-man buses. Number 208 (EDL 637) is seen outside the Sandown Hotel.

RHD/SVOC

'Heavyweight' Bristol coaches followed in 1952–4. This time they were of the then novel underfloor engine layout, designated LS type. The earlier deliveries were Gardner-engined and the remainder Bristol powered, although one vehicle had been delivered incorrectly and was swopped with the correct one that had entered service with Lincolnshire Road Car. Several LS type (No 303, JDL 44, nearest camera) flank a couple of Bedfords in the Carisbrooke Castle coach park.

RHD/SVOC

Opposite top: Deliveries for the 1951 season were three superior 'Queen Mary' Bristol LWL6Bs with full front 37-seat Eastern Coach Works bodies. They lasted until the end of the 1961 summer when all were sold to a dealer – the author's attention was distracted from a school cadet force instruction class when they all passed the window having just been offloaded from the Fishbourne–Portsmouth car ferry! Number 301 (HDL 183) is seen while operating a British Railways inclusive Isle of Wight tour.

RHD/SVOC

Opposite bottom: Most Tilling companies purchased only Bristol vehicles, which at the time were only available to nationalised concerns, but SVOC insisted on lightweight Bedfords for many years as they were cheaper, but adequate, for 'Round the Island' and other local tours. The SBO model was delivered in small numbers from 1955 and Nos 235–7 (ODL 48–50) are seen in Newport depot after the delivery run from Duple, still with builder's labels in the windows. For many years the old established garage firm of Canning Day were agents for the supply of Bedford coaches to Island operators.

RHD/SVOC

Above: The next batch of Bedfords featured more glass, chrome and a stylish curved windscreen. Nos 240 & 242 (SDL 4, 6) are seen at Yarmouth, with the church tower dominating the background, after being offloaded from the car ferry in Spring 1959. This was long before traffic warranted construction of a large car ferry terminal.

RHD/SVOC

Opposite top: The Barley Mow at Shide is the location for No 246 (VDL 854), one of a pair of Bedford SB8 coaches bought for the 1962 summer. This public house was owned by Newport brewers Mew Langton, later to be taken over by Strong then Whitbread. This coach was one of several sold to the Isle of Skye.

RHD/SVOC

Opposite bottom: Duple changed the styling of its bodywork for the Bedford SB from 1964, when the SVOC order was for five coaches. Number 255 (ADL 108B) is seen on a tour to Blackgang Chine, still a popular tourist destination despite the frequent cliff falls on this stretch of coastline.

RHD/SVOC

above: Before the reclamation of the Ryde foreshore for construction of Planet Ice and LA Bowl, the sea wall was the departure point for coach tours and, on Saturdays, express services to holiday camps. Number 252 (ADL 105B) stands at this location awaiting custom.

RHD/SVOC

Opposite top: The next Bedford model was the revolutionary twin-steering VAL 6-wheeler, built to the revised length of 36 feet, thus allowing a capacity of 52 seats. Number 401 (ADL 109B) descends Skew Bridge at Lake (over the Ryde–Ventnor railway). Farmer's Ice Cream factory was located on the opposite side of the bridge at the time.

Author

Opposite bottom: EH Crinage of Ventnor had been one of the coach companies that sold out to Shamrock & Rambler in 1967 and their newest vehicle became No 116 (CDL 698C) after the SVOC takeover. It was a Plaxton-bodied Bedford SB which remained on the Island after sale in 1977 as the Ventnor Middle School coach and later as a caravan. It is seen parked adjacent to Christ Church, Sandown.

Author

Above: After 1969, future coach deliveries were to be shared between SVOC (in cream/green) or Fountain (orange/cream). Bedford VAL No 120 (PDL 351H) was new in 1970 to SVOC but transferred to Fountain in the next year. It became a transporter vehicle, based at Bolton, and may still survive in that form.

RHD/SVOC

Opposite: SVOC continued to maintain a few heavyweight coaches in case mainland work was required. Number 301 (KDL 885F) was built in 1967 although did not enter service until February 1968. It is an unusual Bristol RESH6G with Duple (Northern) Commander body and is seen on a Cotswold tour. In its early days it was embarrassingly underpowered and had to be fitted with a larger engine but has survived long enough to be acquired for display in the IW Bus Museum on Newport Quay.

RHD/SVOC

Above: Later models were of the similar YMT type, such as No 126 (TDL 126S), which was painted in the orange/cream Fountain livery. It almost survived into preservation but was unfortunately broken up at Rookley scrapyard. It is seen descending from Yaverland. A width restriction now placed on this road has denied today's coach passengers the spectacular views across Sandown Bay.

Author

Opposite: From 1973, Southern Vectis purchased the Bedford YRT as its standard lightweight coach. These tended to operate further afield, even on an excursion to a French hypermarket, but Southdown took a dim view of a Bedford sent over to help out in a railstrike! Number 415 (ODL 865M) is seen in pristine condition in National white livery at Shanklin Esplanade.

SVOC

Opposite top: Excelsior Coaches at Bournemouth provided an Isle of Wight tour and contracted with SVOC to provide a vehicle connecting with the boat at Yarmouth. As a result, Bedford YMT No 431 (XDL 431T) was painted in Excelsior cream to operate the daily tour and is seen at Ryde Esplanade with driver Ben Butlin assisting passengers aboard after a lunch stop.

SVOC

Opposite bottom: In the 1970s the coaching business on the Island was doing well enough to require additional secondhand rolling stock. Six Bedford YRQ models came from Maidstone & District in 1976 and No 109 (XKO 196J) is seen at the Cowes (Carvel Lane) coach park. Originally the old Fountain Garage and railway station had occupied the site but now a Co-op store stands there. During the day, when coaches were at work, additional revenue was generated by the parking of cars, for which an attendant was provided.

Author

Above: Further secondhand purchases were made in 1979/80, including a batch of eight coaches from Western National. Number 400 (OOD 360M) had been a Greenslades vehicle and is seen at Havenstreet Station on an excursion for the Summer Steam Show, 1981. The bodywork on these 1974 coaches was good but mechanically they were a disappointment.

Author

Opposite: No more Bedfords bought new after 1980 and because coaches were now undertaking mainland work, including a share of *National Express*, Leyland Leopards were to become standard for a few years. Indeed, SVOC was so keen to obtain a pair for early delivery, they bought them from a dealer rather than through normal NBC ordering channels. Number 307 (RDL 307X) climbs eastward along the Military Road from an idyllic Freshwater Bay, with Tennyson Down beyond.

SVOC

Above: By 1983, the versatile Leopard had been superseded by the Leyland Tiger. Number 314 (C314 TDL), with Plaxton Paramount body, was in the 1986 intake of four coaches and is seen when new with coachman John Frost at the wheel. The centre strip of the bodysides was prone to corrosion, necessitating workshop attention.

SVOC

Opposite: SVOC obtained another Leopard secondhand in 1982. Number 300 (RHY 770M), new to Bristol Omnibus Co, was obtained from Western National. In this official view outside the Nelson Road (Newport) head office, it has just received a variation of the white livery with blue and red stripes. It received cherished registration WDL 142 in 1986 but suffered engine failure a year later and went locally for scrap in 1991 after use as the Ryde depot store shed.

SVOC

Although signwritten for *National Holidays*, the Tigers often performed more localised work. Number 315 (new as C315 TDL) had been reregistered 473 CDL in 1991 and is seen on the Military Road at Brook Chine.

Author

A coach operation, Weypac Ltd t/a Blue Line Coach Hire, had been set up in Southampton but quickly found itself in financial difficulties. Six coaches, owned by SVOC, were returned to the Island and incorporated into the coaching fleet. Number 323 (TND 122X), a Duple-bodied Volvo B58 had been repainted grey by the time it was photographed at Lake, passing the former Co op, which then became a cinema.

Author

A pair of high specification Setra coaches were the last new vehicles for the coaching fleet. Southern Vectis Coaches still exists to arrange tours but Kardan Travel vehicles are used to convey their passengers. Number 901 (H901 EDL) is seen being handed over at Newport to plc MD Gary Batchelor in spring 1991, while the 1992 delivery, No 902 (J902 LDL), is seen at Coppins Bridge, Newport, where the site has been developed as a cinema complex and superstore.

SVOC/Author

Service vehicles

Opposite top: The company's prewar van was DL 8870, a 1-ton Ford new in 1934. It carries the early form of fleetname and is seen at Nelson Road. It was replaced in early post-war years.

RHD/SVOC

Opposite bottom: Old buses could often be converted to serve as service vehicles after their passenger carrying days were over. DL 4468, a Dennis E type, became a lorry in 1933 and worked until about 1946. Seen in Nelson Road, Newport, it had been new to IW Tourist Co., taken over by SVOC in 1930. (See also page 89.)

RHD/SVOC

Above: Dennis DL 4468 was replaced by a Canadian Ford that had been wartime military hardware. It is thought to have been one of 35 similar vehicles that came into the hands of Thames Valley and were resold to Tilling Group companies as lorries or tow-trucks. Number 004 (EDL 554) was the SVOC recovery vehicle for some 17 years from 1947 and eventually passed into preservation with the Island's Military Vehicle Group.

RHD/SVOC

Although this tree cutting vehicle (No 001, BOW 168) never ran as a bus on the Island, it had been used as such by Hants & Dorset. It was a Bristol L5G with Beadle body, so similar to some SVOC buses, and was used to trim the foliage from 1952 until 1966. Seen at Ryde depot, it went to the West of England Transport Collection in Devon after sale but was eventually dismantled for spares.

Author

Two more 'in-house' conversions were of Dennis Ace buses to lorries for the conveyance of chalk to Shanklin Bus Station site in 1954. Number 403 (DL 9013) is seen at Newport depot but, with its consort, was only fit for scrap after the task was complete.

RHD/SVOC

The standard Company van from the late 1970s was the Morris Marina. Six were bought including No 006 (KDL 260P) seen at Shanklin Garage. They were used as engineering runabouts or for publicity work and carried the standard NBC leaf green/white colours.

Author

Lodekka No 565 (TDL 998) became the second driver trainer from 1978 but received only a yellow band between decks rather than the full yellow livery. At the time it was photographed on Newport Bus Station lay-by it had been reregistered ABK 832A but only carried this plate for a short time before the bus returned as part of the Vintage Fleet in 1987 with its original plate. After a loan to the Bus Museum, it was sold for preservation.

Author

Vectis people

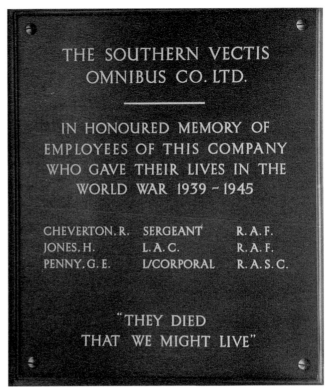

THE SOUTHERN VECTIS
OMNIBUS CO. LTD.

———

IN HONOURED MEMORY OF
EMPLOYEES OF THIS COMPANY
WHO GAVE THEIR LIVES IN THE
WORLD WAR 1939 – 1945

CHEVERTON, R.	SERGEANT	R. A. F.
JONES, H.	L. A. C.	R. A. F.
PENNY, G. E.	L/CORPORAL	R. A. S. C.

"THEY DIED
THAT WE MIGHT LIVE"

Opposite top left: Conductor Don White leans against an almost new AEC Reliance at Ventnor Town Hall. The only item of uniform supplied until 1933 was the cap. In this view the Bell Punch ticket machine is clearly visible.

RHD/SVOC

Opposite top right: Three members of Southern Vectis staff lost their lives on war service during the Second World War. They are remembered on a plaque at the top of the main staircase at the Nelson Road Head Office.

RHD/SVOC

Opposite bottom: Ben Edwards was an early appointment, in the Walter Budd era, from driver to Inspector and was for many years in command at 'The Square' office in Newport. He is seen in the company of fitter Bill Flux at that location in post-war years. Note the wooden seats from a utility bus being put to good use.

RHD/SVOC

Above: Three long-serving members of the Nelson Road depot engineering staff were Harry Green (Foreman, Body & Paint Shop), Wilf Blee (Foreman Fitter) and Stan Larcombe (Chargehand Fitter). The Lodekka behind them displays the luggage racks to allow operation on railway replacement routes.

RHD/SVOC

Opposite top: The crew of 'The Juke Box' (LS type bus No 844), conductor Mew and driver Coburn, pose for the camera at Sandown's Fort Street terminal.

RHD/SVOC

Opposite bottom: A group of Company officers past and present gathered together in October 1971 for a dinner at the Royal Hotel, Ventnor. A silver salver commemorating 50 years from the commencement of the Vectis Bus Co was presented by former officers. The line up comprises (top) Rod Longley (Asst to C Engr, 1953–6), Leslie Duncan (Sec'y, 1932–40; Traffic Manager 1953–7), Robert Hanley (TM, 1957–63), Don Howe (TM, 1965–84), David Searle (Chief Engineer, 1965–9), Arthur Bishop (CE, 1969–85), Gary Batchelor (Secretary, 1970–86), Brian Horner (Asst TM; 1962–6), Brian Hancock (CE, 1963–5), David Dickinson (Asst TM, 1966–9); (front row seated) Reg Augustus, (CE, 1932–62) Ronald Wade (GM, 1970–6), Stanley Bartlett (TM, 1934/39–45) and Leslie Whitehead (Secretary, 1947–65).

CA Bishop Collection

Right: Although several conductresses were trained as drivers in the final days of the war, they were not actually required to take over, as men began to return from war service to resume their former positions. It was not until the late 1970s that Ryde conductress Ann Bartley took her PSV test to become the first lady driver for Southern Vectis.

SVOC

Opposite top: For the Company's 50th anniversary, VR No 650 was repainted in the dark red, cobalt blue and white of the original Vectis Bus Co, together with gold fleetnames in distinctive style. Workshop staff Hughie Hallam, Gary Barton and Alan Cooley (who has been responsible for executing many special liveries and still repaints the buses of the SVOC fleet) stands alongside the completed vehicle.

RHD/SVOC

Opposite bottom: Cecil Perkins, Mechanical Foreman at Shanklin depot, on the day before his retirement in 1973, meets National Bus Company Chairman, Freddie Wood, who was on a tour of Southern Vectis depots and offices.

SVOC

Above: The annual dinner for the presentation of Long Service Awards usually took place at the Royal Hotel, Ventnor. The March 1977 event was attended by (back row) Messrs Burry, Gear, Rayner, Love, Moss, Parker, Savill, Plumbley, Warne, Powell, Wightman, Prowse and Kitcher and (front row seated) FK Poynton (Regional Director), A Boyce, G Langley, E Denness and Ronald Wade (SV General Manager).

SVOC

On the occasion of Cecil Kemp's retirement as Foreman of Newport's Central Works, a large group of engineering staff gather for a farewell photograph. *SVOC*

Opposite bottom: Dick Grabham became the Company's Driving Instructor and was responsible for training countless staff for their PSV test in the 1970s and 1980s. He is seen on the top deck of Lodekka trainer YDL 318 which had been adapted to include a model road layout used for training purposes. *SVOC*

Above: The intake of 1984: six drivers, engaged for the season on crew work, have passed through the autumn conducting school and are visiting Freshwater depot on VR No 673 before taking to the road as one-man operators in the following week. Messrs. Barton, Holmes, Winch, Tittley and Tiltman are seen with the author (far right).

Author

Right: John Hall was well known as one of the service 42 open-top drivers negotiating the tortuous road to the Needles Battery and spent most of his career working out of Freshwater depot. His grandfather had been a West Wight carrier, his uncle, Hilton Hall, started the West Wight Bus Service, later acquired by Brown's, and his father 'Babe' drove for West Wight, Brown's and then Southern Vectis. John's brother Patrick also drove for SVOC for some years while son Gary carries on the tradition as Inspector. John, seen at Alum Bay with a Lodekka, retired after forty-five years service.

Author

Left: Four generations of the Stephens family have worked for SVOC. Fred Stephens was a senior Newport driver while his son George, (pictured here in NBC days), was a Shanklin driver, later promoted to Inspector. The next generation was George's son, Brian, who joined the company as a seasonal driver in 1968, while Brian's daughter, Tracey worked at Ryde as a seasonal conductress in the 1980s.

SVOC

Below: Another long service employee was the late Gordon Butchers, who worked from 1952 until 1997 as conductor and in the Nelson Road Traffic Office compiling timetables and faretables. He imparted much information about the Company and its staff to the author and his quiet humour was much appreciated in the Ryde staffroom when he returned, in semi-retirement, as a seasonal conductor. He is seen at Ryde Bus Station with driver Ken Boulton, one of a good many staff who had previously worked for London Transport, in command of open-top VR No 506.

Author

Above: In NBC days, the driver of the year competition was actively encouraged. It commenced with local heats being held at Plessey's Somerton Works where driver Chris McAlister stands in front of his vehicle while depot clerk Derek Gawn and depot Superintendents Bob Downer and George Farrow awarded marks for performance and fault-finding.

SVOC

Right: Shanklin driver Ron Gatland won the Southern area Driver of the Year competition shield on six occasions (this occasion was in 1977 when VR No 664 was brand new) He won again in a company competition when revived around 2001 and was awarded the George Farrow memorial cup presented by Iris Farrow in memory of the former Shanklin depot superintendent. In 2002 he represented the Company in the National Finals of UK Bus Driver of the Year.

SVOC

Chris McAlister, from Ryde depot, won the TGWU cup by being placed second in the 1979 Southern Divisional Final of the Bus Driver of the Year competition which was held at Chiswick. He is seen with the cup in front of Leyland National No 870 at the Shanklin depot coach house.

SVOC

Left: Brian 'Ginger' Stephens, a Ryde driver, who has now completed 36 years service, is the third generation of his family to work for Southern Vectis. (His father, George, is pictured on page 164.) He is seen here at Ryde bus station with Bristol VRT No 681 (ODL 447) which is now allocated to service 41 *The Downs Tour*, having been displaced from the Yarmouth–Alum Bay/Needles route by the arrival there of Olympians Nos 742/3.

P Savage

Crew operation was retained on the Ryde to Cowes route for many years. Vehicles of the 'Vintage Fleet' were used on this service and the late Robbie Wearn, with his conductor Bob Rayner, are seen about to leave Ryde Bus Station on FLF No 611. This bus is now in the ownership of the Bus Museum and a plaque was placed on the platform in memory of Robbie, for whom the bus was a great favourite.

Author

Operation of the Vintage Fleet meant a continuing need for crews. Driver Russ Jones and conductress Jacqui Steele pose with Lodekka No 573 at Ryde. This particular vehicle is now resident in Scotland.

Author

MD Alan White presents a BCT Driver Instruction Certificate to driver (now Senior Inspector) Pete Garlick in the company of Traffic Officer (later redesignated Commercial Manager) Dave Cham, a second generation busman who started and completed his bus industry career with SVOC, in between taking appointments with Devon General and West Yorkshire.

SVOC

Many of the pictures in this book have come from the collection of the late Reg Davies. Reg worked in the Island bus industry for half a century starting with Yellow Cars of Yarmouth, about 1922, then as a conductor with the Vectis Bus Company, driver for Southern Vectis before retiring in 1972 from the post of wages clerk. For much of that time he carried his camera and the results provide a valuable record of SVOC vehicles and personalities. He emigrated to Australia in August 1994, aged 87, to live with his daughter and is seen here at Portsmouth Hard before the epic journey, having left the Island for the last time.

Author

SVOC Inspectorate in the Newport Bus Station office; Malcolm Johnson, Chief Insp Jerry Rolf and Mick Dyer between them have more than eighty years' service with the company. To the right of the clock is the charging point for the conductors' Wayfarer ticket machine modules.

D Evans/SVOC

As buses 'run in' each night they are swept out, fuelled and receive an oil level check before being put through the wash. One of the ex London Dennis Darts, No 816, in yellow and green livery, receives such attention at Ryde depot from cleaner Roger Lock, who was formerly one of Moss Motors' fitters.

Author

The Isle of Wight Bus Museum

Opposite top: The oldest bus in the collection, housed in a former timber storage shed on Newport Quay, is a 1927 Daimler CK with Marghan body built in Newport and believed transferred from an earlier Vulcan chassis. Number 11 (DL 5084) was sold to a Ryde store before becoming a residence and, later, store shed at Ashey. Rescued in 1966 by John Golding, it was moved into the Bus Museum when it opened in 1997. A former Ryde Pier electric tram is seen in the background.

P Savage

Opposite bottom: The annual Running Day is usually held in October, when resident and visiting vehicles operate local journeys. Bristol LD/Eastern Coach Works No 563 (SDL 268) has just unloaded as *Shanklin's Pony* Bristol RELL6G/Eastern Coach Works No 864 (TDL 564K) prepares to depart with a full load. The visting bus is a King Alfred AEC Renown.

P Savage

Above: The unique Bristol RESH/Duple Commander coach No 301 (KDL 885F) makes a photographic stop opposite Mottistone Manor on an October Running Day. The Museum opens to the public on various days throughout the summer.

P Savage

If you would like further information on the Isle of Wight Bus Museum and its activities, or to enquire about becoming a member, then please write the Membership Secretary at
9 St John's Wood Road, Ryde, ISLE OF WIGHT, PO33 1HP.

A stamped, self-addressed envelope would be appreciated for reply.

Timetables and guides

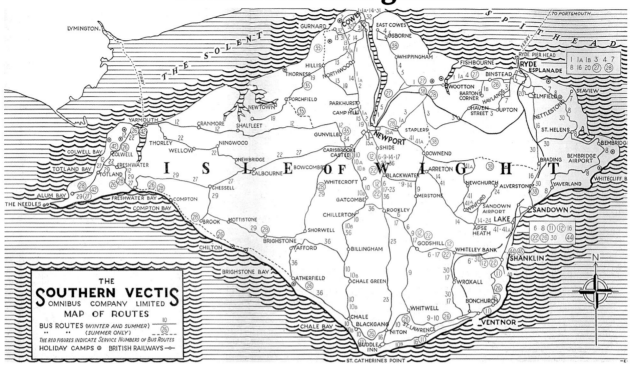

Opposite top: This map of Island bus routes would have been included with timetables of the late 1950s

In 1965 a copy of the summer timetable would have cost you the sum of 1/- (5p). By 1981 the cover price had risen to 25 pence (10/-). 1994 would have seen you handing over 60 pence (12/-) for a copy and by 1997 you would have been paying 65p (13/-). Things have improved somewhat and the 2004 summer issue is priced at 50p (10/-). How far would 13/- have taken you in 1965?

The cover of the summer timetable, since 1989, has featured humourous artwork by local cartoonist Besley, usually lampooning something which has, or is, happening on the Island. The 1994 issue featured an Island Explorer liveried Olympian, running along the Military Road; note the explorers, complete with pith helmets, in the front seats upstairs and the rabbit propping up his burrow on this unstable stretch of coastline. Shanklin Old Village and its traffic congestion was the subject for 1997. All Southern Vectis bus stops are named and on the 2000 cover we see an Olympian, at Ryde, with blinds set for 'Back of Beyond', a stop which does actually exist along the Military Road.

SVOC

Appendices
Southern Vectis Routes
1929/1939/1960/1987/2004

1929

Route (no numbers carried)

Gurnard–Cowes–Somerton–Parkhurst–Newport

East Cowes–Osborne–Binfield–Newport

Newport–Binfield–Wootton–Binstead–Ryde

Newport–Carisbrooke (Village)

Newport–Rookley–Godshill–Shanklin–Sandown

Ryde–Brading–Sandown–Shanklin–Godshill (Station Road)

Newport–Rookley–Godshill–Whitwell–Niton–St Lawrence–Ventnor

Newport–Carisbrooke–Shorwell–Brighstone–Brook–Chessell–Freshwater Bay–Freshwater–Totland–Alum Bay

Newport–Chillerton–Chale–Blackgang–Niton–St Lawrence–Ventnor

Ventnor–Bonchurch–Shanklin

Newport–Cemetery Hill

Shanklin–Sandown

Newport–Wootton Common–Havenstreet–Binstead–Ryde (acquired from Surprise, Sept 1929)

Summer 1939

Service No	Route
1	Ryde–Binstead–Wootton–Binfield–Newport–Four Cross–Cowes–Gurnard
2	Newport–Four Cross–Cowes Pontoon
3	Newport–Havenstreet–Haylands–Ryde
4	Ryde–Binstead–Wootton–Osborne–East Cowes
5	Newport–Binfield–Osborne–East Cowes
6	Ryde (Town Hall)–Airport–Brading–Sandown–Shanklin–Godshill–Newport
6b	Shanklin–Sandown–Sandown Station (Sats only)
7	Seaview–Nettlestone–St Helens–Brading–Sandown–Shanklin (extended to Wroxall & Ventnor, summer)
8	Ryde–Nettlestone–St Helens–Bembridge–Forelands
8a	Ryde–Nettlestone–Seaview (Pavilion)
9	Ventnor–Railway Station–Whitwell–Niton–Whitwell–Godshill–Merstone–Newport
10	Newport–Carisbrooke–Chillerton–Chale–Blackgang–Niton–St Lawrence–Ventnor
10a	Newport–Whitecroft Hospital
11	Sandown–Shanklin–Bonchurch–Ventnor–St Lawrence–Niton–Blackgang (Hotel)
12a	Newport–Carisbrooke–Shalfleet–Yarmouth–Totland–Freshwater Bay
12b	Newport–Carisbrooke–Shorwell–Brook–Chessell–Freshwater Bay–Totland
13	Newport–Marks Corner–Hillis Corner–Four Cross–Cowes
14	Whiteley Bank–Wroxall–Upper Ventnor–Ventnor
15	**Newport Town Service:** Whitepit Lane–Square–Camp Hill
15a	**Newport Town Service:** Whitepit Lane–Nelson Road–Square

Service No	Route
16	Ventnor Town Station–St Lawrence–Buddle Inn
17	Whiteley Bank–Wroxall–Upper Ventnor–Bellevue Road–Ventnor
18	Ventnor Esplanade/Pier–Town Hall–Town Station (or to any part of the town)
19	Newport–Thorness–Porchfield–Newtown–Shalfleet
20	**Ryde Town Service:** Pier–Oakfield–Elmfield
21	Newport–Binfield–Alverstone Farm–Beatrice Avenue–East Cowes (Sats only)
22	Newport–Carisbrooke–Calbourne–Wellow–Yarmouth–Freshwater–Freshwater Bay
23	Totland–Alum Bay (Needles Hotel)
24	Cowes–Park Gates–Woodvale Hotel
25	Newport–Appleford–Kingates–Niton
26	**Coastal Service:** Blackgang–Chale–Atherfield–Shorwell–Brook–Freshwater Bay–Totland–Alum Bay
27	Ryde–Mersley Down–Newport–Carisbrooke–Calbourne–Freshwater Bay–Totland–Alum Bay
28	**Newport Town Service:** Square–Carisbrooke Castle
29	Shanklin–Sandown–Whitecliff Bay–Bembridge (Stn)
30	Ryde–Haylands–Swanmore–Ryde
31	Newport–Marks Corner–Hillis Corner–Gurnard–Gurnard Beach–Round House–Cowes (Floating Bridge)
32	Ryde–Swanmore–Haylands–Upton Cross
33	Newport–Havenstreet–Barton's Corner–Ryde
34	Newport–Carisbrooke–Gunville
35	Newport–Carisbrooke–Porchfield–Thorness–Gurnard Beach & Hotel
36	Newport–Chillerton–Billingham–Shorwell–Atherfield

Summer 1960

Service No	Route
1	Ryde–Binstead–Wootton–Binfield–Newport–Somerton–Cowes
1a	Ryde–Binstead–Wootton Common–Newport–Four Cross–Cowes
1b	Ryde–Binstead (Barton's Corner)
2	Newport–Four Cross–Cowes (Pontoon)
2	**Direct Service** (Summer Saturdays): Sandown–Shanklin–Newport–Cowes (Pontoon)
3	Newport–Blacklands–Havenstreet–Haylands–Ryde
4	Ryde–Binstead–Wootton–Osborne–East Cowes
5	Newport–Binfield–Osborne–East Cowes
5	(Works): Newport or East Cowes–Folly Works
6	Newport–Wootton Common–Havenstreet–Haylands–Ryde
7	Haylands–Ryde–Nettlestone–Seaview
8	Ryde–Nettlestone–St Helens–Bembridge–Whitecliff Bay–Sandown–Shanklin
9	Newport–Rookley–Godshill–Whitwell–Ventnor
10/10b	Newport–Chillerton–Chale–Blackgang–Niton–Whitwell (10) or St Lawrence (10b)–Ventnor
12/22	Sandown–Shanklin–Godshill–Newport–Carisbrooke–Shalfleet (12) or Calbourne and Wellow (22)–Yarmouth–Totland–Freshwater–Freshwater Bay
12a	(Works): Cowes–Somerton–Shalfleet–Yarmouth–Freshwater–Freshwater Bay
12b	(Works): Cowes–Four Cross–Forest Works
13/13a	Newport–Hillis Cnr (13) or Northwood (13a)–Four Cross–Gurnard
14	Sandown–Apse Heath–Arreton–Newport–Four Cross–Cowes
15	**Newport Town Service:** St James's Square–Hunnyhill–Camp Hill
15a	**Newport Town Service:** Whitepit Lane–St James's Square–Pan Estate
16	Ryde–Brading–Sandown–Shanklin–Bonchurch–Ventnor–St Lawrence–Niton–Blackgang
17	Newport–Merstone–Godshill–Wroxall–Upper Ventnor–Ventnor
18	**Newport Town Service:** St James's Square–Carisbrooke Castle
19	Newport–Hillis Corner–Thorness–Porchfield–Newtown
20	**Ryde Town Service:** Pier–Oakfield–Elmfield
23	Newport–Rookley–Leechmore Cross–Niton
24	Sandown–Apse Heath–Alverstone

Service No	Route
26	Sandown–Shanklin–Bonchurch–Ventnor–Whitwell–Niton–Blackgang–Chale–Brook–Compton Bay–Freshwater Bay–Freshwater–Totland–Yarmouth
27/28	Ryde–Binstead–Wootton–Binfield–Newport–Carisbrooke–Calbourne and Chessell (27) or Shorwell and Brook (28)–Freshwater Bay–Freshwater–Totland–Alum Bay
29	Newport–Shorwell–Brook–Chessell–Freshwater Bay–Freshwater–Totland–Alum Bay
30	Seaview–Nettlestone–St Helens–Brading–Sandown–Shanklin–Wroxall–Upper Ventnor–Ventnor
31/32	Cowes–Gurnard
33	(Works): Shanklin–Sandown–Apse Heath–Arreton–Wootton Common–Osborne–East Cowes
34	**Newport Town Service:** St James's Square–Carisbrooke–Gunville
35	Newport–Carisbrooke–Porchfield–Thorness–Hillis Corner–Gurnard–Cowes (Summer Sundays only)
36	Newport–Chillerton–Chale–Atherfield
38	East Cowes–Osborne–Wootton Common–Ashey Down–Brading–Sandown (Summer Sundays only)
40	**Shanklin Town Service:** Oaklyn Gardens–Bus Station–Luccombe Village
41/43	Newport–Downend–Arreton (41) or Knighton (43)–Newchurch–Apse Heath–Sandown
42	Yarmouth–Totland–Alum Bay
44	Sandown Zoo–Lake–Shanklin Esplanade (Open-top, Summer only)
45	**Shanklin Town Service:** Esplanade–Bus Station–Rylstone Corner (Open-top, Summer only)
46	**Shanklin Town Service:** Esplanade–Bus Station–Rylstone Corner–Luccombe Village (Summer only)
47	Sandown Zoo–Shanklin–Bonchurch–Ventnor (Open-top, Summer only)

Express Services

Ryde, Quay Road–Little Canada or Wootton Holiday Chalets

Ryde, Quay Road–Brighstone Holiday Camp

Ryde, Quay Road–Chilton Chine Holiday Chalets

Ryde, Quay Road–Whitecliff Bay Caravan Park

Ryde Esplanade or St John's Road Station–any hotel in Sandown or Shanklin

Cowes (Pontoon)–any hotel in Shanklin

Ventnor Railway Station–St Lawrence (St Rhadagunds)

Sandown Airport–Lake, Sandown & Shanklin

Summer 1987

Service No	Route
1	Ryde–Binstead–Wootton–Binfield–Newport–Somerton–Cowes
1a	Ryde–Binstead–Wootton Common–Newport–Four Cross–Cowes
1b/1c	Ryde–Binstead–Wootton–Binfield–Newport–Carisbrooke–Shorwell & Brook (1b) or Calbourne & Chessell (1c)–Freshwater Bay–Freshwater–Totland–Alum Bay
2	Cowes–Four Cross–Newport–Rookley–Godshill–Shanklin–Sandown
2a	Cowes–Four Cross–Newport–Merstone–Godshill–Wroxall–Upper Ventnor–Ventnor
3	Ryde–Haylands–Havenstreet–Newport–Carisbrooke Castle
4/4a	Ryde–Binstead–Wootton–Osborne–East Cowes

(Early morning 4a journeys via Victoria Grove in East Cowes)

5	*Medinalinx* **Minibus** Newport–Binfield–Osborne–East Cowes
5b	*Medinalinx* **Minibus: Newport Town Service** Bus Station–Priory Park–Gunville
6	*Wanderer* **Minibus: Ryde Town Service** Bus Station–Oakfield–Elmfield–Tesco
6b	Elmfield–Oakfield–Ryde High School
7	Sandown–Apse Heath–Arreton–Newport–Carisbrooke–Shalfleet–Yarmouth–Freshwater
7a	Sandown or Shanklin–Apse Heath–Newchurch–Downend–Newport–Carisbrooke–Calbourne–Wellow–Yarmouth–Freshwater
8	Ryde–Nettlestone–St Helens–Bembridge–Whitecliff Bay–Sandown–Shanklin–Godshill–Merstone–Downend–Newport
8c	Ryde–Nettlestone–Seaview
9	*Medinalinx* **Minibus: Newport Town Service** Bus Station–Pan Estate–Halberry Lane–Bus Station
10	*Wanderer* **Minibus: Ryde Town Service** Bus Station–Haylands–Binstead
13	Yarmouth–Totland–Alum Bay–Needles Battery
14	Yarmouth–Totland–Freshwater–Pound Green–Afton–Freshwater Bay
16	Ryde–Brading–Sandown–Shanklin–Bonchurch–Ventnor–St Lawrence–Niton–Blackgang–Chale–Chillerton–Newport
16a	Ryde–Brading–Sandown–Shanklin–Bonchurch–Ventnor–Whitwell–Niton–Blackgang OR Leechmore Cross & Rookley–Newport
16b	Ryde–Brading–Sandown–Shanklin–Wroxall–Upper Ventnor–Ventnor–St Lawrence–Niton–Blackgang (Certain journeys extended to Chale, Chillerton & Newport)
16d	Ventnor–St Lawrence–Niton–Leechmore Cross–Rookley–Newport
19	Little Canada Holiday Village–Ryde or Newport
25	*Nightclubber*: Newport–Binfield–Wootton–Ryde–Brading–Sandown–Shanklin–Godshill–Rookley–Newport (both directions) (Fri & Sat nights)

Service No	Route
27/a/b/c/28 (School):	Carisbrooke School Site–Freshwater or Totland
30	Newport–Hillis Corner–Four Cross–Gurnard–Cowes
31	**Sandown/Shanklin Community Minibus:** Shanklin–Apse Heath–Winford–Alverstone–Adgestone–Sandown or Shanklin–Sibden Hill or Luccombe
32	Cowes–Gurnard
33	*Medinalinx* **Minibus** Newport–Wootton–Fishbourne
34	Cowes–Gurnard–Hillis Corner–Northwood
35	Newport–Hillis Corner–Thorness–Porchfield
37	Ryde–Bembridge Airport–Sandown–Whitecross–Shanklin–Lower Hyde
42	Yarmouth–Freshwater–Totland–Alum Bay
43	*Viewfinder*: Ryde–Brickfields–Havenstreet–Downend–The Downs–Ryde (Open-top, Summer only)
44	**Shanklin Town Service:** Railway Station–Esplanade–Old Village–Railway Station (*Shanklin's Pony* Open-top, Summer only)
45	Bembridge (Warner's)–Whitecliff Bay–Sandown Zoo–Shanklin–Bonchurch–Ventnor–St Lawrence (Tropical Bird Park) (Open-top, Summer only)
46	Sandown–Shanklin–Bonchurch–Ventnor–Whitwell–Niton–Blackgang–Chale–Brook–Compton Bay–Freshwater Bay–Freshwater–Totland & Alum Bay OR Yarmouth (Summer only)
51/a/b	(School) Newport–Cowes High School
52	(School) Cowes–Carisbrooke School Site

Express Services:

71	Ryde, Quay Road–Little Canada Holiday Village
72	Ryde, Quay Road–Brighstone Holiday Camp or Chilton Chine Chalets
74	Ryde, Quay Road–Fort Warden, Norton, Savoy Holiday Camps & West Wight Country Club
75	Ryde, Quay Road–Gurnard Pines & Thorness Bay
76	Cowes (Coach Park)–Gurnard Pines & Thorness Bay
81	*Medinalinx* **Minibus**: Newport–Ryde Pier Head

Tesco Contracts

82	Shanklin–Perowne Way–Brading–Tesco
83/83a	Bembridge–St Helens–Seaview (83a)–Tesco
84	East Cowes–Wootton–Binstead–Tesco
85	Newport–Wootton–Binstead–Haylands–Tesco
86	Ventnor–Upper Ventnor–Wroxall–Shanklin–Tesco
90	Sandown–Whitecliff Bay–Bembridge–St Helens–Brading–Downend–Newport
91	*Hydrobus* **Minibus:** Whitepit Ln–Newport–Cowes (Hydrofoil terminal)
96	Ryde Pier Head–Brading–Sandown–Shanklin–Bonchurch–Ventnor Esplanade (Summer only)

Summary 2004

Service No	Route
1	Sandown–Whitecliff Bay–Bembridge–St Helens–Oakfield–Ryde–Binstead–Wootton–Binfield–Newport–Somerton–Cowes (Pontoon)
1a	Ryde–Binstead–North Wootton–Newport
1b	(School) Carisbrooke Schools–Ryde
2	*Route Rouge* Sandown–Shanklin–Godshill–Rookley–Newport–Four Cross–Cowes
3/3a	*Route Rouge* Ventnor–Upper Ventnor–Wroxall–Godshill–Rookley (3) or Merstone (3a)–Newport–Somerton–Cowes
3b	*Route Rouge* Sandown–Apse Heath–Winford–Arreton–Downend–Newport–Somerton–Cowes
4	Ryde–Binstead–Wootton–Osborne–East Cowes
5	Newport–Binfield–Osborne–East Cowes
6	Ventnor–Whitwell–Niton–Blackgang–Chale–Chillerton–Newport
7/7a	*Explorer* Ryde–Oakfield–Brading–Sandown–Shanklin–Wroxall–Upper Ventnor–Ventnor–Whitwell–Niton–Blackgang–Chale–Brook–Freshwater Bay–Freshwater–Totland–Alum Bay–Yarmouth–Shalfleet (7) or Wellow & Calbourne (7a)–Carisbrooke–Newport–Wootton Common–Binstead–Ryde
7b	*Explorer* Ventnor–Bonchurch–Shanklin–Sandown–Brading–Oakfield–Ryde–Binstead–Wootton Common–Newport–Carisbrooke–Shorwell–Brook–Freshwater–Bay–Freshwater–Totland
8	Tesco–Oakfield–Ryde–Seaview & Nettlestone
11	Newport–Carisbrooke–Calbourne–Chessell–Freshwater Bay–Freshwater–Totland
12	Ryde–Nettlestone–St Helens–Bembridge–Whitecliff Bay–Sandown
15	*West Wight Tour* Yarmouth–Freshwater–Calbourne–Brighstone–Freshwater Bay–Wilmingham–Yarmouth
18	(School) Godshill–Whitwell–Ventnor
19	Ventnor–Whitwell–Niton–Rookley–Newport
21	Newport–Downend–Newchurch–Winford–Sandown (Joint with Wightbus)
23/25b	*Nightclubber*: Newport–Cowes–Newport
25a	*Nightclubber*: Newport–Shanklin–Sandown–Tesco–Ryde–Fishbourne–Wootton–Newport
25c	*Nightclubber*: Newport–Wootton–Fishbourne–Ryde
	Ventnor Local Services:
31	St Lawrence–Ventnor–Wroxall
31a	Ventnor–Bonchurch
31c	(School) Ventnor–Upper Ventnor–Whitwell–Buddle Inn–Niton–Whitwell–Niton–Blackgang

Service No	Route
32	Cowes–Gurnard
33	Ryde–Haylands–Havenstreet–Downend–Newport–Camp Hill–Northwood–Hillis Corner–Gurnard–Cowes
34	Ryde–Haylands–Ryde
35	Newport–Camp Hill–Hillis Corner–Thorness–Porchfield–Newtown
38	**Newport Town Service** Bus Station–Gunville–Carisbrooke–Whitepit Lane–Bus Station
39	**Newport Town Service** Bus Station–Dodnor Lane–Pan Estate–Bus Station
41	*Downs Tour* Ryde–Wootton Common–Downend–The Downs–Ryde (Open-top, Summer only)
42	*Needles Tour* Yarmouth–Freshwater Bay–Alum Bay–Needles Battery–Alum Bay–Totland–Fort Victoria–Yarmouth (Open-top, Summer only)
43	*Sandown Bay Tour* Sandown (Dinosaur Isle)–Shanklin (Town, Esplanade and Old Village) (Open-top, Summer only)
44	Ryde–Brading–Yaverland–Sandown (Open-top, Summer only)
45	*Nightclubber*: Ryde–Wootton–East Cowes–Newport
47	Newport–Four Cross–Hillis Corner–Thorness Bay–Porchfield–Shalfleet–Yarmouth (Open-top, Summer only)
50	(School) Freshwater Bay–Yarmouth–Porchfield–Cowes High School
51/a	(School) Newport–Cowes High School
52/a	Carisbrooke Schools–Cowes
53/4/5/6/6a/7	(School) Carisbrooke Schools–West Wight
58	(School) Ventnor–Medina High School
59	(School) Wootton Common–Osborne Middle School
60a	(School) Sandham Middle School–Sandown
61	(School) Newport–Chillerton–Rookley–Newport
63	(School) Sandown High School–Merstone–Whitwell
66	*Speedway Flyer*: Ryde–Smallbrook Stadium
68	(School) Newport–Kitbridge Middle School

Tesco Contracts

Service No	Route
83	Shanklin–Sandown–Bembridge–St Helens–Nettlestone–Seaview–Tesco–Ryde
84	Newport–East Cowes–Osborne–Wootton–Binstead–Haylands–Tesco
86	Upper Bonchurch–Ventnor–Upper Ventnor–Wroxall–Shanklin–Perowne Way–Brading–Tesco
90	Sandown–Whitecliff Bay–Bembridge–St Helens–Brading–Downend–Newport

Southern Vectis Omnibus Company Fleet List

Basic details of vehicles, by type, are included in this appendix (except for the miscellaneous fleets acquired with operators, which are listed individually). Chassis type, body manufacturer and seating layout are shown at the head of each batch and lists show, from left to right, (a) fleetnumber (two where renumbering occurred); (b) registration number; (c) date first licensed (which may differ from the date delivered or, in the case of secondhand vehicles, when first used by SVOC and (d) date of sale, as far as is known, or scrapped by SVOC. In many cases the last date of use may be a considerable time before sale. Vehicles marked 'E' are extant, part of the current fleet as at February 2004. The PSV Circle publishes fleet histories from time to time and readers are referred to those publications for comprehensive vehicle details.

Daimler Y/Dodson B28, 29 or 32R

8	DL 2448	1921	1930	4	DL 2760	1922	1932	6	DL 2937	1922	1930
5	DL 2612	1922	1930	12	DL 2784	1922	c1932	9	DL 4489	1926	1932
2	DL 2747	1922	1932								

All ex Vectis Bus Co., 1929; chassis had been reconditioned by Daimler and had probably been World War I lorries.

Daimler CK/Dodson B24 or 26R

17	DL 3346	1923	1934	1	DL 5035	1927	1934	16	DL 5413	1927	1934
18	DL 3369	1923	1934	11	DL 5084	1927	c1934	3	FM 1485	1926	1933
7	DL 4734	1926	1934	15	DL 5411	1927	1933				

All ex Vectis Bus Co., 1929; chassis had been reconditioned by Daimler and had probably been World War I lorries.
No 3 ex Colwill, Ilfracombe

Guy OND/Margham B14R

20	DL 4047	1925	1932	22	DL 4238	1925	1932	23	DL 4475	1926	1935
21	DL 4048	1925	1932								

All ex Vectis Bus Co., 1929; used as 'chasers'

Chevrolet LM/Dodson B14F (19 classed as Ch14F)

24	DL 5235	1927	1932	10	DL 5237	1927	1932	19	DL 5455	1927	1932
13	DL 5236	1927	1932								

All ex Vectis Bus Co., 1929; used as 'chasers'

ADC 416/Dodson B32D

26/300	DL 5536	1928	1935	30/305	DL 5578	1928	1935	34/309	DL 5582	1928	1935
25/301	DL 5537	1928	1935	31/306	DL 5579	1928	1935	36/310	DL 5730	1928	1935
27/302	DL 5538	1928	1936	32/307	DL 5580	1928	1935	35/311	DL 5731	1928	1935
28/303	DL 5576	1928	1935	33/308	DL 5581	1928	1935	37/312	DL 5732	1928	1936
29/304	DL 5577	1928	1935								

All ex Vectis Bus Co., 1929

AEC 426/Dodson B32D

39/313	DL 6155	1929	1936	41/315	DL 6157	1929	1936	38/317	DL 6159	1929	1936
40/314	DL 6156	1929	1936	42/316	DL 6158	1929	1935	43/318	DL 6160	1929	1936

Ordered by Vectis Bus Co.

AEC Reliance/Dodson B32D

49/200	DL 6829	1930	1938	52/206	DL 6835	1930	1938	61/212	DL 7066	1930	1938
50/201	DL 6830	1930	1938	57/207	DL 6836	1930	1938	67/213	DL 7385	1931	1941
51/202	DL 6831	1930	1938	58/208	DL 6837	1930	1938	69/214	DL 7386	1931	1941
53/203	DL 6832	1930	1938	56/209	DL 6838	1930	1938	68/215	DL 7387	1931	1941
54/204	DL 6833	1930	1938	59/210	DL 7064	1930	1938				
55/205	DL 6834	1930	1938	60/211	DL 7065	1930	1938				

AEC Regal/Dodson B32R

70/216	DL 7811	1931	1941	

SM B49A7/Dodson B35R (71/2) or Brush B35R (102-5)

71/100	DL 7991	1932	1941		102	DL 8435	1933	1941		104	DL 8437	1933	1941
72/101	DL 7992	1932	1941		103	DL 8436	1933	1941		105	DL 8438	1933	1941

Dennis Ace/Harrington B20F

400	DL 9010	1934	1956		403	DL 9013	1934	1959		406	ADL 508	1936	1957
401	DL 9011	1934	1941		404	DL 9014	1934	1956		407	ADL 509	1936	1958
402	DL 9012	1934	1941		405	DL 9015	1934	1959					

Nos 403/6 rebuilt as company lorries in 1954

Dennis Lancet/Eastern Counties B36R (500-9/24), Harrington B36R (510-22), Eastern Counties DP32R (525), Auto-Cellulose C32F (526), Dennis (?) B32F (527)

500	DL 9000	1934	1951		509	DL 9009	1934	1951		518	DL 9708	1935	1953
501	DL 9001	1934	1952		510	DL 9700	1935	1954		519	DL 9709	1935	1950
502	DL 9002	1934	1952		511	DL 9701	1935	1950		520	DL 9710	1935	1953
503	DL 9003	1934	1941		512	DL 9702	1935	1952		521	DL 9711	1935	c1953
504	DL 9004	1934	1952		513	DL 9703	1935	1952		522	DL 9712	1935	1952
505	DL 9005	1934	1952		514	DL 9704	1935	1952		524	ADL 506	1936	1953
506	DL 9006	1934	1952		515	DL 9705	1935	1952		525	ADL 507	1936	1952
507	DL 9007	1934	1941		516	DL 9706	1935	1953		526(i)	OV 8100	1932	1951
508	DL 9008	1934	1941		517	DL 9707	1935	1950		527	PJ 5032	1932	1949

Nos 501/2/6/14/5/6 were rebodied by Eastern Coachworks in 1944. No 503 was requistioned in 1941; although returned to SVOC, it never ran again. The chassis was retained for spares at Shanklin garage.   No 526(i) ex City of Oxford Motor Services, 1945   No 527 ex Fountain Coaches, 1946

Dennis Lance II/Eastern Counties H56R

600	ADL 500	1936	1953		602	ADL 502	1936	1953		604	ADL 504	1936	1953
601	ADL 501	1936	1954		603	ADL 503	1936	1954		605	ADL 505	1936	1954

Dennis Falcon/Eastern Coach Works B20F

200	CDL 900	1939	1954		201	CDL 901	1939	1954

AEC Regal/Harrington C31F (17/8), C32F rebodied 1939 (19/20)

17	CDL 94	1938	1940		19	GN 1379	1931	1953		20	GO 1409	1931	1940
18	CDL 95	1938	1940										

Nos 19/20 acquired from Thomas Tilling, 1939

Bedford WTB/Duple C25F

21	CDL 727	1939	1953		22	CDL 728	1939	1953		23/207	CDL 729	1939	1953

Bristol GO5G/Eastern Coach Works H56R

700	BDL 100	1937	1954		701	BDL 101	1937	1954

No 701 rebuilt to L54R by Hants & Dorset Motor Services, 1951

Bristol JO5G/Eastern Coach Works B35R

800	BDL 102	1937	1954		801	BDL 103	1937	1954

Bristol L5G/Beadle B35R (802–8), Harrington B35R (809–22), Margham B35R (823/4), Eastern Coach Works B35R (825–31)

802	BDL 850	1938	1955	812	CDL 603	1939	1955	822	CDL 613	1939	1955
803	BDL 851	1938	1954	813	CDL 604	1939	1955	823	CDL 614	1939	1955
804	BDL 852	1938	1954	814	CDL 605	1939	1955	824	CDL 615	1939	1957
805	BDL 853	1938	1954	815	CDL 606	1939	1955	825	DDL 51	1940	1956
806	BDL 854	1938	1954	816	CDL 607	1939	1955	826	DDL 52	1940	1956
807	BDL 855	1938	1955	817	CDL 608	1939	1957	827	DDL 53	1940	1956
808	BDL 856	1938	1954	818	CDL 609	1939	1955	828	DDL 54	1940	1956
809	CDL 600	1939	1955	819	CDL 610	1939	1955	829	EDL 14	1946	1969
810	CDL 601	1939	1955	820	CDL 611	1939	1955	830	EDL 15	1946	1970
811	CDL 602	1939	1955	821	CDL 612	1939	1955	831	EDL 16	1946	1970

Nos 802–8 converted to B31R standee layout in wartime, later B36R

Nos 829–31 rebodied FB35F by Eastern Coach Works in 1961/2

Bristol K5G/Eastern Coach Works H56R

702/502	CDL 899	1939	E	703	DDL 50	1940	1979

Both vehicles were converted to open-top 1958/9. No 703 became tree-lopper No 001, 1969

Bristol K5G (704), K6A (705–7)/Park Royal UH56R (704/5), Duple UH56R (706/7)

704	DDL 688	1944	1967	706	DDL 764	1945	1967	707	DDL 765	1945	1968
705	DDL 759	1945	1967								

All four vehicles rebodied by Eastern Coach Works,1953 and Nos 705–7 re-engined as K5G

Bristol K5G/Eastern Coach Works L55R

710	DDL 985	1946	1961	721	EDL 657	1947	1964	731	FDL 983	1949	1964
711	DDL 986	1946	1961	722	EDL 658	1947	1964	732	FDL 984	1950	1964
713	EDL 17	1947	1963	723	EDL 659	1947	1964	733	FDL 985	1950	1965
714	EDL 18	1947	1963	724	FDL 292	1948	1964	734	FDL 986	1950	1965
715	EDL 19	1947	1963	725	FDL 293	1948	1964	735	FDL 987	1950	1966
716	EDL 20	1947	1963	726	FDL 294	1948	1964	736	GDL 434	1950	1966
717	EDL 21	1947	1963	727	FDL 295	1948	1964	737	GDL 435	1950	1966
718	EDL 22	1947	1961	728	FDL 296	1948	1965	738	GDL 711	1951	1966
719	EDL 23	1947	c1961	729	FDL 297	1948	1964	739	GDL 712	1951	1966
720	EDL 656	1947	1964	730	FDL 298	1948	1965				

Nos 729/30 loaned to London Transport when new

Bristol KS5G/Eastern Coach Works L55R

740	GDL 713	1951	1967	751	HDL 265	1952	1967	756	HDL 270	1952	1969
741	GDL 714	1951	1967	752	HDL 266	1952	1968	757	HDL 271	1952	1969
742	GDL 715	1951	1967	753	HDL 267	1952	1968	758	HDL 272	1952	1969
749	HDL 263	1952	1968	754	HDL 268	1952	1969				
750	HDL 264	1952	1967	755	HDL 269	1952	1969				

Bristol KSW5G/Eastern Coach Works L55R

759	JDL 33	1952	1969	764	JDL 38	1952	1970	769	JDL 719	1953	1971
760	JDL 34	1952	1969	765	JDL 39	1953	1970	770	JDL 720	1953	1970
761	JDL 35	1952	1969	766	JDL 40	1953	1970	771	JDL 721	1953	1970
762	JDL 36	1952	1969	767	JDL 41	1953	1971	772	JDL 722	1953	1970
763	JDL 37	1952	1970	768	JDL 42	1953	1971	773	JDL 723	1953	1972

Leyland TD1/Leyland H51R (708), Leyland L51R (709), Beadle L52R (712) rebodied 1946, Brush UL55R (743–8) rebodied 1944

708	TF 6821	1931	1954	743	UF 7383	1931	1951	746	UF 7427	1931	1951
709	UH 7175	1929	1954	744	UF 7393	1931	1951	747	UF 7386	1931	1951
712	TK 1854	1929	1954	745	UF 7396	1931	1951	748	UF 7417	1931	1951

Nos 708/9 acquired from Cardiff Corporation, 1945; both rebodied Eastern Coach Works L55R, 1949
No 712 acquired from Hants & Dorset, 1946   Nos 743–8 were on long-term loan 1950/1 from Wilts & Dorset MS

Bedford OB/Duple C29F

208	EDL 637	1947	1958	214	FDL 655	1949	1957	220	GDL 793	1950	1963
209	EDL 638	1947	1963	215	FDL 656	1949	1957	221	GDL 796	1950	1963
210	EDL 639	1947	1958	216	FDL 676	1949	1957	222	GDL 797	1950	1963
211	EDL 640	1947	1959	217	FDL 802	1949	1957	223	GDL 798	1950	1963
212	EDL 641	1948	1959	218	GDL 153	1949	1963				
213	EDL 642	1948	1957	219	GDL 779	1950	1963				

Nos 208–12/8–23 were converted for bus operation as 26 or 27 seaters and fitted with Gardner or Perkins engines

Bristol LL5G/Eastern Coach Works B39R

832	GDL 716	1950	1963	836	HDL 280	1951	1966	840	HDL 284	1951	1966
833	GDL 717	1950	1963	837	HDL 281	1951	1966	841	HDL 285	1952	1966
834	GDL 718	1950	1963	838	HDL 282	1951	1966	842	HDL 286	1952	1966
835	HDL 279	1951	1966	839	HDL 283	1951	1966	843	HDL 287	1952	1966

Bristol LWL6B/Eastern Coach Works FC37F

300	HDL 182	1951	1961	301	HDL 183	1951	1961	302	HDL 184	1951	1961

Bristol LS6G (844, 303–8), LS6B (308(ii), 309–13)/Eastern Coach Works B45F (844), C39F (all others)

844	JDL 43	1953	1970	307/857	JDL 48	1953	1971	311	JDL 759	1953	1967
303/853	JDL 44	1952	1971	308(i)	JDL 756	1953	1953	312	JDL 760	1954	1968
304/854	JDL 45	1952	1971	308(ii)	KBE 179	1953	1967	313	JDL 761	1954	1969
305/855	JDL 46	1952	1970	309	JDL 757	1953	1967				
306/856	JDL 47	1953	1971	310	JDL 758	1953	1967				

No 844 later reseated to B41F; Nos 303–7 converted to DP37F, 1966, for bus operation
No 308(i) exchanged with Lincolnshire Road Car for No 308(ii), 1953
No 313 sold to Shamrock & Rambler, 1968 but returned to SVOC fleet on takeover, May 1969

In line with a trend adopted by fellow Tilling company Hants & Dorset, some LS Type coaches were converted for one-man bus work to extend their working lives by a few years. Number 853 (JDL 44) is seen on Ryde Esplanade on the rural service 3 via Havenstreet to Newport.

Author

Bristol LD6G/Eastern Coach Works H54, 57 or 60R

500	JDL 996	1954	1971	522	LDL 721	1955	1975	544/OT4/500	MDL 954	1956	1979
501	JDL 997	1954	1971	523	LDL 722	1955	1975	545/OT5/500	MDL 955	1956	2002
502	JDL 998	1954	1971	524	LDL 723	1955	1975	546	MDL 956	1956	1977
503	JDL 999	1954	1971	525	LDL 724	1955	1975	547	ODL 7	1957	1977
504	KDL 1	1954	1971	526	LDL 725	1955	1976	548	ODL 8	1957	1977
505	KDL 401	1954	1971	527	LDL 726	1955	1976	549	ODL 9	1957	1977
506	KDL 402	1954	1973	528	LDL 727	1955	1976	550	ODL 10	1957	1978
507	KDL 403	1954	1973	529	LDL 728	1955	1976	551	ODL 11	1957	1978
508	KDL 404	1954	1973	530	LDL 729	1955	1976	552	ODL 12	1957	1978
509	KDL 405	1954	1973	531	LDL 730	1955	1976	553	ODL 13	1957	1978
510	KDL 406	1954	1973	532	LDL 731	1955	1976	554	ODL 14	1957	1978
511	KDL 407	1954	1973	533	LDL 732	1955	1977	555	ODL 15	1957	1978
512	KDL 408	1954	1973	534	LDL 733	1955	1977	556	PDL 516	1958	1978
513	KDL 409	1954	1973	535	LDL 734	1955	1976	557	PDL 517	1958	1978
514	KDL 410	1954	1973	536	LDL 735	1955	1977	558	PDL 518	1958	1978
515	KDL 411	1954	1976	537	LDL 736	1955	1977	559	PDL 519	1958	1978
516	KDL 412	1954	1975	538	LDL 737	1955	1977	560	SDL 265	1959	1978
517	KDL 413	1954	1975	539	LDL 738	1955	1977	561	SDL 266	1959	1978
518	KDL 414	1954	1976	540	LDL 739	1955	1977	562	SDL 267	1959	1981
519	KDL 415	1954	1976	541/OT1	MDL 951	1956	1979	563	SDL 268	1959	1980
520	KDL 416	1954	1969	542/OT2/501	MDL 952	1956	2002	564	SDL 269	1959	1978
521	LDL 720	1955	1975	543/OT3/507	MDL 953	1956	2002				

Nos 541–5 converted to open-top 1973–5 and renumbered OT1–5; OT3/5 originally sold in 1979/8 and repurchased 1994/3 from preservationists (as Nos 507, 500); OT4 on loan to SVOC from preservationist 1986–7 and numbered 500; No 563 returned on loan to SVOC for Vintage Fleet, 1986–97; Nos 500/1/7 reregistered BAS 564/3/2 before sale.

Bristol FS6G/Eastern Coach Works H60RD

565	TDL 998	1960	2001	568	VDL 845	1961	1979	571	YDL 316	1962	1979
566	TDL 999	1960	1980	569	YDL 314	1962	1979	572	YDL 317	1962	1980
567	VDL 844	1961	1980	570	YDL 315	1962	1980	573	YDL 318	1962	2001

Nos 573/65 converted to driver trainers TB1/2, 1977/80 and reinstated as buses 1992/87

Bristol K5G/Eastern Coach Works H56R (781–3/6/7), Brislington Body Works H56R (774–80/4), Beadle L53R (built 1946) (785), Eastern Coach Works L53R (788/9)

774	FHT 260	1939	1957	780	GAE 483	1941	1957	786	GAE 493	1941	c1958
775	FHT 811	1939	1960	781	GAE 492	1939	1957	787	GAE 498	1941	1959
776	FHT 815	1939	1958	782	GAE 497	1941	c1957	788	AFX 757	1939	1959
777	GAE 470	1939	1957	783	GAE 505	1940	1959	789	APR 426	1940	1959
778	GAE 473	1941	1957	784	GHT 140	1941	1958				
779	GAE 479	1941	1957	785	GHU 489	1941	1957				

Nos 774–87 acquired from Bristol Tramways, 1955   Nos 788/9 acquired from Hants & Dorset, 1956/7

AEC Regent/Tilling/BH&D O56, 57 or 58R

900	GP 6244	1931	1960	902	GW 6277	1932	1957	903	GW 6286	1932	1957
901	GW 6276	1932	1961								

All acquired from Brighton, Hove & District, 1955. 902/3 never entered service with SVOC.

Bristol K5G/Eastern Coach Works O56, 58 or 60R (902/3/6–8), Brislington Body Works O56R (904/5), Hants & Dorset FO59R (909–11)

902	CAP 187	1940	1965	906	FHT 112	1938	1966	910	FRU 304	1944	1973
903	CAP 234	1940	1968	907	GHT 124	1940	1968	911	GLJ 969	1947	1973
904	GL 6611	1939	1963	908	FLJ 538	1940	c1974				
905	GL 6612	1939	1965	909	FRU 303	1944	1973				

Nos 902/3 acquired from Brighton, Hove & District, 1960   Nos 904/5 acquired from Bristol Omnibus Co. (via dealer), 1961
Nos 906/7 acquired from Brighton, Hove & District, 1962   Nos 908–11 acquired from Hants & Dorset Motor Services, 1964

Bristol MW6G/Eastern Coach Works C39F (314/5), B45F (later B43F) (801–7)

No	Reg			No	Reg			No	Reg		
314	PDL 514	1958	1975	802	EDL 235C	1965	1977	805	FDL 926D	1966	1977
315	PDL 515	1958	1974	803	EDL 236C	1965	1977	806	FDL 927D	1966	1977
801	EDL 234C	1965	1977	804	FDL 925D	1966	1977	807	FDL 928D	1966	1977

No 315 repurchased 1988 for Vintage Fleet but not restored; resold in 1991.
No 806 repurchased 1988 for Vintage Fleet. Sold to IW Bus Museum 2001 after being on loan from 1997.

Bristol SUL4A/Eastern Coach Works B36F

No	Reg			No	Reg			No	Reg		
845	458 ADL	1963	1975	848	461 ADL	1966	1975	851	464 ADL	1963	1975
846	459 ADL	1963	1975	849	462 ADL	1963	1975	852	465 ADL	1963	1975
847	460 ADL	1963	1975	850	463 ADL	1963	1975				

Bedford VAL14 (401–9); VAL70 (others)/Duple C52F (401–9, 410[i]), Plaxton C53F (410[ii], 411)

No	Reg			No	Reg			No	Reg		
401	ADL 109B	1964	1978	405	EDL 994D	1966	1980	409	HDL 231E	1967	1980
402	ADL 110B	1964	1978	406	HDL 228E	1967	1980	410[i]/120	PDL 351H	1970	1982
403	EDL 992D	1966	1980	407	HDL 229E	1967	1980	410[ii]/110	SDL 743J	1971	1982
404	EDL 993D	1966	1980	408	HDL 230E	1967	1980	411/111	SDL 744J	1971	1982

Bristol FLF6G/Eastern Coach Works H70F (600–21), O70F (OT6)

No	Reg			No	Reg			No	Reg		
600	BDL 576B	1964	1982	608	CDL 476C	1965	1980	616	GDL 771E	1967	1984
601	BDL 577B	1964	1982	609	CDL 477C	1965	1982	617	GDL 815E	1967	1983
602	BDL 578B	1964	1982	610	CDL 478C	1965	1980	618	GDL 816E	1967	1984
603	BDL 579B	1964	1982	611	CDL 479C	1965	1984	619	KDL 143F	1968	1973
604	BDL 580B	1964	1983	612	CDL 480C	1965	1982	620	KDL 144F	1968	1973
605	BDL 581B	1964	1983	613	GDL 768E	1967	1984	621	KDL 145F	1968	1973
606	BDL 582B	1964	1983	614	GDL 769E	1967	1984	OT6	BRX 142B	1964	1979
607	BDL 583B	1964	1983	615	GDL 770E	1967	1983				

No 611 repurchased in 1986 from Shamrock & Rambler for Vintage Fleet. Sold to IW Bus Museum 2001 after being on loan from 1997. Nos 619–21 passed to Scottish Bus Group as part of an exchange for Bristol VRTs. No OT6 was acquired from Alder Valley in 1976, in damaged condition and converted to open-top.

Bristol RESL6G/Eastern Coach Works B43F

No	Reg			No	Reg			No	Reg		
808	HDL 23E	1967	1982	811	HDL 26E	1967	1982	814	NDL 766G	1969	1982
809	HDL 24E	1967	1982	812	LDL 933G	1968	1982	815	NDL 767G	1969	1982
810	HDL 25E	1967	1982	813	LDL 934G	1968	1982				

Bristol RESH6G/Duple C39F (later 41/45 seats)

No	Reg		
301	KDL 885F	1968	2001

Sold to IW Bus Museum, 2001, after being on loan from 1997

Bedford SBO (224–38), SB8 (239–50), SB13 (251–5)/Duple C38F or C41F

No	Reg			No	Reg			No	Reg		
224	LDL 626	1955	1964	238	ODL 51	1957	1967	248	XDL 729	1962	1969
225	LDL 627	1955	1964	239/102	SDL 3	1959	1973	249	XDL 730	1962	1976
226	LDL 628	1955	1964	240/103	SDL 4	1959	1973	250	XDL 731	1962	1976
231	MDL 752	1956	1964	241	SDL 5	1959	1973	251/115	ADL 104B	1964	1978
232	MDL 753	1956	1964	242	SDL 6	1959	1973	252	ADL 105B	1964	1978
233	MDL 818	1956	1964	243/108	TDL 995	1960	1975	253	ADL 106B	1964	1976
234	MDL 819	1956	1964	244	TDL 996	1960	1973	254	ADL 107B	1964	1978
235	ODL 48	1957	1967	245	TDL 997	1960	1976	255	ADL 108B	1964	1978
236	ODL 49	1957	1967	246	VDL 854	1961	1976				
237	ODL 50	1957	1967	247	VDL 855	1961	1976				

Nos 239/40 were sold to Shamrock & Rambler, 1969 but returned to SVOC fleet on takeover, May 1969

Bristol LH6L/Eastern Coach Works B43F (825–9) or Plaxton C45F (AAX)

825	LDL 262F	1968	1977	827	PDL 489H	1970	1982	829	PDL 491H	1970	1982
826	LDL 263F	1968	1977	828	PDL 490H	1970	1982	–	AAX 633K	1971	1990

AAX acquired from Medina Marching Band, 1988, as a source of spares.

Bedford VAM70 (421–6), VAM14 (427, 106)/Duple C45F

421	KDL 162F	1968	c1980	424	MDL 597G	1968	1982	427	EFE 445E	1967	1979
422	KDL 163F	1968	1982	425	MDL 598G	1969	1982	106	EFE 446E	1967	1979
423	KDL 164F	1968	1980	426	MDL 599G	1969	1982				

Nos 427, 106 were acquired from Lincolnshire Road Car, 1974

Bristol LHS6L/Marshall B35F (832–5), Eastern Coach Works B35F (836–9, 200/1), DP29F (DP1) or DP31F (202–4)

832	NDL 768G	1969	1977	837	HDL 413N	1975	1983	201	LFJ 849W	1981	1988
833	NDL 769G	1969	1977	838	HDL 414N	1975	1984	202	KDL 202W	1981	2001
834	NDL 770G	1969	1982	839	HDL 415N	1975	1984	203	KDL 203W	1981	2001
835	NDL 771G	1969	1982	DP1/201	THX 618M	1973	1982	204	KDL 204W	1981	1989
836	HDL 412N	1975	1983	200	FDV 793V	1980	1988				

Nos 200/1were acquired from Devon General, 1986 and both were transferred to Solent Blue Line, 1988. Nos 202–4 were to have been DP2–4. No 204 transferred to Solent Blue Line, 1989. DP1 acquired from National Travel (South East), 1978

Bristol RELL6G/Eastern Coachworks B53F

861	PDL 492H	1970	1988	864	TDL 564K	1971	2000	867	TDL 567K	1972	1988
862	PDL 493H	1970	1988	865	TDL 565K	1971	1988	868	TDL 568K	1972	1988
863	TDL 563K	1971	2001	866	TDL 566K	1972	1988	869	TDL 569K	1972	1982

Nos 861/2/5–8 operated for Badger Vectis 1987/8   No 864 rebuilt to open-top, 1986

Bristol RELH6G/Eastern Coach Works C47F (302), Plaxton C49F (SJB)

302	XDL 122L	1972	1988	–	SJB 114M	1974	1988

No 302 was C45F for a time; SJB was acquired from Alder Valley in 1986, as a source of spares.

Leyland National B52F (870–4/80–2), B44F (875–9/83–8)

870	XDL 794L	1973	1985	877	XDL 801L	1973	1985	884	ODL 884R	1977	1987
871	XDL 795L	1973	1985	878	XDL 802L	1973	1987	885	ODL 885R	1977	1987
872	XDL 796L	1973	1985	879	XDL 803L	1973	1985	886	ODL 886R	1977	1987
873	XDL 797L	1973	1985	880	MDL 880R	1976	1987	887	ODL 887R	1977	1987
874	XDL 798L	1973	1985	881	MDL 881R	1976	1986	888	ODL 888R	1977	1987
875	XDL 799L	1973	1985	882	MDL 882R	1976	1986				
876	XDL 800L	1973	1987	883	ODL 883R	1977	1987				

Bedford YRT/Duple C53F

412	YDL 940L	1973	1982	416	ODL 866M	1974	1987	402	OOD 362M	1974	1982
413	YDL 941L	1973	1982	123	ODL 867M	1974	1983	403	OOD 363M	1974	1987
121	YDL 942L	1973	1982	124	ODL 868M	1974	1983	404	OOD 364M	1974	1987
122	YDL 943L	1973	1986	119	ORU 291M	1974	1982	405	OOD 365M	1974	1982
414	ODL 864M	1974	1984	400	OOD 360M	1974	1982	116	OOD 366M	1974	1985
415	ODL 865M	1974	1988	401	OOD 361M	1974	1987	117	OOD 367M	1974	1984

No 122 reregistered WDL 142, then ABK 116L   No 119 acquired from National Travel (South West), 1979   Nos 400–5, 116/7 acquired from Western National, 1980   No 401 converted to IW Publiclity and Exhibition vehicle PC1, 1983

Bedford YRQ/Duple C45F

107	XKO 192J	1971	1983	429	XKO 194J	1971	1979	109	XKO 196J	1971	1983
108	XKO 193J	1971	1980	430	XKO 195J	1971	1979	428	YKO 562J	1971	1979

All acquired from Maidstone & District, 1976 (new to Streamline, Maidstone)

Bristol VRT/SL6G (619–49), VRT/SL3/6LXB (the rest)/Eastern Coach Works H70F (622–49), H74F (650–85, 711/2, 509/10), CO74F (705–10), H77F (619–21)

No.	Reg	Year	Year		No.	Reg	Year	Year		No.	Reg	Year	Year
619	NGM 168G	1969	1986		647	HDL 409N	1975	1990		675	UDL 675S	1978	1979
620	OSF 305G	1969	1986		648	HDL 410N	1975	1990		676	UDL 676S	1978	1979
621	OSF 307G	1969	1986		649	HDL 411N	1975	1990		671	YDL 671T	1979	1995
622	NDL 490G	1969	1999		650	MDL 650R	1976	1990		672	YDL 672T	1979	1995
623	NDL 491G	1969	1982		651	MDL 651R	1976	1990		673	YDL 673T	1979	1995
624	SDL 634J	1971	1987		652	NDL 652R	1977	1990		674	YDL 674T	1979	1995
625	SDL 635J	1971	1984		653	NDL 653R	1977	1990		675	YDL 675T	1979	1995
626	SDL 636J	1971	1987		654	NDL 654R	1977	1990		676	YDL 676T	1979	1996
627	SDL 637J	1971	1987		655	NDL 655R	1977	1991		677	FDL 677V	1980	1996
628	SDL 638J	1971	1995		656	NDL 656R	1977	1991		678	FDL 678V	1980	1996
629	SDL 639J	1971	1987		657	ODL 657R	1977	1991		679	FDL 679V	1980	1998
630	XDL 377L	1972	1987		658	ODL 658R	1977	1991		680	FDL 680V	1980	1996
631	XDL 378L	1972	1987		659	ODL 659R	1977	1991		681	FDL 681V	1980	E
632	XDL 379L	1972	1987		660	ODL 660R	1977	1993		682	FDL 682V	1980	E
633	XDL 380L	1972	1987		661	ODL 661R	1977	1993		683	DPX 683W	1981	E
634	NDL 634M	1973	1987		662	ODL 662R	1977	1993		684	DPX 684W	1981	2003
635	NDL 635M	1973	1987		663	ODL 663R	1977	1993		685	DPX 685W	1981	2001
636	NDL 636M	1973	1987		664	ODL 664R	1977	1993		705/503	UFX 855S	1977	E
637	NDL 637M	1973	1987		665	ODL 665R	1977	1993		706/504	UFX 856S	1977	E
638	NDL 638M	1973	1987		666	ODL 666R	1977	1993		707/505	UFX 857S	1977	1998
639	NDL 639M	1973	1987		667	ODL 667R	1977	1993		708/506	UFX 858S	1977	1998
640	NDL 640M	1973	1988		668	UDL 668S	1978	1994		709	UFX 859S	1977	1983
641	NDL 641M	1973	1990		669	UDL 669S	1978	1994		710	UFX 860S	1977	1983
642	NDL 642M	1973	1990		670	UDL 670S	1978	1995		711/507	RFB 614S	1977	1991
643	HDL 405N	1975	1990		671	UDL 671S	1978	1979		712/508	RFB 615S	1977	1990
644	HDL 406N	1975	1990		672	UDL 672S	1978	1979		509	PTT 98R	1977	1992
645	HDL 407N	1975	1990		673	UDL 673S	1978	1979		510	VOD 595S	1978	1992
646	HDL 408N	1975	1990		674	UDL 674S	1978	1979					

No 619 acquired from Central SMT, 1973; Nos 620/1 acquired from Eastern Scottish, 1973; No 622 converted to tree-lopper 009, 1986; Nos 624/6/7/9–40/53/4/60–9/76–80 transferred to Solent Blue Line; No 641 sent to SBL, 1990 returned 1991. Nos 681–3 converted to open-top, 2000/1 and reregistered ODL 447, VDL 744, 934 BDL; Nos 705–10 acquired from Hants & Dorset, 1979, in exchange for Nos 671–6 (UDL 671–6S); Nos 705/6 (as 503/4) reregistered XDL 872, WDL 655 in 2000 and converted to permanent open-top for 2003 season. No 503 had also carried reg nos 473 CDL and VDL 613S; Nos 711/2 acquired from Bristol Omnibus Co. in exchange for Nos 709/10. Nos 509/10 acquired from a dealer, ex-Devon General, 1987; three vehicles of the 1970 delivery were diverted to City of Oxford Motor Services as OFC 901–3H.

After over 13 years service on the Island 1973-built Bristol VRT No 637 was sent to Southampton to work for Solent Blue Line. It was later acquired, by the author, for preservation and is pictured here leaving Yaverland, with Culver Down in the background, when on loan to Westbrook Travel. It carries an early version of Solent Blue Line livery, applied during preservation.

P Savage

Bedford YMT/ Duple C46 or 51F (125–7, 303, 417–20), Plaxton C51F (431/2, 304), Willowbrook C46 or 53F (305, 433, 128)

417	ODL 174R	1977	1988	303	TDL 303S	1978	1991	304	XDL 304T	1979	1991
418	ODL 175R	1977	1988	419	TDL 419S	1978	1988	305	EDL 267V	1980	1989
125	ODL 176R	1977	1988	420	TDL 420S	1978	1988	433	EDL 268V	1980	1990
126	TDL 126S	1978	1990	431	XDL 431T	1979	1991	128	EDL 269V	1980	1990
127	TDL 127S	1978	1988	432	XDL 432T	1979	1996				

No 304 reregistered TDL 998, then BDL 65T and transferred to Solent Blue Line as driver training vehicle, 1991.
No 432 reregistered WDL 748, then WXI 6291, then BDL 301T.

Leyland Leopard PSU3/Plaxton C46, 47, 48, 49 or 53F (all except 308(i)/9), Eastern Coach Works C49F (308(i)/9)

300	RHY 770M	1974	1991	308(i)	RDL 308X	1982	1983	–	PPM 888R	1977	1989
302	WJM 811T	1979	1997	309	RDL 309X	1982	1991	–	WJM 809T	1979	1990
306	RDL 306X	1981	1991	308(ii)	LUA 276V	1980	1991				
307	RDL 307X	1981	1997	–	MPM 389P	1976	1989				

No 300 acquired from Western National 1982, reregistered WDL 142, then TPO 935M
No 302, MPM 389P, PPM 888R, WJM 809T acquired from Bee Line, Reading, 1989. Only No 302, reregistered CXI 5971, was used by SVOC.
Nos 307/9 reregistered LXI 4409, VDL 263 (later TDL 483X)
No 308(ii) acquired from Aldham Coaches, Wombwell, 1987 (new to Wallace Arnold)

Leyland Olympian ONLXB/1R/Eastern Coach Works H75F

686	RDL 686X	1982	2003	692	WDL 692Y	1983	2002	698	A698 DDL	1984	2002
687	RDL 687X	1982	2003	693	WDL 693Y	1983	2002	699	A699 DDL	1984	1989
688	RDL 688X	1982	2003	694	WDL 694Y	1983	1989	700	A700 DDL	1984	1989
689	RDL 689X	1982	2003	695	WDL 695Y	1983	2002	701/101	A701 DDL	1984	1991
690	RDL 690X	1982	2003	696	WDL 696Y	1983	2002	702/102	A702 DDL	1984	1992
691	RDL 691X	1982	2003	697	A697 DDL	1984	1989				

Nos 686–93/5/8 refurbished to CH70F, 1994/5; Nos 701/2 rebuilt as CH64F, 1987/8, renumbered Nos 101/2 and reregistered WDL 748/142, later A110, 295 FDL.
Nos 694/7/9, 700, 102 transferred to Solent Blue Line.

Leyland Tiger TRC/Plaxton C49, 51 or 53F

310	WDL 310Y	1983	1977	315	C315 TDL	1986	1999	320	E320 JDL	1988	1999
311	WDL 311Y	1983	1997	316	C316 TDL	1986	1997	321	E321 JDL	1988	1997
312	A312 BDL	1984	1997	317	C317 TDL	1986	1997	326	A780 WHB	1984	1996
313	A313 BDL	1984	1997	318	A588 RFR	1984	1992	327	A781 WHB	1984	1992
314	C314 TDL	1986	1999	319	A589 RFR	1984	1991				

310–4 reregistered TJI 8780–4 (310/4 also carried WDL 142, 748)
315–7 reregistered 473 CDL, 390 CDL, VDL 263 later reverting to original numbers
318/9 acquired from Cosgrove, Preston, 1987. Reregistered 390, 473 CDL later becoming A111 FDL, KDZ 8761.
326/7 acquired from Blue Line Coach Hire, 1988. Reregsitered 934 BDL, VDL 263 (later LDZ 3474)
320/1 reregistered TXI 7520, WXI 6291

Ford R1114/Plaxton C53F

434	BFH 900N	1974	1989	436	TKH 209R	1977	1989	437	VNK 547S	1977	1988
435	LVS 231P	1976	1988								

Acquired from West Wight Motor Co, Freshwater, April 1987

Volvo B58-61/Duple C53F

322	TND 121X	1982	1991	324	TND 124X	1982	1991	325	TND 131X	1982	1991
323	TND 122X	1982	1991								

Acquired from Blue Line Coach Hire, 1988

Ford Transit 160D (249–52), 190D (253–70/81)/Carlyle B16F (on Dormobile frames)

No	Reg	From	To	No	Reg	From	To	No	Reg	From	To
249	B922 BON	1984	1988	257	B257 MDL	1985	1993	265	C265 SDL	1985	1998
250	B250 LDL	1985	1988	258	B258 MDL	1985	1992	266	C266 SDL	1985	1996
251	B251 LDL	1985	1988	259	B259 MDL	1985	1991	267	C267 SDL	1985	1997
252	B252 LDL	1985	1988	260	B260 MDL	1985	1991	268	C268 SDL	1985	1998
253	C253 SDL	1985	1996	261	B261 MDL	1985	1991	269	D269 YDL	1986	1991
254	B254 MDL	1985	1991	262	C262 SDL	1985	1996	270	D270 YDL	1986	1991
255	C255 SDL	1985	1993	263	C263 SDL	1985	1996	281	C220 XRU	1985	1989
256	B256 MDL	1985	1992	264	C264 SDL	1985	1998				

No 249 initially operated as a demonstrator and was acquired in 1985   Nos 252/62/6/70/81 were transferred to Solent Blue Line
No 262 was returned from Solent Blue Line, fitted with coach seats and reregistered WXI 6291, later C606 CTP
Nos 264/8 were converted to engineering runabouts 1996/4   No 265 was converted for use as a publicity vehicle in 1996
Nos 269/70 operated variously as 16, 18 or 20 seaters   No 281 was transferred to SVOC from Solent Blue Line (after working for Badger Vectis); it was later returned to SBL.

Iveco 49-10/Robin Hood B23F (271–5/9), Phoenix B23F (283–9), Car Chair B23F (234–8), Carlyle B25F (GCC)

No	Reg	From	To	No	Reg	From	To	No	Reg	From	To
271	E271 HDL	1987	1997	283	F283 SDL	1989	E	234	J234 KDL	1992	2001
272	E272 HDL	1987	2001	284	F284SDL	1987	2002	235	J235 KDL	1992	1999
273	E273 HDL	1987	2001	285	F285 SDL	1989	2001	236	J236 KDL	1992	2002
274	E274 HDL	1987	1998	286	F286 SDL	1989	2001	237	J237 KDL	1992	2001
275	E279 HDL	1987	1997	287	F287 SDL	1989	2001	238	J238 KDL	1992	2001
276	E276 HDL	1987	1997	288	G565 YTR	1990	E	–	G246 GCC	1989	1992
279	E275 HDL	1987	1997	289	H289 DDL	1990	E				

Nos 272/3 were franchised/leased to B Isaacon and Traditional Motor Bus Co. 1997–2000.
No 279 (E275 HDL) was transferred from Solent Blue Line, 1994; the fleet number was then exchanged with No 275 (E279 HDL).
Nos 283–7 were leased to Traditional Motor Bus Co. 1998–2000; Nos 283/4 leased to Alpha, 2001.
Nos 283/6/7 were reregistered to ODL 447, WDL 655, XDL 872 in 1999/2000, later reverting to original numbers.
No 288 was built as a Phoenix demonstrator but may not have been used as such
Nos 236–8 were sold to M-Travel in 1999 but returned to SVOC later the same year.
Nos 276, 234/5 were transferred from Solent Blue Line 2000/1999 respectively. No 235 was used for spares
G246 GCC was acquired for spares in 1992 from Amberline, Speke; it was new to Crosville Wales

Leyland Olympian ONCL10/1RZ (710–2), ON2R50C13Z5 (all others)/Leyland CH68, 70 or 72F

No	Reg	From	To	No	Reg	From	To	No	Reg	From	To
710	F710 SDL	1989	E	716	G716 WDL	1989	E	724	G724 XDL	1990	E
711	F711 SDL	1989	E	717	G717 WDL	1989	E	725	G725 XDL	1990	E
712	F712 SDL	1989	E	718	G718 WDL	1989	E	726	G726 XDL	1990	E
713	G713 WDL	1989	E	719	G719 WDL	1989	E	727	G727 XDL	1990	E
714	G714 WDL	1989	E	720	G720 WDL	1989	E				
715	G715 WDL	1989	E	723	G723 XDL	1990	E				

Nos 710/1 were delivered as Nos 701/2 (F701/2 RDL) but were altered before entering service. All were reregistered TIL 6710–20/3–7 in November 2001 and were subsequently refurbished and painted in *Route Rouge* livery.

Kassbohrer S215 HD (Setra)/Kassbohrer C49FT   (902 later C47FT)

No	Reg	From	To	No	Reg	From	To
901	H901 EDL	1991	2002	902	J902 KDL	1992	1997

Nos 901/2 were registered WDL 142, 748 but later reverted to original numbers

Leyland Olympian (735–43), Volvo Olympian (744–59)/Northern Counties CH70F

735	K735 ODL	1993	E	743	K743 ODL	1993	E	752	R752 GDL	1998	E
736	K736 ODL	1993	E	744	M744 HDL	1995	E	753	R753 GDL	1998	E
737	K737 ODL	1993	E	745	M745 HDL	1995	E	754	R754 GDL	1998	E
738	K738 ODL	1993	E	746	M746 HDL	1995	E	755	R755 GDL	1998	E
739	K739 ODL	1993	E	748	M748 HDL	1995	E	756	R756 GDL	1998	E
740	K740 ODL	1993	E	749	M749 HDL	1995	E	757	R757 GDL	1998	E
741	K741 ODL	1993	E	750	M750 HDL	1995	E	758	R758 GDL	1998	E
742	K742 ODL	1993	E	751	M751 HDL	1995	E	759	R759 GDL	1998	E

Nos 742/3 were converted to open-top (74 seats), 2003/4

Leyland Tiger TRCTL11/3R/Marshall DP53F

865	F86 TDL	1983	2001

Originally Ministry of Defence, reg no 20 KB 78, later A550 DPA. Acquired via a dealer, 1995 for use as a driver trainer but regularly used in service

Iveco 59-12/Marshall DP23F (239–47; 239 also B25/27F), Mellor B27/29F (255–62), Dormobile B25F (263/4)

239	K172 CAV	1992	E	246	P246 VDL	1997	E	260	L445 FFR	1994	E
240	N240 PDL	1996	E	247	P247 VDL	1997	E	261	N261 FOR	1996	E
241	N241 PDL	1996	E	255	K702 UTT	1993	E	262	N262 FOR	1996	E
242	N242 PDL	1996	E	256	K713 UTT	1993	E	263	L936 KSG	1993	2003
243	N243 PDL	1996	E	257	K724 UTT	1993	E	264	L937 KSG	1993	E
244	P244 VDL	1997	E	258	K823 WFJ	1993	E				
245	P245 VDL	1997	E	259	K804 WFJ	1993	E				

Nos 239/55–60 were acquired from Stagecoach Devon, 2001   Nos 261/2 were transferred from Solent Blue Line, 1996
Nos 263/4 were acquired from Traditional Motor Bus Co, 2002; No 263 was used for spares only.

Dennis Dart 8.5SDL/UVG B31 or 33F (810–5), Duple (Carlyle) B31F (816/7), Reeve Burgess B31F (818), Plaxton B31F (819), Plaxton B29F (300)

810	N810 PDL	1996	E	814	N814 PDL	1996	E	818	J382 GKH	1992	E
811	N811 PDL	1996	E	815	N815 PDL	1996	E	819	K244 PAG	1992	E
812	N812 PDL	1996	E	816	G516 VYE	1990	E	300	HW52 EPX	2002	E
813	N813 PDL	1996	E	817	G526 VYE	1990	E				

Nos 816/7 were acquired from London United in 2000   Nos 818/9 were acquired from a dealer in 2003

Volvo B10M-62/Plaxton Excalibur C53FT

903	N667 VJB	1996	2000	904	N668 VJB	1996	2000	905	P618 FTV	1997	2000

Nos 903/4 were acquired from Horseman, Reading in 1997 and were reregistered WDL 142, 748 later reverting to original numbers.
No 905 was acquired from Ralph's, Langley (via a dealer) in 1999 and was reregistered 473 CDL. It, too, later regained its original number.

Dennis Javelin/Plaxton C41F (converted from C53FT)

575	MIL 9575	1989	E

No 575 was acquired from Brighton & Hove, via Fleetmaster (dealer), Horsham in 2002 and was originally registered F505 LAP. It is used primarily as a driver trainer.

Volvo B7TL/Plaxton (Transbus) President H73F

100	HW52 EPK	2002	E	103	HW52 EPO	2002	E	106	HW52 EPV	2002	E
101	HW52 EPL	2002	E	104	HW52 EPP	2002	E				
102	HW52 EPN	2002	E	105	HW52 EPU	2002	E				

Vehicles acquired with other operators' businesses

SV Fleet No	Reg No	Chassis	Body	Seats	New	Wdn	
Ex-FW Casey, Ryde – January 1929							
45/600	DL 5277	Guy BA	Strachan & Brown	B20R	1927	1935	
46/601	DL 5278	Guy BA	Strachan & Brown	B20R	1927	1935	
602	DL 6220	Guy OND	Guy	B20D	1929	1935	
Ex-Surprise, Havenstreet – September 1929							
405	DL 4802	Dennis 30cwt	?	B19F	1926	1934	
406	DL 4982	Dennis 30cwt	?	Ch14	1927	1934	
401/413	DL 5290	Dennis F	?	?	1927	c1935	
404/406	DL 5387	Dennis 30cwt	Short	B16F	1927	1936	later B14F
400/410	DL 6432	Dennis 30cwt	?	B19F	1929	1937	
Ex-Creeth, Nettlestone – January 1930							
–	DL 1463	Dennis	Creeth	Ch26(?)	1919	1930	
–	DL 1614	National (steam)	Creeth	Ch32	1920	1930	
–	DL 1779	Dennis	Creeth	Ch23	1920	1930	
–	AF 2582	Dennis	?	Ch20	1920	1931	
–	DL 2782	Dennis 50cwt	London Lorries	Ch20	1922	1931	
–	DL 3202	Fiat	Chelsea MB	Ch14	1923	1930	
Ex-IW Tourist Co, Ryde – June 1930							
62/402	DL 4467	Dennis ES	Margham	B26F	1926	1933	
63/403	DL 4468	Dennis E	Margham	B26F	1926	1947	
64/407	DL 5500	Dennis 30cwt	Margham	B20F	1928	1936	
65/408	DL 5501	Dennis 30cwt	Margham	B20F	1928	1935	
66/409	DL 5524	Dennis 30cwt	Margham	C14	1928	c1937	
Ex-Supreme, Ryde – July 1933							
800/20	MY 7937	GMC T30	Grose	B20F	1930	1938	
700/30	DL 7607	Bedford WLG	Grose	B20F	1931	1937	
Ex-Brown's, Carisbrooke – March 1935							
414	DL 5191	Dennis E	Dennis	B26D	1927	1935	
411	DL 5611	Dennis G	Margham	B20	1928	1937	
900	DL 5709	Dodge TDX	Strachan & Brown	B20F	1928	1935	
–	DL 5873	Dennis G	Dennis	B20	1928	1937	
1	DL 6435	Star Flyer VB4	Margham	B24F	1929	1935	
415	UW 6827	Dennis EV	Dennis (?)	C32	1929	1952	
603/3	DL 7051	Guy ONDF	Guy	B20F	1930	1937	
10	DL 7144	Chrevrolet LQ	Hoyal	B14F	1930	1938	
11	HX 9466	Chevrolet U	Waveney	B14	1930	1937	
701/31	DL 7552	Bedford WLG	Grose	B20F	1931	1937	
523	DL 7990	Dennis Lancet	Margham	B32R	1932	1941	
413	DL 8530	Dennis GL	Margham	B20F	1933	1941	
Ex-Walkden, Sandown – March 1936							
–	DL 5585	Morris Z	Strachans	B20	1928	1937	
–	DL 6302	Morris TX	Margham	B20R	1929	1937	
12	DL 6569	Chevrolet LQ	Grose	B14F	1929	1938	
300	DL 7569	Morris Viceroy	Strachans	B26D	1931	1938	
301	DL 7570	Morris Viceroy	Strachans	B26D	1931	1938	
302	DL 7995	Morris Director	Strachans	B20D	1932	1939	
50	DL 9086	Leyland SKP3	Strachans	DP26F	1934	1950	later 20 seats
51	DL 9680	Leyland SKP3	Strachans	DP26F	1935	1950	

SV Fleet No	Reg No	Chassis	Body	Seats	New	Wdn	
Ex-Coffen, Ryde – March 1937							
–	TP 7181	Morris	Wadham	B14F	1929	1937	
–	UV 9121	Guy OND	?	B20	1929	1937	
–	IA 9363	Thornycroft A12	Thornycroft	B20F	1931	1938	
32	DL 8014	Bedford WLB	Duple	B20F	1932	1939	
303	DL 8475	Morris Dictator	Thurgood	B20	1933	1939	
408	DL 9043	Dennis Ace	Harrington	B20F	1934	1941	
Ex-Eames, Shanklin – July 1937							
4/412	DL 5189	Dennis F	Dennis	Ch26	1927	c1945	
5	DL 5746	Dennis F	London Lorries	C26F	1928	c1947	
6	DL 7515	Dennis Arrow	London Lorries	C28F	1931	by 1953	
7	DL 7961	Dennis Lancet	London Lorries	C28F	1931	1950	
8	DL 8495	Dennis Lancet	Duple	C28F	1933	by 1953	
9	DL 9077	Dennis Lancet	Duple	C28F	1934	by 1953	
10	DL 9104	Dennis Ace	Duple	C20F	1934	1941	
11	DL 9719	Dennis Lancet 6	Duple	C32F	1935	1953	
12	ADL 401	Dennis Lancet 6	Harrington	C32F	1936	1952	
14	ADL 629	Dennis Lancet 2	Harrington	C32F	1936	1953	
15	BDL 313	AEC Regal	Harrington	C32F	1937	1940	
16	BDL 314	AEC Regal	Harrington	C32F	1937	1940	
–	BCG 995	Armstrong Siddeley limousine		7 seats	193?	1947	
Ex-IW Tourist, Ryde – June 1938							
–	DL 5117	Dennis 50cwt	London Lorries	C26	1927	1939	
–	DL 5707	Dennis 50cwt	London Lorries	C26	1928	1939	
–	DL 6449	Dennis 30cwt	London Lorries	C14F	1929	1939	
–	DL 6450	Dennis 50cwt	London Lorries	C26	1929	1939	
–	DL 7524	Dennis Dart 6	Margham	C20F	1931	1939	
–	DL 7525	Dennis Dart 6	Margham	C20F	1931	1941	
15	DL 8362	Dennis Lancet	Margham	C30R	1933	1953	
–	DL 9727	Dennis Ace	Margham	C20F	1935	1941	
–	DL 9728	Dennis Ace	Margham	C20F	1935	1941	
17	ADL 309	Bedford WTB	Margham	C26R	1936	c1949	
16	ADL 400	Dennis Lancet	Margham	C30F	1936	1952	
18	BDL 278	Bedford WTB	Duple	C25F	1937	1954	
Ex-Colson, Carisbrooke – March 1939							
–	DL 6210	Dennis 30cwt	?	B20	1929	1939	
–	DL 6997	Chevrolet LQ	?	B14F	1930	1939	
30	ADL 392	Bedford WTB	Duple	B20F	1936	1954	
31	BDL 287	Bedford WTB	Duple	B20F	1937	1954	
Ex-Enterprise, Newport – June 1951							
900/700	BRD 754	Guy Arab I	Strachan	UL55R	1942	1956	
901/701	BRD 816	Guy Arab II	Strachan	UL55R	1943	1956	
32	DDL 532	Bedford OWB	Duple	UB26F	1943	1954	
33	DDL 706	Bedford OWB	Duple	UB26F	1944	1954	
526	AJH 870	Dennis Lancet	Auto-Cellulose	B35F	1935	1954	
34/207	GDL 226	Bedford OB	Duple	B30F	1949	1963	later 28 seats

SV Fleet No	Reg No	Chassis	Body	Seats	New	Wdn	
Ex-B Groves, Cowes – May 1955							
227	EDL 808	Bedford OB	Duple	C29F	1947	1957	
228	FDL 240	Bedford OB	Duple	C29F	1948	1957	
229	GDL 102	Bedford OB	Duple	C29F	1949	1957	
230	HDL 570	Bedford SB	Duple	C33F	1951	1960	
Ex-Nash, Ventnor – June 1956							
100	EDL 715	Dennis Lancet III	Duple	C33F	1947	1960	
101	FDL 216	Dennis Lancet III	Duple	C35F	1948	1960	
102	GDL 32	Crossley SD42/7	Whitson	C33F	1949	1960	
103	GDL 33	Crossley SD42/7	Whitson	C33F	1949	1960	
104	HDL 304	Commer Avenger	Harrington	C33F	1951	1960	
Ex-Shamrock & Rambler – May 1969							
–	YEL 773	Bedford SB3	Duple	C41F	1959	1969	
101	PDL 611	Bedford SB3	Duple	C41F	1958	1970	ex-Randall
104	YYV 488	Bedford SB1	Duple	C41F	1960	1975	ex-Fountain
105	XYO 10	Ford 570E	Duple	C41F	1960	1975	ex-Fountain
106	660 NKK	Ford 402E	Kenex	B11F	1961	1973	ex-Fountain
107	VDL 841	Bedford SB3	Plaxton	C41F	1961	1971	ex-Crinage
108	XDL 783	Bedford SB3	Plaxton	C41F	1962	1971	ex-Crinage
109	516 ABL	Bedford SB8	Duple	C37F	1962	1976	ex-Fountain
110	517 ABL	Bedford SB8	Duple	C41F	1962	1976	ex-Fountain
111	518 ABL	Bedford SB8	Duple	C41F	1962	1976	ex-Fountain
112	65 BDL	Bedford SB3	Plaxton	C41F	1963	1971	ex-Crinage
113	527 CER	Bedford SB5	Duple	C41F	1963	1978	
114	100 BRU	Bedford VAL14	Harrington	C52F	1964	1978	
115	ADL 300B	Bedford SB3	Duple	C41F	1964	1971	ex-Randall
116	CDL 698C	Bedford SB3	Plaxton	C41F	1965	1977	ex-Crinage
117	MTD 559C	Ford 676E	Duple	C52F	1965	1978	ex-Fountain
118	PEL 994G	Bedford VAL70	Duple	C53F	1969	1982	

Additionally taken over were Nos 102/3 (SDL 3/4) and JDL 762 which had previously operated in the SVOC fleet and are listed elsewhere. Nos 113/4 and YEL 773 were transferred from the Bournemouth operation; the others had been based at Cowes. Nos 109–111 were new to Thames Valley. No 118 was taken over new.

As a part of the National Bus Company formation, the Fountain Coaches organisation, which had been acquired by Shamrock & Rambler at Bournemouth, was placed under the management of SVOC in 1969. The name was retained for many years although the bulk of the fleet was between five and ten years old so was replaced in due course. Number 110 (517 ABL) was a Bedford SB8, new to Thames Valley in 1962; it eventually ended its days on the Scottish island of Benbecula.

P Relf

Service Fleet

(excluding Staff Cars and Motorcycles)

Fleet no	Reg no	Type	New	Sold
–	DL 2609 [1]	Model T Ford lorry	1922	c1931
–	DL 4851 [2]	Model T Ford van	1926	1934
–	DL 8870	Ford 1 ton van	1934	c1952
–	DL 4468 [3]	Dennis E lorry	1926	1947
–	UW 6827 [4]	Dennis EV tree cutter	1929	1952
–	RX 3494	Austin 12 van (ex-taxi)	193?	1947
006	EDL 213	Bedford van	1946	1963
005	EDL 292	Bedford 30cwt lorry	1946	c1965
004	EDL 554 [5]	Ford (Canada) recovery	194?	1967
007	FDL 18	Bedford van	1947	1960
002	GDL 880	Fordson van	1950	1964
006	HDL 726	Bedford van	1952	?
001	BOW 168 [6]	Bristol L5G tree cutter	1938	1966
003	KGX 645 [7]	Morris 10cwt van	194?	1960
403	DL 9013 [8]	Dennis Ace lorry	1934	1959
406	ADL 508 [8]	Dennis Ace lorry	1936	1956
008	VDL 613	Bedford CAV van	1961	1969
009	VDL 614	Bedford CAV van	1961	1970
010	234 ADL	Bedford CAV van	1963	1972
004	GXX 785 [9]	AEC Matador recovery	1945	1986
011	ADL 724B	Bedford CAV II van	1964	1975
012	CDL 952C	Bedford-Hawson lorry	1965	1974
013	EDL 602D	Ford Anglia 5cwt van	1966	1976
008	NDL 58G	Bedford 10/12cwt van	1969	1978
001	DDL 50 [10]	Bristol K5G tree cutter	1940	1979
009	PDL 942H	Bedford CF van	1970	1977
010	VDL 298K	Bedford HA 8cwt van	1972	1977
007	ADL 705L	Bedford HA 8cwt van	1973	1981
002	GDL 343N [11]	Bedford CF 35cwt lorry	1974	1988
003	GDL 654N	Morris Marina 7cwt van	1975	1981
011	KDL 217P	Bedford CF van	1975	1983
005	KDL 259P	Morris Marina 1300 van	1975	1986
006	KDL 260P	Morris Marina 1300 van	1975	1988
TB 1	YDL 318 [12]	Bristol FS6G trainer	1962	2001
TB 2	TDL 998 [12]	Bristol FS6G trainer	1960	2001
003	WDL 464T	Morris Marina van	1978	1989
007	MDL 578W	Morris Marina 575 van	1981	1990
008	ODL 805X	Morris Marina 10cwt van	1981	1989
011	XDL 506Y [13]	Ford Transit 16cwt van	1983	1989
PC1	OOD 361M [14]	Bedford YRT	1974	1987
009	NDL 490G [15]	Bristol VRT tree cutter	1969	1999
004	BCW 146R [16]	ERF PCM386 recovery	1977	E
020	D 304ADL	Ford Granada hire car	1986	1992
021	D 305ADL	Ford Granada taxi	1986	1988
31	RDL 603X [17]	Mercedes 308 van	1982	1991
32	UDL 607Y [17]	Mercedes 308 van	1982	1989
33	VDL 700Y [17]	Mercedes 207D van	1982	1990
34	UDL 608Y [17]	Mercedes 308 van	1982	1990
35	C332 RDL [17]	Mercedes 308 van	1985	c1994
36	VDL 287Y [17]	Mercedes 308 pick-up	1983	1991
37	VDL 651Y [17]	Mercedes 310 van	1983	1990
38	WDL 550Y [17]	Mercedes 310 van	1983	1990
39	VDL 652Y [17]	Mercedes 310 van	1983	1990
(249)	B922 BON [18]	Ford Transit minibus	1984	1988
(TB 2)	CKH 780C [19]	AEC Renown	1965	1989
40	A980 XOK [20]	Ford Transit minibus	1985	1989
253	C253 SDL [21]	Ford Transit minibus	1985	1996
005	F376 MDL	Austin Maestro van	1988	1995
006	F893 ODL	Ford Transit pick-up	1989	E
011	F699 RDL	Ford Transit 100 pick-up	1989	E
32	F102 SDL [22]	Mercedes van	1989	1994
003	G659 VDL	Bedford Astromax	1989	1997
–	G521 XDL [23]	Leyland DAF 400	1990	1994
–	G522 XDL [23]	Leyland DAF 400	1990	1994
–	G523 XDL [23]	Leyland DAF 200	1990	1994
–	G524 XDL [23]	Leyland DAF 200	1990	1994
007	G628 YDL	Ford Transit van	1990	E
005	M533 GDL [24]	Ford Escort van	1994	2002
002	B827 VBK [25]	Volvo F7 artic tow truck	1985	E
010	D696 YDL [26]	Vauxhall Astra van	1986	1998
008	J581 JDL [26]	Leyland DAF van	1991	2002
012	R839 BDL	Ford Transit 120 van	1997	E
014	M461 TTV [27]	Iveco 35.10 van	1995	E
016	M209 DDU [28]	Iveco Cargo tree cutter	1994	E
015	S710 BDL	Ford Transit van	1999	E
017	HW02 KDX	Renault Kangoo van	2002	E
009	W868 YPX [29]	Renault Master van	2000	E
020	R491 HDL [30]	Renault B120-60D bus	1993	2003

1 Ex Vectis Bus Co; new to Fountain Garage
2 Ex Cheverton, Newport, 1931
3 Converted from bus No 403, 1933
4 Converted from bus No 415, 1945
5 Ex Thames Valley, 1947; originally War Dept.
6 Ex Hants & Dorset bus No 735, 1952
7 Ex Pickfords, Road Haulage Executive, 1953
8 Converted from buses, 1954
9 Ex North (dealer), 1964
10 Converted from bus No 703, 1969
11 Transferred to Solent Blue Line, 1988
12 Converted from buses Nos 573 and 565 in 1978, 1980 respectively
13 Transferred to Solent Blue Line, 1989
14 Converted from coach No 401, 1983; new to Greenslades
15 Converted from bus No 622, 1985
16 Acquired 1985
17 Ex AB Wadham (Rentals) Ltd, 1987; No 38 transferred to SBL, 1990
18 Ex bus No 249, 1987; transferred to Wadham hire fleet
19 Ex East Yorkshire via Carl Ireland (dealer), Hull, 1988. Not used.
20 Ex SBL No M80, 1988; new as demonstrator, used for Wadham hire fleet
21 Ex bus No 253, 1988; transferred to Wadham hire fleet
22 Purchased for Wadham hire fleet
23 Purchased for Southern Vectis Rentals
24 Transferred to Solent Blue Line, 2002
25 Ex Vectis Transport, 1994
26 Ex Island Group 90, 1996
27 Acquired 1998 from an engineering firm
28 Acquired from dealer, 1999
29 Originally registered on Guernsey as a parcels delivery van
30 Left-hand drive demonstrator, formerly registered 7883 RK 58